The Ladies of Low Arvie

The Ladies of Low Arvie

◆

Living the Farming Dream

Linda Watson

iUniverse, Inc.
New York Lincoln Shanghai

The Ladies of Low Arvie
Living the Farming Dream

iUniverse books may be ordered through booksellers or by contacting:

iUniverse
2021 Pine Lake Road, Suite 100
Lincoln, NE 68512
www.iuniverse.com
1-800-Authors (1-800-288-4677)

Cover: Low Arvie Farmhouse 2002, Beauty, Lady Olga, Lady Catherine

ISBN-13: 978-0-595-35837-3 (pbk)
ISBN-13: 978-0-595-80300-2 (ebk)
ISBN-10: 0-595-35837-3 (pbk)
ISBN-10: 0-595-80300-8 (ebk)

Printed in the United States of America

~

With thanks to

The Ladies of Low Arvie

Richard

the kind Galloway folk who appear in these pages

Catherine

Jane P. Lindsay for her encouragement and opinions

Martin of 'Douglas Books' for his encouragement

Andy for the photography

Zvonko for the cover and photography

~

In memory of

Hughie

23

~

Contents

Introduction

Low Arvie, June 2005

Hello,

Have you ever had a dream?

A dream of living life to its fullest extent.

A dream where life is varied, exciting, perhaps not always carefree but where there are no problems, just challenges which you meet head on, with joy in your heart and the determination to succeed in your head…where there is no one standing over you ready to criticise or harass…where you wake every morning happy to greet the day, whatever the weather…where you know that there may be hard work ahead, but that when you reach your bed again at night, the chances are much better than even that you will be looking back upon a day of fulfilment and satisfaction. A life that means that when you are too old to work any more and you can only sit by the fire and re-live your yesterdays, all the memories will make you smile.

A farm, a small piece of land that we could call our own, where we could live out the second half of our lives in harmony with nature and at peace with the world, perhaps grow corn or rear cows, whatever the land we bought dictated. This was our dream. We were lucky. We found it and we live it.

It wasn't easy, it took a lot of searching, a long time to realise, but this is the story of what happened when we did.

I hope you enjoy sharing our journey and that it will give you pause for thought about the life you live now and, if you find that it is less than perfect, that you will be inspired to follow your dream, whatever that might be…

1

Buying the farm

The first time we saw Low Arvie, it was pouring with rain and we had just driven two hundred miles, with raindrops beating against the windscreen all the way from Ferrybridge. The sky was dark, and the light beginning to fade. The house looked sad and forlorn, and the farmyard empty and unkempt, with the rivulets running down its length, joining together like the veins of an arm and collecting into a large pool at the far corner. We were singularly unimpressed, and our mood, as gloomy as the sky, was in deep contrast to the one we had set out with that morning, in the bright spring sunshine, full of high hopes that this would be our dream home.

We had been searching for a farm for three years, but the criteria had become somewhat less stringent over that time, as our available capital was ever diminished by the falling stock market and the subsequent continuous lowering of interest rates. We wanted somewhere away from the hurly-burly that life had become, somewhere with enough land to be genuinely called a farm, situated in a green and pleasant land. Somewhere isolated enough to satisfy Richard's desire for privacy, but not too isolated so that it could suit my intermittent gregariousness, somewhere with long views and the large farmhouse kitchen that I had been dreaming of for a long time. The price of such places was rapidly going away from our limited resources but, on paper, Low Arvie had seemed to fulfil most of these conditions and looked to be a reasonable buy at the guide price. We had seen so many places over our three-year search, and I had always felt that I would know the instant we walked into *the one*. We had agreed that both of us needed to like the property and, after the two false starts where one of us had had to compromise, we set off that day, Saturday 18th May 2002, with hopes as high as the weather was beautiful.

Within fifteen miles, the sunshine has gone and the rain began, and with it our hopes and mood became more and more dour until, on our arrival, it seemed to sink towards despair. The house, though entirely habitable and nicely decorated with plain colours…although perhaps too much pink…was small. The views to the east and west were fairly long, but all the windows in the house faced south towards the road, some seventy metres away. The nearest village, Corsock, was one and a quarter miles, but there was a small cluster of houses half a mile up the road, whose chimneys could just be seen by peering around the corner of the window. The only criteria that were fully met was that this was certainly a very green and pleasant land, and, with one hundred and twenty acres of land, Low Arvie was definitely a farm. On closer inspection, however, only twenty of them were covered in grass, with the rest growing lush flushes of rush. In the gloomy daylight and the incessant rain and after such a dreary journey, it seemed far from the idyllic place we had hoped for.

The system of purchasing a property in Scotland is entirely different to England, where one is not committed to the purchase until the contracts are exchanged. Up here, when there are more than one interested prospective purchaser, it is usual for a closing date to be set and the request for sealed bids, properly drawn up by a solicitor, to be handed in to the estate agent. Once the bid is entered, you are committed to the purchase, if yours is the one that is chosen. The vendor gives no guarantees to sell to the highest offer, but can take time to investigate the ability to pay, which has to be included in the bid. If you are not the chosen bidder, there is no recourse to 'gazumping' or re-negotiation. If your bid is the accepted one, then you are committed to go ahead or be penalised. The previous week we had been beaten into third place on another farm, not far away from Low Arvie…I had liked it and Richard had compromised…and had tasted the disappointment that being the loser under this system brings. We had hoped to find, in Low Arvie, a property that would remove this disappointment and replace it with joyful anticipation. It was, therefore, with heavy hearts that we left the little house to its lonely, rainy evening and drove away to find the B&B that I had booked.

The next morning it was still raining hard, but we decided to drive back to the farm for a further look, before heading back south. We drove slowly along the mile of road frontage, past the myriad rushes with the relentless rain dripping from them. As I looked between the raindrops on the car window, I began to think how the brown of the rushes contrasted attractively with the patchwork of grass that grew on the higher drums between the low-lying areas. As we approached the far end of the farm's land, I saw that there was a small stretch of broad-leaved woodland, where the burn flowed under the road and wended its way, roughly marking the north-western boundary of the farm. Amongst the trees I could see the bright yellow flowers of kingcup growing along its banks.

There were dry stone walls snaking across the land that appeared to bound some reasonably grassy fields, where the rushes only grew around the low perimeters. The higher domes were covered with tall, green, spring grass, crying out to be grazed. We turned the car round and gazed in silence at the land. When we were level with the house, Richard stopped the car and we sat, each one lost in our own thoughts. The house, sitting slightly higher than the road, at the end of a short track, was small, but, nevertheless, seemed friendly and attractive in the morning light. It had new windows, and the decor, even though mostly pink, was such that we could move in and live, without doing any work first. The buildings grouped around the back were modern in design…there were no old stone byres…and, though they had not been erected recently, they were weatherproof and serviceable. The conifer plantation behind the house was planted on the much lower ground there and provided an attractive backdrop to the house, rather than overshadowing it. As I sat there, I knew that Richard was running through the different criteria with which he would be concerned, what kind of farming he could follow here, what work would be required before a start could be made, what kind of life we could make for ourselves. I waited, without any idea of what he would say when he eventually spoke, but I knew that, whatever it was, it would be ok for me. I could drive away from here, either to continue the search or to work out a realistic bid to buy this place, with complete equanimity of mind. We had looked at so many farms over the preceding three years and had actually only bid on the one that I had liked, that I had come to face the prospect of life as being a constant search, without any resolution. In some ways, this was a far less scary proposition than actually finding and buying somewhere!

The silence went on for a long time and I could not tell what Richard was thinking. I think I was quite surprised when, eventually, he said, "I think we have to have a go for this." I gulped hard, and immediately my mind went into panic. I can't remember any of the drive back home, as a whirl of figures and half-formed ideas floated around in my head. There was such a lot to decide if we were going to 'have a go'.

The farm we had bid on and lost was in the same area, and we learned that our bid had been beaten by ten thousand pounds. This gave us something to work with, as the final price of that farm had been about twenty percent higher than the guide price. We worked around this figure, adding twenty percent to the guide price of Low Arvie, and decided to bid at that level. We had three weeks before the closing date, when bids had to be in and, having decided the price we wanted to offer, we got on with the daily routine of our life. I am no good at coping with suspense, and every moment that I relaxed, my mind flew to Low Arvie, and all that it meant and would mean to us, whether we got it or not. Richard suffered one of his migraine attacks during the next week, brought on, no doubt, by the stress of his thoughts around the event, but I knew that once he had said that we should bid on the place, he would not change his mind. This was some comfort to me, as it gave me a focus for my thoughts. At least I knew that we would 'have a go.' Fortunately, I had things to occupy my mind, as the course I was following at the local college was now more than two thirds of the way through, and there was work to be completed for that.

Over the next few days, the estate agent's brochure of Low Arvie stayed within easy reach on the coffee table, and I watched Richard pick it up periodically and sit working out different things with the calculator, making plans in his head for the farm he would create, if we were successful. From time to time, he would discuss some point or other with me, either acreages of woodland, numbers of livestock that the land would support or the machinery he would require. As time went by and we chatted about these various points, we decided that our original idea of the price we would bid was too high for the opportunities that the farm gave. There was a lot of work needing to be done, the land was very wet, indeed, one of the fields was actually called the Bog of Allan and filled over fifteen acres of the hundred and twenty, and we kept coming back to the size of the house. It had only two rooms of any size downstairs, with a small lean-to kitchen at the back, and one other room, which was tiny. The two bedrooms were of reasonable floor area but had coombed ceilings, which took away much useful space. The only other room was the bathroom, which was just big enough to hold the usual offices of bath, basin and toilet. On the plus side, it was carpeted and curtained, the Esse range had been left on, making the atmosphere warm and welcoming when we had gone in, and keeping any damp at bay while the house was empty; and the decor was of a reasonable standard. Putting all this together, we decided to downsize our offer by seven percent. This gave us a figure that was still substantially above the guide price, but left a bigger slice of our capital to use. With a week to go to the closing date, Richard rang our Scottish solicitor and asked him to put in our offer on the due day.

There were many things that had to be done down in Yorkshire before we could really think about moving and, now that we had put our offer in, we felt a fresh impetus to get on and complete a few of them. The next few days were spent working hard to move these projects on, and we had little time to think about Low Arvie. I deliberately tried to think philosophically about the offer, having been disappointed before, and carried on with my college work. I had been fortunate enough to be offered a place at Strathclyde University for the following October, to do a Postgraduate Diploma in Counselling. I had begun a Foundation Course in Counselling the previous year, as it was something that I found interesting and I had time on my hands. What I hadn't expected was the very great enjoyment that the course gave me, and I went on to follow a course in Bereavement Counselling, and then enrolled on two Certificate level courses in Counselling Skills and Theory. I was thoroughly enjoying them both and had also met and made several new, very good friends, something I had lacked for several years, after changing the course of my life. I had decided to apply to Strathclyde because it had an excellent reputation in Counselling Training, it was in Scotland and the Course was only one year. I had reasoned that we would not find a farm too quickly, and I could spend a year gaining a qualification that might prove useful in the future. I could not have foreseen then that it was not to be and I was busy making plans to leave my mother, who was 90 years of age at this time, with sufficient support whilst I was away in Glasgow during term time.

Thus, every time Low Arvie crept into my mind during that week, I was almost successful in being able to push it away, as I got on with some of the more pressing jobs around me. The days passed by quite quickly, but as we hadn't told anyone about putting in a bid, and Richard was not disposed to indulge in 'what ifs' and 'maybes'. I found it increasingly difficult to 'stay in the gap' (as counselling jargon has it), and I became more and more aware that it was ever present at the back of my mind. It would have been easier if I could have spoken about it, but I felt that to break our silence would somehow jeopardise our chances, and so I kept my own counsel and suffered in silence.

The previous time we had bid on a farm, we hadn't heard the result until the day after the closing date, and so I was somewhat unprepared for the solicitor's call when it came through at about 4 p.m. on the closing day itself. "You seem to be the owners of Low Arvie Farm," he said, in his clipped and cultured Scottish accent. For a moment the room seemed to spin and I was unable to speak. Eventually, I stammered something like, "Oh, what do we do now?" His terse tones were uncompromising in their peremptory, "Do nothing until you hear from me!" With little more ado he rang off, and I sat quite still by the fire for a long time, mesmerised by its flames, and unable to think of anything remotely sensible, except that we had a farm.

2

Completing the Deal

We were unable to think much about the whole event for the next twenty-four hours, as a little while after receiving the phone call and telling Richard, we learned that his mother had suffered a stroke and we rushed off to be with her. Richard stayed with her that night, and our concern was for her rather than the farm, which we both knew we would have the time to think about later, and in any case we had to 'do nothing' until we heard again from Mr Kellie.

It was in fact two days before we heard again, and then the call brought us some concern. We had paid scant attention to the water supply on our visit to look at Low Arvie, merely noting that the estate agent's brochure stated that it had a private water supply. We had seen that the bathroom and kitchen possessed the usual features and had tried the taps and found water in them that looked normal. We did notice that the toilet took rather a long time to fill, but then found that the water storage tanks were under the coomb, and thus almost level with the cistern inlet, which was explanation enough for that. However, Mr Kellie had made enquiries about the water supply and had been unable to get a satisfactory explanation from the agents or the solicitors. He could find no one who knew anything about it, and he was concerned. The lady who had lived in Low Arvie, had died the previous year, and her daughters were living away. The farmer himself had died several years before, and, for the last few years, the land had been rented out. Mr Kellie was, therefore, unable to satisfy himself as to the rightness of the water and drainage systems. This was quite worrying to us, as these things can run away with precious resources if they need putting right. I didn't understand the problems, which probably made me worry more; but then there came the first of several remarkable coincidences that happened around this time, and about Low Arvie, which may lead one to think that we were really meant to live here.

A few weeks before all this took place, we had won a holiday in a Scottish Country Cottage, and, because I was planning to go to Glasgow in the autumn, we had chosen to go to the nearest cottage to that city. This belonged to Mac and Julie and was situated up a glen near Loch Lomond. We had spent a very enjoyable few days there and had become friendly with Mac and Julie, and they had been very kind to us. They had mentioned that they wanted to go to Spain in June, but had no one to look after their animals, (one cat, two dogs, several ducks and hens and a goat), and to do the 'swapover' for new guests in the cottage on the Saturday. Being 'footloose and fancy-free' at the time, we had offered to come up for the ten days or so and oblige. It was at the time of the 'water question' at Low Arvie that we were in contact with them, making the final arrangements for this trip, and, during one of the resultant phone calls, Richard mentioned to Mac the problem about the water system as we knew it. Mac was able to be very reassuring to us, as they also have a private water supply, taking water from the burn near the house, and he told us of their experiences when they moved there some years before. Since we had already spent five days using their system and not noticed any difference to our own in England, we began to worry less about Low Arvie's water and drainage system. We reasoned that a family had lived and prospered there for many years, and that there were other houses in the vicinity that must have a similar system, where people were living quite satisfactorily. We settled back into preparations for the trip to Mac and Julie's, to making plans for the farm and to await Mr Kellie's next instructions. For a while we heard nothing, and I began to wonder if I had dreamed the whole thing, but then, early the following week, I took a call from Mr Kellie. He told me that he had still been unable to satisfy himself over the water and drains and he wished to see the place for himself. "Would you be able to meet me there?" he asked. Once again coincidence came into play, as that was the very week that we were to go up to Mac and Julie's, and Low Arvie was very little out of the way. Indeed, we had planned to call in on our journey and have another look for ourselves anyway. The arrangement was, therefore, quickly made and we agreed to meet at 12 noon on Thursday 20th June. Mr Kellie said he would ring the agents and ask for a key to be available.

It was just on 12 as we drew into the farmyard that Thursday to find Mr Kellie's car already parked in the yard, and the man himself enjoying the spring sunshine. Together we went into the house, and the two men applied themselves to investigating the drains and water. It was then that I noticed for the first time that the sink in the kitchen had a third tap mounted beside the usual hot and cold ones. Mr Kellie turned this on and water ran from it for a short time, and then dribbled to a stop. He turned the others on, and they gave a thin but continuous stream of clear water. He left them running for a while, and then, suddenly, from the cupboard at the side of the sink, there came the sound of a motor whirring. Opening the door, we saw the noise was coming from a pump in the bottom section of the cupboard, and, rushing upstairs, we could hear the water running into the two cold water storage tanks under the coomb in the west bedroom. Underneath one of these was situated a small, but hot, copper cylinder that obviously housed the water warmed by the Esse range. In a minute or two the pump stopped whirring, and we realised that the tanks must be full. We retraced our steps and went outside, where we identified what we felt must be a well situated about four metres from the east wall of the house. A concrete slab of unidentifiable shape, with grass growing towards its centre from every edge, was the only part of it that could be seen, and, having stood and looked down on it for a while, we re-entered the house. Apparently Mr Kellie was reassured by what he had found, because he said no more about the water systems in the house, and went on to take out a sheaf of dusty papers, tied with a pink ribbon, from his bag and began to discuss with Richard, in (to me) incomprehensible legal language, various clauses that were contained in the deeds to the property. There appeared to be nothing of any great moment in these papers to cause us any concern, and I wandered off to look around the other rooms and began to mentally place our furniture.

This did not take long. The east room downstairs was obviously the lounge and would take the settee and two armchairs, TV and perhaps one of the nests of tables and that was about all. The two bedrooms would only need bed, one wardrobe and one dressing table to fill the available space, leaving the west room downstairs to be a dining/cooking room (using the Esse), with the wet work done in the lean-to at the back. The small room downstairs would have to suffice as office space for the time being, and we would just have to see how much we could fit in there. The centre portion of the house contained the hall, stairs and landing; and, in the roof above the S-shaped stairs, which wound up left to right, was a Velux roof window that was allowing the June sunshine to fill the space with golden light. It made the whole house feel light and airy, and I felt that we were going to be all right in this place.

When I came back into the kitchen, Richard and Mr Kellie had finished looking at the deeds and had moved outside into the farmyard. They were standing talking by Mr Kellie's car. As I approached, I heard Richard ask, "What will happen now?" "Well," said Mr Kellie, "We have a completion date of the 10th July, and I have to pay your ten per cent deposit on the 3rd." I could tell by the look that spread across Richard's face that he was as taken aback by these words as I was. This was already the 20th June, and we were just off to do Bed and Breakfast at Mac and Julie's for ten days. We had the purchase money for the farm, but it was spread out amongst various investments and needed gathering together, before any cheque would clear! We were completely surprised by Mr Kellie's words, having relaxed and 'done nothing' for the preceding ten days, as per his earlier instructions. There was further consternation to come, when we realised that Mr Kellie would want the money in his bank account even earlier, to give it time to clear, before he had to pay it to the agents' solicitors. After a few minutes discussion, it was decided that Richard should write out two cheques for Mr Kellie, one for the deposit to be banked in time to clear by July 3rd, and one, for the balance, to be paid in to clear by the 10th. We explained that we needed time to get the money into the correct account, and asked him not to present the cheques earlier than was necessary, to which he agreed.

Time has eclipsed from memory all the machinations we had to go through to comply with the criteria, but suffice to say that Richard managed to get all the correct amounts of money into the correct bank account by the due dates, and the purchase of Low Arvie went through with no hitches after that.

3

Strone House

Apart from a niggling worry about leaving my native village after fifty-four years of living there and moving one hundred and ninety-three miles away to an area where I knew no one, the main concern exercising my mind throughout this process was my mother. I had been the main carer for her for five and a half years, since the death of my father. Although I had told her of the plans that Richard and I were making as soon as we had formulated them some four years previously, I knew it would come as a big wrench to her when I left. I had arranged a care call every day for her some time before, when we went off to Spain for a holiday, and she had a treasure called Karen, who came twice every week to clean and shop for her and take her to visit her sister, my aunt, in the local residential home. She received the modern equivalent of 'meals on wheels', which took the form of frozen dinners delivered once a fortnight, to be microwaved on a daily basis. They weren't very appetizing, but were nutritious and saved her from slipping into the habit of missing meals and eating badly followed by so many people who live alone. She also had a 'dispersed alarm' attached to a call centre, run by the council, which was manned twenty-four hours a day, but, even when she fell and shook herself up very badly, once when I was away for the day, she had never used it, not wishing to put the ladies to any trouble! The people from the church she had attended regularly for sixty-three years were also very good, sometimes visiting her and always supplying lifts to Sunday service. But in spite of all this, I knew that, without me close at hand to sort out queries and problems for her, she would pass many lonely hours and have many worrying moments. It was a considerable cloud on my otherwise very bright horizon, and I could see no way through it.

We thought of her going into the home where her sister was living, and, on her weekly visits, she tried to imagine herself there, but she just wasn't ready for that kind of life. Although ninety years of age and somewhat wobbly in the leg department, she had deteriorated very little. The main problem was a lack of confidence, because she had always had someone 'who belonged to her' there to sort out problems and cope with her affairs. The one thing that she was always adamant about was that she never wanted to live in the same household as either my brothers or me. She had carved out for herself a nice routine after the death of my father, where for the first time in her life she did exactly as she wanted to do, and she firmly believed that to join up with any of us would not only spoil our independent existence, but hers too!

There then occurred another of the coincidences that played such a big part in this episode of my life.

After saying goodbye to Mr Kellie in the farmyard, we continued on our way north. We arrived at Strone House, in Glen Fruin, late in the afternoon. Mac and Julie had already left for Spain, so we were plunged immediately into our duties as animal sitters, and Richard went off to feed the various creatures, whilst I got out the meal 'I had prepared earlier' and began to find my way around the kitchen. We were totally unfamiliar with the house and so it took a little while to get sorted out, but sometime before midnight, all the mouths had been fed, and we had unpacked sufficiently to get ourselves to bed. There were many thoughts (not least the problem of my mother) buzzing around in my brain, but, before any resolutions could be found, I fell into a deep sleep.

Two days later found us changing three double beds in the cottage, putting up the cot that had taken us a while to locate, cleaning, hoovering and generally making it ready to receive the new occupants. I am hopeful that we achieved a good standard for them and gave them a warm welcome when they arrived. After showing them 'the ropes', we withdrew, and I proceeded to fill the washing machine with the first of many loads, as the washing seemed just endless.

The next day was Sunday and we were expecting a Mr and Mrs Tickle to stay for three nights' bed and breakfast and evening meal. They had stayed in the house for one night on their way further north, before we took over, and they were now on their way back south, but having a longer stay. We spent the day cleaning and polishing ready for their visit, getting their room ready and preparing the evening meal. It was the first time I had ever done bed and breakfast 'for real', let alone an evening meal, and the cooking facilities in Strone House consisted of a super four-oven AGA cooker. Before going to Strone House, my only experience of an AGA-type cooker had been at the home of my best friend, when I was growing up in Yorkshire. They had had a solid fuel model and, far from cooking on it, our only use of it had been to put large cushions on the hot-plate lids and sit there, whilst painting our nails and discussing the current range of boyfriends. It had been fortunate, therefore, that I had had two days to get used to using it before our guests were to arrive. I had pre-cooked several dishes before we went up to Scotland and had taken them up frozen. They had stayed frozen on our journey north, and now was the time to get them out to thaw, and to peel the fresh vegetables that were to accompany the steak and kidney pie that I had decided was to be the first night's dinner. I soon learned the enormous pleasure of cooking on the AGA range, and it is my ambition to have one in Low Arvie as soon as possible.

We had just finished our preparations and were sitting down to a well-earned cup of tea, when a middle aged couple appeared around the corner of the house and introduced themselves as Dennis and Eileen Tickle. Since they had been to Strone House the previous week, they knew their way around, and I made them a cup of tea whilst Richard helped them with their luggage. When they had freshened up, they joined us in the conservatory and we chatted amiably for a while. Inevitably the chat turned to personal histories and current life styles, and we learned that Dennis was retired from his long-term career, but had taken on charity work to fill some of the spare time he now enjoyed. He was, he said, chairperson of the local Abbeyfield Society in his home district of Ormskirk, in Lancashire. Having never before heard of the Abbeyfield Society, I politely enquired as to what it might be. Something, I gathered, to do with an old people's home and overseeing the repairs and finances of the home. Though interested, I did not spend a lot of time thinking about it, having more concern at that moment for the soup, steak and kidney pie and apple crumble that I was about to serve up to them.

Later, after the meal had been served and, I hope, enjoyed, we repaired once again to the conservatory to enjoy our coffee, more chat and the evening sunset in equal measure. Now it was our turn to tell of our situation, as Dennis and Eileen obviously knew that we weren't the owners of Strone House, and the talk turned to Low Arvie and the embryo of our future plans.

We enjoyed our time with Dennis and Eileen very much, they were very forgiving about my inexperience of bed and breakfast, and any problems that arose were quickly sorted out. We slipped into the same routine of sharing the day's experiences over coffee in the evenings, and it was a very pleasant interlude. I can't remember at what point my situation viz a viz my mother entered the conversation, but when it did, Dennis said "You ought to get in touch with the local Abbeyfield Society and see if they can help." Thus, I began to take more interest in what this Abbeyfield Society was and quizzed him more closely about it. It is an International organisation that is Christian in foundation and has the aim of providing older people with a home where they can follow an independent life, whilst at the same time being 'overseen' in a fairly distant, but friendly manner. Each town or district has their own Abbeyfield Society that is administered by a local committee under a Chairperson, and the only paid official is the Executive Secretary, who has overall view of the dealings of the Society. The Society owns a house (or houses) in the area that are large enough to house a small number of single elderly folk, each with their own room and living space, but under the same roof. Breakfast is taken independently in one's own room, but a house-keeper prepares and serves lunch and tea in a communal dining room. Residents are totally free to follow their own life and interests as though they were in their own home, and in some cases, even carry on with their employment. It is a stage in between living independently and living in a residential home, and it sounded to be an ideal solution to my problem.

Dennis and Eileen left Strone House to return to Lancashire on the Wednesday morning, and, when they had gone, we began to gather up our things and make the house clean and tidy for Mac and Julie's return. Because of our need to get all the money for Low Arvie into the correct account before Mr Kellie presented the cheque, we had to return home on the Thursday. We had not taken all the necessary bank account details to Scotland with us, and, although we had managed to cover the first cheque, there were still some financial movements to make to cover the second, which could only be done with the correct details to hand. In order to allow sufficient time for transactions to be completed, we had to make them on the Thursday afternoon. Mac and Julie were not returning until Thursday evening, and so we gave the animals enough food and water to last them the day and left Strone House about 10 a.m.

We arrived home in Doncaster with time to complete the necessary arrangements and began to relax for the first time in ten days. Richard's mother had been taken into the hospital, in the hope that she could recover sufficiently well from her stroke to continue living in her own little house in the village, and that evening we went to visit her.

It was, therefore, quite late before I had time to open up my computer and send for my email messages. There were several that had been piling up, waiting for my return, and scanning the list of bold type, I was quite surprised to see that there was one from Dennis Tickle. I opened it up and found that it contained the information I needed to log on to the Abbeyfield website, and how to find the appropriate part for Dumfries and Galloway. As it was so late and it had been a long day, I decided to leave logging on until the next day and, closing down the computer, I went to bed.

4

Low Arvie

Low Arvie is a farm that has no arable land. It forms an almost perfect isosceles tri-angle, with the mile of road frontage being the base and the house and buildings situated right in the middle, about seventy metres back from the road. The house is in front of the farmyard, which is square, with the buildings around the other three sides. About thirty of its one hundred and twenty acres are grass of a reasonable standard called, in agricultural parlance, 'Improved Grassland.' This is a mixture of good grass and wild flowers, which will make into hay or, in Galloway with its unpredictable and fairly wet climate, haylage, a product somewhere between fully dried hay and silage. The grass is mowed and baled and then wrapped in plastic to 'pickle' and preserve it for winter feed. Around eighty-five acres are made up of what is called 'Rough Grazing'. This is land which grows only rough grass inter-spersed with weeds such as nettles and thistles, which are no good for preserving, and, on Low Arvie with its low lying boggy land, rushes and wetland plants. Several of the nine fields that we have are made up of Improved Grassland on the higher knolls or drums, and this Rough Grazing wetland around the perimeter in the lower parts. We only have one field which is all good grass, and even that has a small amount of rush creeping in, due to the lack of good husbandry over the last few years. The two largest fields, which happen to be situated at either end of the farm, are both predominantly Rough Grazing. The remaining acreage is used up by buildings, tracks, open water and rock. There are no lakes and only one small pond which dries up in hot weather, but, marked on the map, there are several drains, or ditches, which criss-cross the land. When we arrived at Low Arvie, these were only marked by lines of thriving rushes that had all but blocked the drains with their roots and, when the water could not get away, held it static in their strong shoots. The tracks were barely discernible across the fields, as parts had sunk and become waterlogged and, in other places, the stones that had once been ordered were now dispersed across the land. Low Arvie's land undulates between 145 metres and 155 metres above sea level, and there are several high spots, which are marked by rocky outcrops of grey stone. The lowest land lies at the point of the triangle furthest from the road, and this is the Bog of Allan, almost twenty acres of land covered by rushes, wetland plants and wet peat, and is unsuitable for grazing cattle except in the driest times. The two equal sides of the isosceles triangle are formed by the Crogo Burn, which delineates, for the most part, the boundary of the farm. The northwest edge is bounded by the Wilson's farm at Auchenvey and by the forestry plantation that begins there and stretches away to the west. The northeastern side adjoins another farm, which has the higher land and grazes cattle on it. The road, which is the A712, runs from Crocketford to New Galloway, and, in spite of its being an 'A' road, is fairly quiet and peaceful, except for the logging lorries that come up empty and go back full on a fairly regular basis. Fortunately, the house is far enough back from the road for these not to be a problem. Across the road we look out onto a wooded hill-side and sometimes see the cattle from Tom Corsan's farm grazing the grass at the top of the hill. This farm is Arvie and must once have been called Upper or High Arvie.

From outside the house, we can enjoy the long views to east and west that, unfortunately cannot be seen from inside. To the west, we can see Dot and Willie Wilson's sheep grazing the White Hill, which adjoins our Low Knowe field, and beyond that the forestry land. Looking down on this peaceful scene is the dark, heather clad Black Craig Hill some five or six miles away, over which we watch some beautiful, summer sunsets. This view will never be visible from inside the house but, hopefully, once the new extension is built and we move in, we will wake to the sun rising over the hills to the east. This is an even longer view and, when the sun is shining, we marvel at the patchwork of greens laid out before us, as the land climbs up through the fields of Drumhumphry farm on the other side of the village and rises up over Craig Adam, in the distance.

Richard's idea for the farm was to have a herd of suckler cows and produce beef from the grassland. There were alternatives but, although he had been in agriculture since the age of sixteen, he had never been concerned with calving cows and wanted to experience it. The land at Low Arvie seemed tailor made for this system, and most of the farms roundabout ran suckler herds and sheep. There is no arable land in the area. The thought of raising sheep did not appeal to Richard and so he decided to go with the sucklers. The idea is that the farm supports a herd of cows that are put to the bull yearly, and the bull calves produced, if of good conformation can be raised entire as bulls and sold for work as such, or can be castrated at an early age and raised for beef. The female, or heifer, calves can be raised to become part of the herd and produce more calves, or they can be sold as breeding cows to other farmers, or they can go into the food chain as beef with the castrated bullocks. It takes somewhere between one and two and a half years to produce a beef animal ready for slaughter, depending on the breed and the regimen followed in raising it.

Having decided on the type of farming Richard wanted to do, we then had to decide on the breed of cow to buy. With this in mind, we had decided to go to the two agricultural shows that were taking place at this time, and Monday 1st July found us at the Royal Show in Warwickshire. This was the first time I had been to such a large show, but it was somewhat lacking in animal numbers, having not quite fully recovered from the foot and mouth outbreak that had devastated large areas of British farming the previous year and had caused all agricultural gatherings to be cancelled for the entire season. However, there were a fair few representatives of many breeds, and we set off to look at them and talk to the farmers with them, if we could. Since the farm was in Scotland, and more particularly in Galloway, we thought that the best breeds would be those traditional ones that were bred to the terrain and climate. There were several possibilities, and I rather favoured the noble Highlanders with their shaggy red-brown coats, gentle features and long curved horns. The little ones were so cute and cuddly and they were so much a symbol of Scotland, a country I had known and loved since my first visit as a small child in the early fifties. They seemed so solid and sturdy as they waited patiently in the big sheds for their turn to go into the show ring, and, although I hadn't fully accepted the reality that we owned a farm, and everything was tinged with a dream like quality, I was thrilled to think that we might soon be owners of such beautiful animals. Another possibility was the Galloway breed itself. Born and bred precisely for the land and climate that we were to move to, they seemed a very sensible option. There are several different Galloway breeds, differing in colour though not in conformation. Probably the best known, and certainly the most distinctive, is the Belted Galloway with a broad white band around its middle sandwiched between black front and rear portions. Then there are the Black Galloways and the Duns, which are a beautiful soft fawn colour. We made our way to the Galloway section of the shed, and immediately our eyes went to the Belteds. The farm was to be our pathway into eventual retirement, both of us having retired early from careers in education, and, therefore, we were at liberty to choose first for pleasure rather than profit, although we would want the farm to be somewhat self-supporting. We had read of a farmer who had done the same thing as us some years before and had chosen to produce Belted Galloway beef and was doing very well. He had virtually the same system as we were hoping for, and it seemed appropriate to consider these animals as a good bet for us, too. They were smallish, sturdy and attractive, with just a soupcon of idiosyncrasy about them. Richard was a little concerned about the Highlanders' horns in a one-man operation, and so it began to look like the Belted Galloway was the favourite.

We now had slightly more than one week left before the deal to buy Low Arvie was completed and we had no vehicle to transport any of our stuff up there. But then came another of those coincidences. I was involved in charity work at this time and I just happened to be talking to one of the ladies that I came into contact with during the next afternoon, and mentioned that we had to get some kind of van before the next week. "We've got a van for sale at the moment," she said. We arranged for Richard and me to go over the next morning and, when we got there, we found that her husband was by way of being a general dealer, and not only had a van for sale, but several trailers as well. Before long we were the owners of a very serviceable van and a fourteen-foot trailer with a bright yellow framed cover that made it into further weatherproof transport for our stuff!

The next week we went to the Great Yorkshire Show to confirm our choice of cattle. The first stall we came to on entering the show ground was selling beef from Highland cattle, and the man said it was the best beef bar none. He admitted that it was closely followed by the Galloway beef, and that both left other kinds far behind. Having never knowingly eaten Highland beef, we decided to purchase some on our way home, and then went off to find the cattle. Nothing we saw there that day persuaded us to change our minds, and we went home planning to find some Belted Galloway cows to inhabit our acres. It would, of course, be some time before we were ready to get some cattle, as we had plenty of issues to settle in Yorkshire before we could stay for long periods of time in Scotland. However, it seemed to bring a bit more reality to the dream, now that we had decided on the cows we would eventually have. We did buy some of the Highland beef, and it was absolutely beautiful, but they still had big horns!

The day after the Yorkshire show, the 10th July, was *the* day when the farm would actually become ours. We had decided to go up on the 11th, as we had had a hectic week and needed a bit more time to get enough stuff together to enable us to 'support existence' at Low Arvie. I had commitments to fulfil in Yorkshire the next week and would have to return by then, but Richard was concerned that the grass on the good land at Low Arvie was very high and needed mowing and baling for winter feed. He was going to stay until he had arranged for that to be done. The only farm equipment he possessed was one 1953 Fordson Major tractor, known as Bluebell, that had definitely seen better days, one cattle crush, one fertiliser spreader and a few gates. It was obvious that he would need to find a contractor to come and make the haylage for us, and, as yet, we knew no one in the area.

5

Abbeyfield

After I received the email about Abbeyfield from Dennis Tickle, I lost no time in contacting Mrs Stanley, the executive secretary for the Abbeyfield Society in the Stewartry, which is the region of Dumfries and Galloway in which Low Arvie is situated. I was not at all certain that Mother would be eligible for accommodation in that area, coming from so far away, and if she was, then surely there would be a long waiting list. I placed the situation as succinctly and as clearly as I could in an email and clicked on the send button, with much hope but little expectation of such an easy answer to my problem. At this stage I had not mentioned the Abbeyfield Society to my mother, as I wanted to know if it was a possibility, before broaching the subject. We spoke together about the situation, and I knew that the residential home, where my aunt was, had some attraction for her, but neither of us really felt that it was a good solution. I knew that if this were the outcome, I would not go to Low Arvie very happily. Everyone agreed that I could not put my life on hold, waiting for a more convenient solution to mother's loneliness and geriatric deterioration, but I felt very much responsible for her well being and, with one brother in Canada and one in Birmingham, the hundred and ninety-three miles from Yorkshire to Low Arvie seemed an awfully long way. I had already made enquiries about trains between Dumfries and Doncaster and discovered that I could do the return journey in one day, leaving very early and getting back very late, giving me five hours in Doncaster. I was not confident of my ability to drive all the way there and back in one day, but I had resigned myself to the idea that I would be spending a fair amount of time travelling one way or another, for the foreseeable future, unless something else turned up.

This was the situation, then, as I clicked my email on its way to Mrs Stanley's mailbox. Her reply was almost immediate, and what she wrote was balm to my troubled spirits. She said that Abbeyfield seemed to provide the perfect answer to my problem. Implicit in this was the message that Mother would be eligible to enter an Abbeyfield house in Galloway. She told me that there were three Abbeyfield houses in the area providing 'very sheltered' accommodation for elderly persons, and there was also an Abbeyfield residential home, such as the one my aunt was in, which was used for the residents of the three other houses when they needed more care. She said that she was mailing some information for me to show my mother, together with an application form, and suggested that, when Richard and I went up to Low Arvie, we gave her a call and went to look at the house in Castle Douglas, our nearest town.

I decided to wait for the information to arrive before speaking to Mother, but Mrs Stanley again did not keep me waiting long, and, in the next day's post, I received a large brown envelope containing all the information required to gain a good insight into what Abbeyfield was, and what an Abbeyfield home was like. I wasted no time in taking it to Mother, telling her how I came to have it and what little I knew of the system. As I spoke, I could see a large weight lift from her shoulders. We looked together at the leaflets and it did, indeed, seem absolutely perfect. From the minute she first heard of Abbeyfield, in spite of her ninety years of age, her attitude was positive and eager.

We learned that the Abbeyfield Society was instituted specifically for people in her situation, those who faced spending their declining years in loneliness, but who weren't ready to give up their independence and rely for all their needs on others. The houses are very much a 'halfway house' between independence and total dependence. Each resident has their own room and, mostly, en suite bathroom, which they furnish and clean themselves. They are provided with basic kitchen facilities where they get their own breakfast and look after the necessary implements. Each room contains an alarm system to call for help, should it be necessary, and this is connected to a call centre in Dumfries during the hours when the housekeeper is not on duty. Thus, each person has 24-hour cover for emergencies. The housekeeper cooks the midday and evening meals, which are taken in the communal dining room with the other residents. These are varied and plentiful and always beautifully cooked and presented. The housekeeper also makes a short morning and evening visit to each resident to check out needs and help with problems. In all other ways the inhabitants act entirely as they would in their own home, coming and going as they please. The more she learned about Abbeyfield, the more Mother became convinced that it would provide an answer for her. She never once uttered any form of regret at having to leave South Yorkshire after living there all her life, but, as the days went by, she began to look forward to this new challenge with its built in security.

Of course, there was just one drawback to her being able to embrace this new found future with complete composure, she would be leaving her sister, now ninety-seven years of age, in the residential home in the village. They had always lived within the boundaries of Doncaster and had visited each other regularly throughout their lives. The relationship wasn't what I would have called close exactly, but was underpinned by family ties and was, therefore, very strong. Ethel had been widowed twice in her life and each time she had relied heavily on my parents for support. As she grew older, she had continued to live alone in the bungalow she had shared with her second husband. Life became more and more of a burden to her, as it does with the elderly, and in 1992 I had taken over responsibility for her and her affairs, visiting every week and overseeing things for her. However, it was the kindness and generosity of one of her neighbours, the local doctor's wife, who called in to see her every morning and generally kept an eye on things, that had really allowed Ethel to remain for so long in her bungalow. Between the two of us, we managed to support her there for a further five years. The time came, though, when it was obvious to us all that Ethel needed more than this and, after a protracted process of liaison with the local Social Services, she eventually moved to the residential home where she now resided. She had been there for almost five years, by this time, and was fully settled and integrated into the home. In spite of her great age, she did not suffer from any illness, but her memory had begun to fail some time before and she had now lost the will to read or occupy herself in any way. She had always been happy in the home and only showed slow deterioration. Mother visited her once a week, and thus they kept up their lifelong connection. The heavy burden of duty which we, and more particularly Mother, felt towards her, now became the one blot on the landscape. I felt I could cope with organising a move north for Mother, if that was what she decided to do, but the thoughts of moving Ethel as well was too mind-blowing to be contemplated with all the other things that I had going on at the time. However, I said that we should sort Mother out first and then, if she moved and settled, I would give my attention to Ethel and see what could be done. Thus, I felt I had done what I could to lift some of the burden for Mother. It would all depend now on the Abbeyfield Society in the Stewartry, and I could do no more for the moment until I got to Low Arvie. I once again emailed Mrs Stanley and made an appointment to meet and discuss the situation with her at Bothwell House, in Castle Douglas, during the first week of our occupancy.

6

Moving In

Even with all this going on in the background, it was with mounting excitement, only just tinged with apprehension, that I followed the bright yellow cover of the trailer that Richard was towing, in my little green car, packed almost to the roof with our first consignment of goods and chattels, as we made our way slowly but steadily north on July 11th 2002. I had very little experience of moving house, only having ever lived in three houses in my life and they were all within three-quarters of a mile of each other, and I was unsure how daunted I ought to be by this gigantic step that we were taking. This last month had seen things move so quickly that I had hardly had time to really worry about anything, only occasionally stopping to wonder at it all.

I was, therefore, quite surprised to find that, between our arrival at 2 p.m. and going to bed that first night around 10.30 p.m., we had managed to change Low Arvie farmhouse from a slightly forlorn and empty building into quite a cosy and comfortable home. The fact that the Esse range had been left working all through the selling process and was still warming the house and the small tank full of water, was in no small measure responsible for some of this; but we had worked hard for the hours we had been there, putting chairs, tables and beds in place and unpacking boxes of the smaller items of home making equipment. My initial visit was to be for a week, as I had things to do back in Yorkshire after that, and it was spent continuing the process of settling in.

The farm that we had first bid on and lost was about twenty miles from Low Arvie. The day we went to look at that one, we were met there by the man who was the executor of the deceased owner's estate, one Jack Macauley. We had liked him from the early moments of our acquaintanceship, and he had proved very helpful on our second visit to look at that farm, helping us to decide what kind of an offer to put in. We had spent quite a while speaking with him on that occasion, and he had given us his card, for if we needed any more information. He worked for a national oil company and, in the course of his work, he visited all the farms in the area. Also, he had had stock of his own on the farm he was selling, so he was cognisant of the farming scene in Galloway. Richard decided to trade on his good nature now we were at Low Arvie and ask his advice about contractors in the area. Jack seemed genuinely pleased to hear from us and also to learn that we had been successful in our second effort to purchase a farm. He told Richard that he would give some thought to our contractor problem and get back to us.

A day or two later he appeared at the door with the telephone number of a Mr Brown, who lived and farmed not far from us and did contract mowing and baling. Jack was on his way to Stranraer but, like everyone around here, had time to come in for a cup of tea and a chat. It was the first of several visits that he made to see the progress we were making. He assured us that Mr Brown was reliable and honest and would sort us out and that he was expecting us to phone him. Accordingly, Richard rang at once.

It was soon arranged that Mr Brown would come and mow our twenty acres of grass and organise the baling and wrapping of the resulting haylage. Now that was sorted out, we could relax a little and concentrate on getting settled in.

I was to be in charge of the 'inside' farm work, which was much more to my liking than the thought of going out into the cold wind and rain to feed animals and mend machinery. I knew there was a lot of paper work connected with farming these days and that there were procedures which had to be followed very strictly. Since it was all new to me, I had decided to start right at the outset working 'on line' with the government department responsible for the administration of British farming. In England this department now goes by the new name of DEFRA: Department for the Environment, Food and Rural Affairs, but in Scotland it is called SEERAD: Scottish Executive, Environment and Rural Affairs Department. Our local office, through which most of our contact would be made, was in Dumfries, and we had called in there to pick forms up to register our ownership of Low Arvie. SEERAD administers Scottish agriculture according to the rules laid down by the European Union, and we have found a number of them to be illogical in concept and unfair in execution. There is a date, May 15th, each year by which every farmer in the land must hand in a form to their local office, stating the nature of their farming activities for that year. The penalty for missing this date is dire: access to European Union subsidies, which keep farming afloat, is lost for that year. Of course, we were unable to comply with this regulation because the farm did not become ours until July 10th. It would be natural to assume that there would be some contingency for farmers who begin farming after May 15th, and that they would have access to some compensatory fund for their first year. It shows how naive we were, when we duly filled in the form and handed it in to the Dumfries office on July 11th. We received a reply from the Principal Agricultural Officer informing us that it did not constitute a claim under any Scheme for 2002, but that they had amended their address list to show that Richard was now the occupier of the farm. However, it added, as it takes a year for their lists to be updated, should we have need for any forms in the meantime, we should go into the office and get them. Having thus discovered that we were 'locked out' of the system for the year through no fault of our own, we began to make enquiries about what we could do.

In the latter part of the twentieth century, European agriculture produced too much of certain foods, and this led to the creation of the 'butter mountain', the 'beef mountain' and the 'wine lake'. So the EU decided to limit the amount that farmers were producing by the use of a subsidy system, which compensated them for producing less. They were paid to take land out of production, and plantations of young trees began to spring up all over the country on this 'set-aside' land. Each farm animal was given a value and people started to talk in 'Livestock Units'. If farmers limited the number of these 'Livestock Units' they had on their land to a certain level, they were again compensated for so doing. A bovine animal above the age of two years has a value of 1 Livestock Unit, and between 6 months and two years a value of 0.6 of a Livestock Unit. Sheep are valued at 0.15. The amount of production required was divided by the acreage of agricultural land, and a national quota thereby created. Farmers were granted portions of this quota according to the amount of grazing land that they owned. Newcomers to farming can apply to a national reserve of this quota, which is strictly administered by DEFRA and SEERAD, and any spare quota is distributed each year in a very regimented fashion. It is also possible to buy quota from farmers who are reducing their numbers but it is very expensive, the remaining alternative being to lease units of quota for one year. Each unit of quota owned or leased, backed up by an animal on the farm, leads to a subsidy payment that year on each animal. The system is highly complicated, and even some of the people in SEERAD seem to have difficulty interpreting the rules.

It appeared that, since we had been unable to get our base form in by May 15th, we would only be allowed to claim subsidy on a maximum of 15 Livestock Units in 2002. This was the number available each year to small farmers with little land and few animals, who did not have to submit the base form. Richard fixed on this number as the beginning of our herd. We, therefore, decided to 'lease in' 15 units of suckler cow quota, and this would mean that we had to get the 15 animals onto the land before the closing date for this scheme, which was December 6th. We now had something to work towards, a framework upon which to pin the beginning of our farming life.

In order to interact with SEERAD and the other Government Departments more efficiently, I had ordered a new computer with plenty of memory and processing ability and a farm business software package already loaded. This was due to arrive on Monday 15th July, and a man was coming to set it up on the following day. These events duly happened, and the little man unpacked the four boxes and fixed up the computer on the table we had put into the smallest room downstairs. This room would have to serve as the 'office' until we could do some building, which we hoped would be as soon as possible. As soon as the man switched the computer on, I knew something was not quite right. He had told me that the disc, with the Internet connections on, had already been programmed with my name, but when it started, it came up with an entirely different name. I said to the man that surely that was not correct, and he immediately changed his story and said, "Oh, that's just for demonstration purposes!" He proceeded to change the name to mine and attempted to get the programme started. Nothing would work properly, and it soon became obvious that the man had no more idea than me how to make it right. He pressed buttons and typed different things in and, when he had eventually got an email screen, he said, "It'll be ok now," and hurriedly left.

Suffice to say that it wasn't! Every time I logged on it was calling me Mr Webster, and neither the internet nor the email worked correctly and, when I attempted to get into the farm programme, the pass number I had been given didn't work at all. It was clear that I had been sent the wrong computer. I contacted the company, and, very soon, they verified that my computer had been sent to a Mr Webster in Cheshire and I had his. Fortunately for me his little man hadn't yet been, and they were able to prevent it from being opened and corrupted; it could simply be collected and re-delivered to me. Poor Mr Webster, however, would have to wait for the computer I had to be collected, sent back to the company and re-programmed. My computer arrived on the Saturday, but then I had to wait until the following Wednesday for the same little man to come and start all over again. I was very worried because I had no confidence that he knew what he was doing, but, fortunately, things went better this time and my name came up and my pass number worked. However, I was disappointed to find that the Internet was no faster than my previous computer, in spite of all the extra gigabytes and pixels or whatever I had bought, because, of course, out here in the sticks, our telephone exchange is the one that Noah used to order the wood for the ark, and an internet connection is only as good as the telephone line that operates it. Nevertheless, it was one more step along the way and, at least, I felt in touch with the world once again.

7

Bothwell House

Our visit to Bothwell House took place during this first week of occupancy. We were invited to go for morning coffee and meet with Mrs Stanley and the house keeper, whose name is Norma. We drew up outside the large, white, double-fronted house and sat, for a moment or two, taking in the surroundings. The road led out from the town centre towards the village of Auchencairn and the Solway Coast. The houses that bordered the right hand side of the road were town houses fronting directly onto the pavement, whilst on the other side they had fairly long front gardens. On both sides the houses were big and well cared for. Next door to Bothwell House stood a new church hall and adjoining that was a small church. The sign said that it was Episcopalian in denomination, and I had discovered that that was the nearest in spirit to the Anglican Church that Mother belonged to. Here was a very good sign: she would be able to walk there under her own steam, instead of relying on others to take her, as she had to do now. We read the sign on Bothwell House door and complied with the instructions to press the 'clear' button and then 'call' and we heard a brrr brrr ringing inside, letting someone know we were there. Suddenly, the buzzing stopped, to be replaced by a high-pitched peep peep, and the door clicked open. We entered the entrance hall and were immediately impressed by the ambience created by the elegant furnishings and the tall clear window in front of us, filling the place with sunshine. A dark-haired lady appeared from the right hand hallway and introduced herself as Ivy Stanley. After we had introduced ourselves and shaken hands, she led us along the hallway into a very large and yet more elegantly furnished room. Near the door stood an oval table, large enough to seat ten or twelve people easily. There was a sideboard to one side, and the walls were hung with many pictures. At the far end, where a large window looked out onto the broad, lawned garden, the Carlingwark Loch could be seen glistening in the sun beyond the garden wall, on which several white doves hopped around and flew periodically into their cote.

A second lady came into the room carrying a tray on which were four cups, a coffee pot and cream jug and a plate of biscuits. We sat down by the window and as we drank our coffee, Ivy explained all about Abbeyfield in the Stewartry. The four homes were run under the same 'umbrella', but each one had its own committee of voluntary ladies who administered their own particular house. The three sheltered houses were situated here in Castle Douglas, in Kirkcudbright about ten miles away and one in Gatehouse of Fleet, which was about 20 miles away. The fourth, which was the residential care home, was in Dalbeattie, about six miles to the east. The three houses had rooms for seven or eight residents, each with a housekeeper who lived very near or, as here in Castle Douglas, in a separate flat in the same building. A relief housekeeper came two days a week and stayed overnight in a room that doubled as a single guestroom, when she didn't require it. There were also ancillary staff members who came in part time to clean and do the laundry. Bed linen and towels were laundered weekly by the house but personal washing and cleaning of the resident's room was their own responsibility.

Finishing our coffee, we went to look around the rest of the house. Work was being carried out to convert three rooms into two en suite ones and this was still very much in progress. Because of this, the residents were being moved around to other rooms at the moment and this was why Ivy couldn't tell me whether there was a place available or not and, if not, when it was likely that there would be. She assured me that she would place Mother on the waiting list, which in any case was quite short! The only room that we could see on this trip was the one that the relief housekeeper was using on the first floor and, as we climbed the stairs, I noticed the stair lift running alongside. The room was about four metres square, with one corner walled off to provide en suite toilet and washbasin facilities. There was no bath or shower in this particular room but there was one of each located just along the landing, which was shared with the two other rooms on this floor. Just next door to the room itself was a small kitchen containing fridge, kettle and toaster, a sink and table and chairs in one corner. This was also a shared facility where breakfast was prepared. The room itself contained a single bed, wardrobe, a set of drawers, a reclining chair and two small tables, one housing a television. The room was comfortably full with these items, though not cluttered, and, with Mother's main requirements at this stage in her life being her bookcase, reclining chair and television, we could see that she would probably feel that this was adequate. The furnishings were all in very good condition, and everywhere was spotlessly clean. Furthermore, there was a very good atmosphere in the whole place. I told Ivy that I was almost certain that Mother would like to come, and she promised to put her name down on the waiting list. I said that Bothwell House would be the preferred choice but that any of the houses would be fine, while she was waiting for a room to be available here. The system gave opportunity for the resident to go and stay in the house for a four week 'probationary' period, where both sides would make up their minds about each other, and, at the end of that time, the decision would be taken about future permanence. We all felt that this was a very necessary benefit for everyone contemplating such a move, but more particularly so for Mother, when it meant total upheaval at such an advanced age. Ivy said that as soon as she received Mother's application form, she would add her name to the waiting list at Castle Douglas and she would be in touch by email with me the moment she had news of a vacancy anywhere within the three Stewartry houses.

We left, feeling that this was indeed going to provide a perfect solution. Castle Douglas is ten and a quarter miles from Low Arvie and is our nearest town. The only other shops nearer to us are both about seven miles away anyway, so it would be easy for me to make Castle Douglas my main shopping place and call in to Bothwell House at the same time. I could see that the whole system of Bothwell House, the people who administered it and those who worked there, would provide Mother with everything that she required, and, as far as I could see, there were no snags or drawbacks. I could not wait to get back to Yorkshire the next day and tell her all about it.

She was still very positive about the whole idea and, although she must have had the same misgivings as I had about leaving South Yorkshire, she never once showed them. We discussed the whole situation over and over again and we always came up with the same conclusion. She was delighted that we should want her to come and be near us, she was as sure as she could be without seeing the property that she would like it, and, above all, she was relieved that she didn't have to face the rest of her life living alone.

I had hardly had time to do anything other than have a cup of tea on my arrival home than Mother was telling me to get the application form and "Let's have it filled in!" With no more ado, I did just that, and we sat together answering the questions about health, reasons for wishing to join Abbeyfield and religion. As soon as it was done, Mother was out of her chair and putting on her coat. The post box was just within walking distance for her deteriorating leg muscles and, whilst I sat back to catch my breath, she was off 'double-sticking' her walking stick up the road to post the form.

8

Making Haylage

The day after my second computer had been delivered, Mr Drew Brown had come to Low Arvie and mowed our haylage fields for us. I had been down in Yorkshire at that time and so wasn't able to meet him until he called again to make arrangements to come and bale the drying grass. His farm is larger than Low Arvie and is about three miles away on the other side of the village. Drew has proved to be a good friend to us since we have been here, helping us with advice, and allowing Richard to borrow equipment from time to time. We were very pleased to be getting the grass mowed and dried without it being rained on, as Drew said that another local farmer, Tom Corsan (of Arvie), would come the next afternoon to 'row up'. Drew and his team of baler and carters would be along in the evening to complete the job. The 'rowing up' was necessary as the grass had had no fertiliser that spring and was, therefore, not as lush as it could have been. Drew's mowing had left the cut grass in long, narrow lines snaking around the fields, and he said it would be a good idea to add three of these lines together to make the baling quicker and more efficient. This was the 'rowing up' which young Tom Corsan was to do. It is necessary to specify 'young' Tom Corsan because there is also 'Father' Tom and 'wee' Tom. They are the current 'Toms' in a long line of six or seven generations of Tom Corsans who have lived at Arvie Farm. Young Tom, who is son of Father Tom and father of wee Tom, lives with his wife, Linda, wee Tom and younger son, Ross, in a house just out of the village, while Father Tom and 'Mother' Ibby inhabit Arvie Farmhouse.

Duly around three o' clock the next afternoon, I was sitting at the table in the small 'office' just getting to know my computer, which had been fixed up that morning, when I first of all heard and then saw a red tractor go past the window and stop. Going out to greet the driver, I found a young, good-looking man seated in the cab and I saw that he had the hay turner attachment fixed to the back of the tractor. The man smiled shyly and introduced himself as "Tom Corsan, come to 'row up'." Richard appeared around the corner to speak to him and, having said 'Hello', I returned to my computing. Later I went out to watch, as Tom worked away up and down the rows of grass. He went one way up the field turning the first row onto the second and then went back the other way turning the third row on top of them. Up and down he went until all the rows had been stacked in threes ready for the baler.

We were just finishing our evening meal, when we heard more tractor noises coming into the yard, and young Dougie Brown, Drew's eldest son drove up with his baler. After speaking with Richard for a minute or two he went off into the fields and began to drive up and down Tom's rows, 'eating up' the grass and stopping briefly every now and again to drop off the large round bales into which the grass had been rolled. When the bale was complete the baler wound three or four layers of stretchy nylon 'net wrap' netting tightly around it, before opening up to let the bale roll into the field.

Soon, there was a further sound of engines and machinery coming up the track into the yard, and four more tractors appeared, the first three with long prong like appendages attached to the front, and the fourth towing the bale wrapping machine. Drew was driving this last and he dismounted to introduce us to the three tractor drivers. They were his younger son, Peter, and another local farmer, David Porteous and his son, Colin. There was no time for more than the usual pleasantries, and the three tractors with the front spikes were soon plying back and forth, spiking the bales which Dougie had made and carrying them back to In-bye field, where Drew got to work with the wrapper. The weather had held so far, and we watched with mounting relief and pleasure as Drew worked steadily up and down the row of green, net wrapped bales, which the three tractors placed in just the correct position for him. It was fascinating to watch as each one was lifted onto the machine's bed and then whirled round and round, each turn covering a fresh section of green with shiny black plastic, until there was no green left. The machine then stopped whirling, and the bale was released back onto the field, before the next one was lifted on, and the process begun again. At the end of three hours non-stop work by the five men, there were one hundred and four large, and one small, shiny black parcels of winter feed neatly arranged in the field.

Because we were only planning to have fifteen head of cattle that first year, Richard and Drew had worked out that fifty bales would be enough to see us through the winter, and we had agreed to sell the remaining bales to David Porteous. The next day, Colin came and took them away, whilst Peter Brown came and stacked our fifty neatly, in the compound near to the large cattle shed, to 'pickle' away over the remainder of the summer, ready for use when the time came. The chemistry of the process depends on all the air being removed from the grass, hence the tight wrapping of plastic, and then, in these anaerobic conditions, bacteria get to work preserving the dry matter in the grass, and with it, as much nutritional value as possible. The best haylage requires making before the flowers of the grass turn to seeds, and we were too late for that this year, but, nevertheless, it was a reasonably good product, when we eventually began to use it.

This dealt very nicely with the 'Improved grassland' and it looked neat and tidy now that it had been cut, but the 'Rough Grazing' land was looking decidedly sorry for itself, with the long fronds of grass waving in the wind. It all looked very unkempt and uncared for. Once again, Drew Brown was able to suggest a solution. Since we weren't able to put our own cattle on the land until much later in the year, he and David Porteous would rent the grazing and bring some of their own herds onto the land. Over the next few days, twenty-six cows with their calves arrived on the field at the west end of the farm, which we had now called Aunchenvey after the Wilson's farm that adjoined it. They set to with a will to eat down the grass that had not seen a cow for the previous few months. David brought twenty-five young stock and loosed them into Eastside, the field at the east end of the farm. Very soon that land, too, began to take on a neat and tidy appearance. These cattle stayed on our land right through to September, when the grass growth began to slow, and both Drew and David came regularly to check that they were all right. Although, of course, we saw the cattle and sometimes watched them for a while, Richard was not allowed to perform any official duties as stockman, because he was registering his business with the VAT office and, if you perform a service for someone, then you must charge VAT. He could rent out the grazing—in effect he would be selling the grass—and this would be classed as a tax-exempt sale. The whole process did everyone a favour, as the two men got some good extra grazing for their cattle, and Richard was able to provide the VAT office with concrete proof of trading as a farmer, in the form of the invoices he sent to Drew and David.

The other incidental benefit to this process was that we saw a lot of them and got to know them quite well, over the course of the summer. Drew usually came very early in the morning to see his stock, and sometimes we were still in bed when we heard his car draw into the yard. Other times, we would be able to have a few words with him, either as he set off, or on his return. David mostly came in the evenings, when his day's work was over. His wife, Kathy, worked some evenings in the local hotel, and so David had much more time to spend with us. He would come in and sit at the table over a mug of tea, and we enjoyed getting to know him and hearing the things he told us of the region that was now our home. I was quite sad when the time came for the cattle to go home and hoped that we could continue our friendship with David and Drew.

9

Land, Garden and Rubbish

We had some friends in the locality, met whilst we were all house hunting in the area and staying in the same Bed and Breakfast establishment the previous November. They had been moving from London and required a bungalow, thus their search had been a little easier than ours, and they had moved to Hightae, a village about 30 miles from Low Arvie, the previous April. We had kept in touch for the intervening time, and, when they came over to make their first visit to 'inspect' the farm three days after we moved in, things were fairly well organised, and we were able to spend the afternoon walking with them over some of our land. This was my first look at the further points of the farm and, although the grass was high and the going rough in places due to long years of neglect, I could hardly believe that all this natural beauty was ours. We walked down to where the burn formed our boundary with the Forestry Commission land along the north-western edge, and there we found beautiful water lilies floating on the clear brown water that babbled and gurgled over rocks and stones. We walked across the Bog of Allan, and I began to realise that not only had we bought a farm, but it was also a ready made nature reserve. With the movement away from productive farming to farming for the environment that is prevalent in this twenty-first century, this farm was tailor made for the new agri-schemes that people were talking about.

I made a mental note of the plants that I saw and, when I had a spare moment, I began a diary of flowers, birds and animals that I have seen on the land or in the skies over it. The list is still growing, as each year I find more and more to add. Among the many treasures we have, are ragged robin, several species of wild orchid, both colours of loosestrife and the delicate marsh violet and pink purslane. The burn is decorated at various times of the year, not only with lilies, but mimulus and water violet, and we always know that spring is on its way, when the pale mauve flowers of lady's smock and the bright golden ones of marsh marigold begin to peep out from between the rushes.

In the Bog, heather and Erica, bog asphodel, heath bedstraw, milkwort and bog myrtle all flourish amongst the wetter patches of sphagnum and dicranium. Down there, also, we found several areas where the peat had been cut to provide winter fuel in years past, and I was pleased that things had moved on, and our fuel was now delivered by tanker! However, I did cast a slightly envious backward glance at those days, remembering the sweet smell of burning peat, that filled the evening air, on my visits to the Outer Islands, and just for a second, wondered if…

At the eastern end of the Bog, we found one of the many drains, which cross the land, flowing quite freely into the burn. This was the main drain into which all the others flow, and there was a fair volume of water coming down it, keeping this one open when so many of the others had ceased flowing and become clogged with the roots of the rushes. It was possible to trace the course of these drains by the lines of rush that grew so profusely in straight lines all over the low-lying land, and this was where we would start to improve the land, by clearing the rushes and letting the water drain away. It would take a very long time to achieve this in all hundred and twenty acres, but we had decided to make a start in the garden in front of the house and work outwards from there.

At the moment, the garden was indistinguishable from the fields. Where the level was above the water table, it was knee high in grass, and where the land fell sharply away towards the road, there were nettles and rosebay willow herb, in abundance. Lower still, in the last four or five metres this side of the fence, grew the ubiquitous rush. The land there was waterlogged and, for the moment, impenetrable. Just the other side of the fence was one of the clogged up drains, where the water merely glistened stilly amongst the needle-like stems of rushes, instead of flowing swiftly away to meet the drain to the burn. This was why the land on either side for several metres, including the end of the garden, was so very waterlogged. When it rained, the water just spread out over the surface of the peat and stayed until the next shower joined it.

To give life to the wilderness that was the garden in the early days, we bought and put up several bird feeders. Almost immediately these attracted flocks of small birds. Chaffinches vied with great tits and blue tits to get a free meal. Gradually, other species joined them, and, soon, we had quite a variety to watch from the kitchen window. Bright yellow siskins are regular visitors, along with the great spotted woodpecker, and both these add to the colour of the scene. We have a regular resident in Philip the pheasant, who, with his cohort of females, patrols the garden under the feeders, waiting for the crumbs that the other birds let fall. To date, forty seven different species of birds have been seen through this one window of the farmhouse, probably the most exciting of which was a female hen harrier hawking stealthily along about six feet above the rushes, between here and the road. Among small visitors have been tree creeper, reed bunting and long tail tits, black caps, bullfinches and fly catchers, wheatear, stonechat and grey wagtail. Winter visitors included redwing, Mistle thrushes and, one day, a sparrow hawk graced us with his presence in the tree outside the window. Barney the Owl lives quite happily alongside us in the granary store at the far side of the farmyard, and we see him regularly fly out at dusk to begin his night's work, just as we are finishing ours.

One dark evening before the end of the winter, Richard came into the house to fetch me to the workshop, where an owl had blundered in, in the fading light. Richard had turned on the light, when he went in for something, and found him, blinking hard and very disorientated, sitting on a high shelf. I looked at him in quiet excitement and saw sticking up, above each of his eyes, a tuft of orange brown feathers. He was sitting upright on the shelf, and these tufts gave the appearance of extreme alarm. Of course, I had no idea where to find my camera and, as he was becoming extremely agitated, I did not feel inclined to prolong his discomfiture, and so we switched off the light and stood back. Immediately reorientated and in his own element once again, he located the door with unerring accuracy and, swooping low once over our heads as if in thanks, he disappeared on silent wings into the night. Checking in the bird books later, I discovered we had had our first sight of a long-eared owl. The book says his call is like that of a tawny owl, the familiar to-wit to-whoo sound, only more haunting, and we often hear such a sound in the night. I cannot be sure, though, whether this is Tufty or not, as we also see a tawny owl perching on the electricity pole outside the bedroom window just after dusk.

In order to follow our plan to start at the house and work outwards, one of the necessities for the first load to be brought up from Yorkshire had been the ride-on lawn mower we had bought two seasons before. It had the ability to leave the cut grass anything from one to six inches long; and the second evening of our occupation saw Richard cutting the level area of lawn to a six-inch length. It was slow going, but a tribute to the mower that he was successful, and the view from the window was much improved. There was a row of small conifers, in the middle of this patch of grass, that were browning and unattractive, so we pulled those out and felt satisfied that we had, at least, made a start. It took most of the summer to work our way through the rest of the garden, which is about thirty metres wide by about the same deep and diamond in shape, but, slowly, we cut the grass and weeds down to size. I unearthed several flowering plants down the wall side, which had been completely invisible when we arrived. The main culprit in covering these was a thick carpet of green moss that spread outwards from the wall. It was growing to a thickness of four to six inches in most places and a lot of it just lifted off the top of the ground. The ground sloped upwards for about one metre from the level surface of the lawn to meet the wall, and it was here that the moss was thickest and here that I found the few flowering plants that there were in the garden. I have continued to build this strip as a kind of poor man's herbaceous border, pushing in the few plants I brought from the south. Some of them have at least survived, and I intend to continue to add to them over time. The main body of the lawn has several levels, possibly due to the contours of underlying rock that has been covered over, and our aim is to try and grade this more evenly down to the fence at the bottom and leave it as lawn. I am purposely using the word lawn instead of grass, as I find the myriad plants that make up the sward to be attractive and I would like to keep them. Also, as the year progresses—we are now in May—I am finding a similar attraction in the wetland down by the fence. I am fighting a running battle with the nettles, rush and Rosebay and I think I am winning at the moment. I know from experience that nettles give up the fight fairly easily if one is persistent, but I have still to learn about the other two. I suspect they may be more tenacious! This is allowing other, more attractive wild flowers to establish themselves, and we now have kingcups, several ferns and meadow sweet appearing down there. In the centre of this area rise two or three rowan trees, and, around the eastern edge, grow willow bushes, and, together, these give a framework, in which the smaller plants fill the centre. I shall see how things progress before making final decisions about this area.

The west side of the garden houses a copse of small trees, mainly blackthorn and damson, and, beneath these, grows a tangle of bramble and nettles. Every few days I attacked a different part of the garden, pulling out nettles and Rosebay willow herb by the hundred, some much taller than me, but I decided to leave the little wood alone and let it do what it would. Eventually, by our first winter, I had cleared the whole garden, except for this wood, and, although I am no Alan Titchmarsh, at least it now looks tidy, and the lawn, though made up of moss and sedge, buttercup and dandelion, lady's smock and daisy and very little actual grass, is green and short. We were pleased to find a huge patch of snowdrop and daffodil on the slope this spring, and they last much longer here than down in Yorkshire, as the spring is much slower to get going and the summer much shorter.

At the northern end of the wooded section, there was a large patch of Rosebay willow herb and, one day, I attacked this with vigour, pulling up the plants and throwing them onto the grass, where Richard was scooping them up and carting them off to the bonfire. There were hundreds of them, and it was a very therapeutic exercise to grab the wretched things and wrench them out of the earth. Slowly, I uncovered an inlet into the wood of about ten square yards. Between this inlet and the house, there grew some weedy damson trees, and, fetching his chain saw, Richard began to thin these out, leaving the sturdier ones with air around them, in the hope that they would bear fruit (so far forlorn). As we worked away clearing this space, I became aware that, every now and again, there was a glass bottle lying among the roots of the Rosebay. Rather than being an odd one, they were increasing in number the nearer I got to the wall, which was the boundary of the garden and the farmyard. As I cleared the last of the long green stems away, I saw why I was finding bottles. About five metres from the house wall, previously hidden by the damson trees and the Rosebay, was a mound of household waste. The mound was about three yards across and probably two yards deep. Its height was unfathomable, as the land undulated here and there, but it was level with the top of the wall. We had cleared half of its perimeter, and the other half was screened by tall and spindly snowberry bushes. Previous occupants, apparently, came from the house and threw empty bottles, tins of all kinds and other rubbish literally over the garden wall! I suppose it was because there were no dustbin collections in the country in those days, and this appeared to be all the things that wouldn't burn. Tins would be put in the range oven to burn off all the food remnants, and bottles would be washed clean, in order not to attract unwelcome wildlife, and then this inaccessible corner of the garden used to house the waste.

"Goodness me," I said to Richard, "The next fine afternoon, we have to come here and clear all this lot up!" To date, we have filled forty-three fertiliser sacks with the contents of this heap, and processed them six a week in the wheelie bin. At a rough estimate, we have cleared perhaps a quarter of it. We have found lemonade bottles, such as we knew in our youth, with the black and orange rubber stopper, by the dozen, and can only assume that this has been the family rubbish heap for sixty or more years—perhaps even longer than that. We are still working away each week, filling our six sacks. Richard is shovelling the contents straight into the sack now, as it is all solid tin or glass with occasional plastic toys and washing up liquid containers (remember Squezy?) mixed in. The snowberry bushes were not in front of the pile, as I had first thought, but are actually growing through it, their roots and lower branches deformedly cradling jam jars, shampoo bottles and china cups and plates. Most of the jars and bottles have been broken, and there are sharp shards of glass all around. We will never be able to get every piece up, but when we have cleared the heap, we shall cover the surface with a layer of topsoil and grass it over for safety. I have grave suspicions that some of the undulations may be other, older rubbish heaps but I don't intend to find out!

So much for my fine afternoon's work!

10

Electrics and Plans

The first weeks that we were at Low Arvie were naturally very busy. Getting the haylage harvested so easily was a huge bonus to us, instead of the major worry that it had promised to be, and it left us time to get other projects under way. The electrical system in the house was obviously quite old, and, as there was no central heating, the single socket in each of the bedrooms and the lounge promised to be inadequate for our needs, if not now, then certainly when the weather began to turn colder. Although we had formulated plans to extend the house and put in heating, we were aware that this would take time, as planning permission would be needed, and, fortunately, at this stage we had no idea just how difficult this would prove to be. We decided to have the electrics overhauled and extra sockets put in, at least upstairs, so that we could have additional warmth when necessary. We reasoned that downstairs was quite well catered for, with the Esse a permanent source of heat in the kitchen, and, when we got the fireplace operating in the lounge, that would help the overall temperature in the rest of the house, as well as providing a cosy venue for our winter evenings. When we arrived, this last housed an electric fire, but, with the large supply of free wood around the farm, we would soon remove it and re-instate the log fires that we were accustomed to.

I arranged for two local firms to come and give us quotes for the electrical work, and, with just a hint of the lackadaisicalness that we have found to be so prevalent in Dumfries and Galloway, managed to get their quotes at only the second time of asking. We arranged for Paul Mitchell to send his workman, whose name was Rob, on September 23rd. This was four weeks ahead and, as Paul had been vacillating about how long present jobs would take and telling me it could be ten days or it might be twelve days, I felt that a firm commitment, so far in advance, was by far the best way to arrange things for both of us. Nothing, I felt, could go wrong! We were to have a panel heater and several sockets fitted in each of the bedrooms, wiring for towel rail, shower and wall heater put into the bathroom ready for the extension work, and a new circuit board downstairs. The original wiring in the downstairs rooms would be checked for safety, but the work required here would wait until the extension.

The Friday before the work was due to begin, I debated with myself whether to ring Mitchell's and check that all was well for the Monday. In the end I decided that, having made such a firm arrangement with Paul, all would be well, and that it would look like paranoia if I phoned, and so I left it. I know better now! On the morning of Monday 23rd September, we got up early and moved all the furniture we could out of the way, took up carpets and generally prepared for the electrician to start work when he arrived. We had breakfast and Richard went off to work outside, whilst I cleared away the pots and waited...and waited...and waited.

When the clock got round to 9 a.m. and still no workman, I could stand it no longer and rang the firm's headquarters in Castle Douglas. The lady on the other end of the line had clearly never heard of Low Arvie and the work that was waiting here. It was plain from her prevarications that the workmen had all gone off to their specified jobs for the day, and she had no idea what to do. She was Paul's aunt and was only in the office temporarily, she said, as Paul's wife had just returned home the previous day from the hospital with a new baby, and Paul was having a few days off to settle the newcomer in. She also said that he had turned off all telephones in his house, and was, thus, incommunicado. Begging me to 'bear with her', she rang off to see what she should do.

It was not long, however, before she rang back, full of apologies and told me that they would have someone out to do the work by 11 a.m. They were as good as their word and Rob appeared just on 11. He turned out to be an excellent workman, who did a very good job, and, by the end of the week, we had bedrooms equipped for the use of clocks, hairdryer and electric blankets, and the chilliness of the autumn evenings could be taken off by the two smart new heaters on the walls under the windows. Downstairs the new circuit board catered for this new loading, and we felt the wiring in the house was safe.

At the same time as this was going on, we were making enquiries into people who could draw up the plans we needed for the large extension we planned. We had worked out what we thought was a good idea for the house, making it convenient for us and large enough to house our guests in the present bedrooms with the bathroom for their own private use. This entailed practically doubling the size of the house, building what almost amounted to a second house at right angles to the original. I would have the large farmhouse kitchen that I had so longed for, with living room space at the far end, and we would have bedroom, bathroom and dressing area for our own use above. We planned to build this at conventional height, so that Richard would not bump his head on the coombs as he did now, and to place new water tanks in the roof space to give enough head of water to run showers, which was impossible at the moment, and fill the toilets at normal speed. The upstairs of this new part would not be connected to the upstairs of the old house, thus keeping both guests' apartments and ours' private. At the moment we were unable to accommodate any overnight guests, as the second bedroom was used as storage space for all our accoutrements that did not fit into the rest of the house. We were trying to keep this as uncluttered as possible, just setting out what was essential for daily use. We knew that we would have to live in the house as it was for quite a long time, before the new part could be built, and we had enough furniture to furnish the new part as well as the old. This needed to be stored for the duration, and, what was not needed at the moment and would not deteriorate, was presently cluttering up Richard's workshop, but the rest had to be accommodated in the house.

We planned to link the old house to the new part along the back of the house, making the old wet kitchen into a 'boot' room for wet coats, wellies and dirty farm clothing, if possible leaving the sink, washing machine and dishwasher that were already installed for farm use. The central heating boiler would be housed in here and the far end would become a toilet with washbasin. The 'dry' kitchen would become office space and the small room that we used as an office now would be knocked through into the lounge area and house bookshelves for all, or if I had my way, the more useful of Richard's many books. The link between the 'boot' room and the new kitchen/living room would be useful space for freezers and tumble dryer. At the front, our idea was to knock the small porch off and replace it with a larger conservatory—another dream of mine—and join this to the living room end of the new kitchen. Thus, we could close off the original upstairs, when we had guests giving them a large area to themselves—two rooms and bathroom—and this would be ideal as Bed and Breakfast accommodation, if we decided to do that at some point in the future. We realised that it was an ambitious plan and would be expensive, but decided to go ahead with the plans and costing and then see how we could reduce it, if we needed to.

Exactly two weeks after moving in, we opened the door to another Rob, the surveyor, and, welcoming him in and providing tea and cake, we told him of our idea. I wonder now if we would have started this, if we had known how difficult and long the process was to be. Ten months after that first surveyor's visit, we were still waiting for the Building Warrant, which grants consent for the work to begin, and it looked like being some months more before a start could be made.

We had had to alter our idea considerably along the way. We had several specimen plans drawn up before we got what we wanted, and then, just as they were about to be presented, Rob spoke with the planning officer 'off the record' and was told that no way could the new part be higher than the old part, no way could we build in front of the original building line and no way could we have a large conservatory on the front of the house. We wondered why Rob had allowed us to go down this line for so long, without finding these things out first. Anyway, the size of the new build was reduced to conform to these specifications, and Richard would just have to learn not to bump his head! In general, we were still be able to have the conformation that we first planned.

At the same time as Rob applied for the building warrant, he put the specifications and plans out to four builders, all of whom expressed their interest in the project. We didn't know any builders in the area and could find nobody who would recommend one, so we were once again in Rob's hands, except for one that we could offer. When we had bid on the first farm that we didn't get, we had driven into the nearest village, Thornhill, and had seen a small cottage being renovated. Over the course of our two or three visits, we had watched the progress and decided that the work was being well done. The name on the van parked outside was A. McMeekin, and we had written this down with the accompanying telephone number. We now gave this to Rob as our only offering. Rob thought that we should get six quotes, and we left it to him to find the other five. A week later, he got back to us, saying that he had found only four builders who wanted to quote, but these were all keen to get the work. He had given them the deadline of 12 o'clock on March 24th to have their quotes here to us. This was five weeks away. Two weeks later we had a visit from John Donnelly of Cornerstone Builders in Dumfries. He had been asked to quote for the building work by one of the four, Alex Campbell of Kirkcudbright, who was a joiner and needed to get quotes from plumber, builder and electrician to make up his final offering. Two other people visited from Robison and Davidson, another local building firm, but we saw no one from the remaining two. Just before the deadline, we received an email from Rob saying that Robison and Davidson had asked for a further week to get their quote in, and he had agreed.

At 11.40 a.m. on March 24th the postman brought one large brown envelope, which proved to be the quotation from Alex Campbell of Kirkcudbright. It was satisfactorily presented, with each workman giving his quote for the work, but the joinery work to be done by Alex himself was only an estimate! We felt we really needed to know how much the work was going to be. However, as he had been the only one of the four to get his quote in on time, we felt very kindly disposed towards him. As 12 o'clock passed, we received no more quotations that day.

The next day an orange and black van drew into the farmyard, and a young man presented us with another envelope, which Richard opened. He extracted from it a single sheet of paper with a large amount of money written on it. There was no breakdown and no detail of any kind. This was the offering of the Trades Team, a firm amalgamated from local joiners, electricians, plumbers and builders, all working together. We began to quiz the man about the figure written on the paper. Yes, it was a quotation for the work, but that was all he could tell us. It was obvious that he was only the postman for the quote and knew nothing about it. He went away promising to return the next day, with more information about what was included. We are still waiting!

Ten days later we heard again from Rob. Robison and Davidson begged to be excused from quoting due to pressure of work. Not one word had been heard from Mr McMeekin of Thornhill, although Rob said he had been very keen to quote for the work when he had spoken to him. After ringing him three or four times and getting no reply, I was eventually able to speak to him, and he assured me that the quote was coming. On being asked when, he replied, "About a week!" I spoke to him again about three weeks later, and he said he was still working on the quote, and it would be in the post. Since we are now in mid-May and have still heard nothing, even if, by the remotest chance, he did come up with something, I don't think we would be inclined to go with him. I like to be able to trust the word of people who are going to work for me.

In the end, none of these people built the extension. It took several months for us to get the building warrant, and, during this time, we heard of another builder who may be interested in the work. The building control people asked for several changes to the original plans, and, when these were drawn up, they were sent out to Mr Campbell of Kirkcudbright and, also, to the new builder who had expressed a willingness to quote. His name is Andy Harrison and he had shown himself to be much keener than any of the previous people. Within a week of hearing about the work, he had made three visits to us, one to discuss the work in general terms and twice with joiner, Alan McMorran, plumber Alan McCaig and electrician, Kenny McBride, to go through the fine detail of each section of the job. Within two weeks of receiving the new plans, he came again and brought us his quote, spending time with us going through the details. We waited for the deadline that Rob had given to Mr Campbell to pass, and, when we heard nothing from him, I rang Andy and told him to begin the work as soon as he could. Obviously, he had ongoing work to finish first, but mid-September saw him arriving with his lad to begin the work. Because all his 'gang' are small firms, it has taken longer to do the work than a big firm would. Three months down the line we have the shell completed but nothing done inside, however, we are very pleased with everything that Andy has done, and I am sure that by next winter we shall be in a much more comfortable building.

11

Kirkcudbright

One day towards the end of July, I was busy getting the office space organised, when the phone rang. It was Ivy Stanley calling to tell me that they had just had a meeting of the Abbeyfield Society Committee and they had identified a vacancy in the Kirkcudbright House. She was happy to offer it to my mother, if she wanted it, until a room should become vacant in Castle Douglas. Ivy still had no idea when this might be, as the work was still going on in Bothwell House, and they wouldn't be able to sort anything out there until this was finished. She suggested that if Mother wanted to take the Kirkcudbright room, she should come up on 21st August for a four-week trial period. This was for the benefit of both parties, to see if the arrangement was suitable. It was, after all, community living, and there has to be a degree of fitting in, if life is to be of a reasonable quality for all concerned. Ivy said there was no hurry to decide, and Mother should think about it carefully. We were all aware that it was a huge decision for her to have to make at 90 years of age.

Richard and I had planned to make a trip back to Yorkshire for another load of furniture the next weekend, and I decided not to tell Mother of the offer until I was with her in person, so that it could be discussed properly, and I would be there to support her through the decision making process. Her hearing was not very good on the telephone, and I did not want her to have additional worries of mishearing and forgetting what I had said. It was something that she had to decide for herself, without persuasion or coercion from anyone, and she needed to be clear about the options. For this reason, we had decided not to say anything to my brothers either, until the decision was made one way or the other. I did not know what they would say about it, but Mother was capable of being swayed on occasions, and I didn't want any body else's opinion to make her mind up for her. I saw this move as one possible solution to our problem, but I knew that it was not my decision and I tried to be as impartial as I could, in putting the pros and cons to her.

When I got back to Yorkshire that weekend, I found that she had been talking to a few people in the village about the plan. Some of them were very positive, some were urging caution and some were downright against. However, I found that Mother was still as positive as ever, and her answer to those who were against never altered. She was going and that was that. And so I told her the news. She had just three weeks left to wait before the big move to Scotland. Naturally enough, now that it was a reality, it was at this point that her mind began to waiver a little. I had been unable to get into the Kirkcudbright house and so couldn't tell her about the room she would be moving into. I had run over one afternoon, but there had been no reply to my knock. I had walked around the outside and looked through as many windows as I could and I described what I had seen to her. It was a large double fronted house, with a pleasant garden in front, where there were benches for sitting outside, and there was a largish back garden. What I had been able to see of the rooms looked very similar to Bothwell House in Castle Douglas, but the downside to this house was that it was situated on the main road into the town, which was very busy, and there was nowhere pleasant to walk. Mother had got into the habit of taking a daily walk to keep the weakness she was experiencing in her leg muscles from getting worse, and this would not be terribly interesting from the Kirkcudbright house. The alternative was to wait for a room to come available in Castle Douglas, which I was almost certain she would like very much. I left her to think over these things for a while. At twenty miles, it was also twice as far from Low Arvie to Kirkcudbright than to Castle Douglas, but as it would only be short term, I didn't think this mattered too much. It would not really make any difference to Mother, but just make my journeys to see her longer.

When I returned, she said that she was going to come to Kirkcudbright. After all, it was for a four-week trial and, if she was unhappy, she could always return to Yorkshire until there was space in Castle Douglas. She was very unhappy about staying in the village, so far away from me, and coming north would solve this major problem.

Whilst I was down in Yorkshire, I helped her to make all the necessary arrangements for her departure, letting the social services know that she wouldn't need her care call or the frozen meals after the 21st. Ivy had said that the room would be furnished by Abbeyfield for the four-week period, but Mother had to decide which of her own things she would want to take if she stayed. She said that she thought she wouldn't want to go back to Yorkshire even to get her things, and so all had to be decided upon now. When I left her for the last time to go back to Scotland, I knew that she had some anxious days ahead of her until

August 21st. I arranged to come back as soon as possible to support her through this time and I promised to try and see the room in Kirkcudbright before my next visit.

Circumstances transpired to prevent this, and, when the day came for us to go north, we were both in fairly anxious mood. We had told my brothers about the projected move and they had expressed some concerns and reservations about the scheme. With hindsight, I can understand why this was. Mother and I had been discussing my move to a farm for three years, and possible solutions for her almost as long, but it had come out of the blue for them and it took them a while to come to terms with it. Also, they had never heard of Abbeyfield. Their concern was that Mother was doing the right thing for her and, when they contacted me and began to give their opinions, I asked them to contact Mother and let her tell them about it. When they had done this and heard how positive she was about the process, they seemed to be happier about the affair.

The day was fine and the journey went well, although Mother found it long and quite tiring. We stopped for coffee at Mains Gill Farm Shop, just past Scotch Corner, and for lunch at the Farm and Coffee Shop, just off the M6 at the border. It was about 3.30 p.m. when we pulled up outside Strathdee, as the Abbeyfield House in Kirkcudbright was called. We were met by Ann Middleton, who was the House Chairperson, as it was during the hours of the housekeeper's off duty period. She led us into the dining room, where she introduced us to a gentleman, who was seated in one of the easy chairs, and left us while she went to make a pot of tea. We chatted to the gentleman, and, soon, Mrs Middleton came back carrying a tray of tea and biscuits. It was purgatory to have to sit and drink tea and make social chit-chat, when all I wanted to do was to see the room and get Mother settled in. I knew that Mother would be feeling exactly the same, and the next ten minutes seemed longer than the entire journey from Yorkshire.

Eventually, the tea drinking was over, and Mrs Middleton led us up the stairway and through a dark landing, where there was a large refrigerator standing beside a sink and worktop. There was a loud television playing in a room off to the right. We passed along the landing and round a corner and saw a door, through which we could see a large bathroom with a shower cubicle at the side of the bath. Then we came to what Mrs Middleton said was the room Mother was to have. We pushed the door open and stepped in. It was fairly big and lit on two sides by large sash windows. In one corner, there was a door leading to the en suite toilet and washbasin, and the room was pleasantly furnished with bed, wardrobe, easy chair and bookshelf. Over by the window was a table, with a kettle and crockery enough for one person to use for breakfast and drinks. There was a container with tea in, and one with sugar. One of the windows looked out onto the back garden and it was open slightly at the bottom, and the gentle breeze that entered, wafted the green striped curtains to and fro. We peered into the toilet and saw that it was plenty big enough to house its two fittings, several shelves and the towel rails, where two blue towels were hanging. I looked at Mother and could see the relief on her face. She sat herself down in the easy chair and declared that she was very pleased with the room. So was I.

Feeling well satisfied with the way things were going, I went down to the car and began to unload Mother's possessions. They were few in number, but of vital importance to her existence. A box of books—she was an avid reader and devoured books at the rate of two or three a week, a box of videos—since my father's death she had become very fond of watching television, and, when there was nothing on that suited her, she used videos as an alternative to her books, a box of writing paper and envelopes—never one for using the telephone very much and too old for the electronic mail of today, she still spent many hours writing letters to her friends. These things catered for her leisure hours and, apart from these, we had just brought her summer weight clothes. Mrs Middleton very kindly helped me to bring these things up the stairs, and then she left Mother and me to sort them out and find places for them all.

I had rung Richard, who had stayed at Low Arvie whilst I went down to fetch Mother, and he soon arrived to carry up the television and video for us. In a short while, we had the clothes stowed away in the wardrobe and drawers, and the books and videos on the bookshelf. The room was beginning to take on a homely appearance. I plugged in the bedside clock and put it right, and had just tuned in the television and got the video working, when there was a knock on the door, and a slight, youngish woman with fair hair entered. She introduced herself as Paddy, the housekeeper, and we all chatted amiably for a few minutes. She then said that it was teatime, and would Mother like to come downstairs to the dining room.

There, we found the table had been covered with a snowy white cloth, and was laden with plates of cakes and biscuits. Several elderly people were seated around the edge, and there was one place left, which was obviously for Mother. Richard and I crept away at this point, and left Paddy to make the introductions and help Mother to settle into to her new home. We felt that she would be ok, if a little strange at first, and I had told her that I would visit her again the next day, to see how she had got on.

I found her sitting in the easy chair in her room, which was bathed in the sunshine coming through the windows. She was slightly bemused, and still clearly in a state of anxiety, but the positivity was still very apparent. She liked her room, and the house, and had been very comfortable. The housekeeper had been up to see her just before bedtime and again first thing in the morning, and the meals she had had so far had been beautifully cooked and a vast improvement on the frozen meals of the past two years! The one thing that had caused her a problem was that the local accent was very difficult to understand and had prevented her from communicating terribly well with the other residents. However, they too had been very kind and welcoming. There were three men and three other ladies in the house. She began to talk about these fellow residents and, at this moment, there was a knock on the door, and a very dapper gentleman, wearing a navy blue pinstriped suit, came in carrying a small book. He introduced himself as Willie, and said that his room was just along the landing. He had been there just a few weeks and was finding it very good. He said that he was eighty-eight years old, and still worked as a journalist on the local newspaper, attending local events and sending his copy in from the fax machine installed in his room. The little book was the local guide he wrote and produced each year about Kirkcudbright and the events that were happening, and he had brought it for Mother, to help her learn about her new environment. Over the time that Mother stayed in Strathdee, Willie was very solicitous of her, and she was woken every morning to his knock on her door, as he left her copy of the Daily Telegraph on the other side.

This was the other essential ingredient of Mother's daily life. She had been an avid reader of the Telegraph as long as I could remember and even before that, and she and my father completed the cryptic crossword every day. Since Father's death, her breakfast of bran flakes had been accompanied by her first look at the crossword. On a recent but rare trip to the doctor's back in Yorkshire, he had urged her to keep using her brain in order to prevent the onset of any kind of dementia, and he suggested the use of puzzles as one possible option. "Oh yes, Doctor, I do the cryptic crossword in the Telegraph every day", she replied. To which the doctor had proclaimed his astonishment, and admitted that he had been thinking more in the way of children's puzzle books! She was now rarely able to finish the crossword, a fact attributable to her 90 years, (but she liked to blame the crossword setters), and it was always an essential part of the day to do as much as she could. (And still is!)

All in all, then, I felt that this change of lifestyle had got off to a good start, and I drove back to Low Arvie feeling very relieved

12

The Rural Stewardship Scheme

The land at Low Arvie is so wet and has such a small amount of good agricultural land, but the current trend in agriculture is to farm productively, but with the environment very much in mind; and the EU is promoting schemes that encourage farmers to follow this line. The coming years will see a drift away from subsidising production, which has been so prevalent in the past, towards these 'greener' ideals. When we decided to buy a farm, it was always with the intention of running an extensive operation—in agricultural parlance this is the opposite of intensive, rather than having the more usual connotation. We had both retired from mainstream careers and wanted a unit that would provide occupation and, hopefully, some fun, without too much hassle and aggravation. Richard was the practical side of the equation, having been in agriculture in one form or another since he was sixteen, and I was—as I always put it—the mental side (probably in all nuances of the word!). Over the previous ten years, since ill-health forced my early retirement, I had, very fortuitously as it now turned out, done a course in computer book keeping and accounting to keep my brain active, and this would prove very useful and save us the cost of an accountant. Since we had made the decision to buy a farm, I had also been researching the system of subsidies and rules and regulations that pertain to agriculture in the twenty-first century—of which there are considerable amounts; and I told Richard that, whilst I would be of no help whatsoever on the practical side, I would do all I could to help in this area. This really suited us both very well, in a Jack Sprat way, because he had no patience with forms and accounting. I told him that the state of my brain, after two breakdowns in the early nineties, was unreliable, and would require him to check everything I did carefully, as mistakes had a habit of cropping up on a very regular basis. If he could cope with this, then I would do my best to help wherever I could.

As well as the land being very wet and, in places, very dangerous for both man and beast, the tracks and roads that led into the various fields, were also very badly deteriorated, and, in some places, it was difficult to see even where they had been. It was apparent that no maintenance had been carried out for years, but, as we began to sort out these problems, we started to realise that there must once have been a very comprehensive network of drains and ditches. Instead of growing haphazardly, as had first appeared, we found that the rushes were almost always in straight lines running across the land and, thus, marked the courses of the original drains. On every track, there were several low spots, where the runoff rainwater of years had collected and formed large soggy patches several metres across, making it impossible to walk on. Once, when I tried to cross one of these, my welly sank into the mud to a depth of at least a foot, and was immediately clamped fast, as if held in bands of steel. I had been alone at the time, and had been very much afraid that I would have to leave my welly boot to sink slowly into the morass, and return home in my sock. After trying for several minutes and getting muddier by the second, I did eventually retrieve my boot and was able to get home, but it was a salutary experience, and one that I did not wish to repeat. A friend who came to visit in the early days fared even worse, being heavier than me and in a worse place, he got both feet clamped in the vice of the mud, and it took all Richard's considerable strength to extricate him. There was at least one of these patches on every track, and several on most, and so I was unable to explore the land very much, as I was too afraid.

At the time, I didn't worry too much about this, as I was so busy with other things, trips back and forth to Yorkshire, getting Mother sorted out and, always in the back of my mind was the thought of the place waiting for me at Strathclyde University. I had not gone to University as a teenager, and I had been pleased to receive a place at this stage in my life. Prior to getting Low Arvie, I had been looking forward with pleasurable anticipation mixed with only slight apprehension to going now. We had been to 'suss' out the campus at Jordanhill, where the Counselling department resided, during our first visit to Strone, and I had decided to apply for a room in the Hall of Residence next to the Lecture room block. The course I was to follow was very prestigious in the Counselling world, as the director was Professor Dave Mearns, who had written many books and was very highly thought of. It had been reading his work that had inspired me to apply to Strathclyde in the first place, and I knew that I would meet people on the course from all around the world, anxious to learn from such a master. The course ran from October to June, and, after the first four weeks, I would only need to be in college from Wednesday to Friday, as Mondays and Tuesdays were spent on placement, and I could probably find a place for this somewhere local to Low Arvie. The problem was the written work that would need to be done. I had done really well in the previous courses, but had spent many hours reading and then writing the required essays. That was at the local college and at Certificate level, this would be University and a higher plane altogether.

I spent time taking a long hard look at the situation, and, when I found it too difficult to make a decision, I pushed it to the back of my mind. There were plenty of distractions. But when, at the end of August, the reading list and other information to do with the course began to arrive, I knew I could put it off no longer. There would be plenty of people on the waiting list ready to take a vacant place, but they would need time to make plans, and it would be unfair for me to delay longer. So I took one final look at the picture. The farm we had bought was sadly neglected and needed a lot of TLC to make it into something to be proud of. Richard was committed to putting fifteen suckler cows on the land by December, and would need help with paperwork. Mother was just installed in Kirkcudbright, and still needed a lot of support to settle in to her new life. On top of all this, my daughter had rung, early one morning in late August, to say that her marriage of two years was in difficulty. She was living in Banbury and travelling forty-five miles each way to her job as a forensic scientist in Birmingham, which put her under enough stress when life was going well. Now, with this major problem on top of that, I thought that she would also need plenty of support to get through it all. When I added all this together, I realised that there was no decision to be made. With all of these things going on, I knew that I would never be able to do justice to the course in Glasgow, and, reluctantly, I wrote to the course director giving back word. I received no reply from her, so I don't know whether she understood or not, but I hope that whoever took my place has enjoyed the course and has done well.

Having written the letter and posted it, I vowed to put counselling behind me for the time being, and get on with helping Richard to make something of Low Arvie.

Even though I had not been able to walk all the land—still today there are parts that I haven't got to—I knew that it was beautiful, it was full of natural history and it had a variety of ecological habitats. We decided to call in the Farming Wildlife Advisory Group to have a look, and give us their advice on joining one of the Countryside Schemes. I had heard of some of these whilst visiting various parts of the United Kingdom on holiday, and knew, for instance, that the farmers on the island of Islay were given grants to leave some of their grass uncut to provide winter feeding for the thousands of geese that arrive each year. Also, in the

Outer Islands, crofters are helped with grants to farm sympathetically for corncrakes and other rare birds.

When I had been researching the rules and regulations of farming, in the previous years, I had come across the Rural Stewardship Scheme, and we had been given a pack of their literature. Looking through this, it appeared that we had several of the habitats that this scheme sought to preserve by grant aid, and it was this that we were particularly interested in.

We duly made an arrangement for the FWAG representative to come and see us and, in late July, a slim girl pulled into the yard in a green Peugeot 106. She introduced herself as Kirsty Hutchison, and we sat in the kitchen drinking coffee, whilst she began to explain the RSS to us. As I have found with all schemes to do with farming, it is never as easy as it seems to be, and we had hard work to follow all the ramifications that Kirsty was telling us. However, she said the first thing was for her to look at the farmland and produce a preliminary report for us about the natural habitats, outlining how we could be sympathetic to the wildlife in the area. This would tell us, she said, whether it was a suitable candidate for the RSS. As with all funding, there is a limited amount of money, and some way has to be devised to choose the recipients. With the RSS, this was done on a points system. The farm received points based on the number of habitats, the number of species that would benefit and various other criteria.

Kirsty asked for a map of Low Arvie, which I was able to provide for her, having made several copies of the one in the estate agent's brochure, and then she and Richard donned wellies and jackets and went off to look at the land.

When her report came, it said that we could claim around 43 points for the RSS. The previous year 43.5 points had been sufficient to get into the scheme, but there had been a lot of complaints about this, as all the money had gone to just 196 of the 612 applicants, at an average rate of £72,000 each, for the five year plan. It looked as though things might change to allow more people to get in this year. Also, we had a large nipple-shaped knoll in Auchenvey, which was marked as a Cairn on all the maps, even the one dated 1850, and Kirsty had not included this in her report as an archaeological site, for which we could claim a further two points. This would give us 45, so it began to look as though we could give serious attention to applying to join the scheme for the five-year period 2003 to 2008. Our scheme would come to less than £20,000 for the five years, and this would not in anyway be clear profit, but it would help towards getting some of the dry stone walls repaired, and the land put back into shape. In return, we would have to plant some new hedgerows and protect them with fencing, fence off the riparian woodland to protect it from damage by grazing cattle and create a pond—this would be in front of the house and would enhance the view from the present windows and the new conservatory. One area was designated as species rich grassland, and the haylage fields contained both mown grassland and wetland and these would provide habitats for nesting birds. In return for a payment of £100 per hectare each year, we had to undertake not to mow the grass before July 1st—this was no hardship as the grass was not ready here before then, and also not to graze these fields after April 1st, again no hardship since we would want the grass to be left to grow then anyway. The species rich area was to be ungrazed from May 15th to August 15th and would require fencing, as it was part of the grazing field of Auchenvey, but this should not cause too much difficulty, as it was not large. It could be grazed when the flowers had seeded, after the middle of August, and would be useful then. The riparian woodland would only be available for grazing for a very short time in the autumn, just to control the vegetation. We would have to undertake not to drain the wetland, but we could keep the present ditches cleaned out, and the rush growth had to be prevented from becoming rank. We very much doubted whether it would be possible to drain the wetland anyway, but we wanted to clear out the ditches and try and get the rush growth under control. One of the wettest areas was earmarked to become the pond and, like the riparian woodland, this would have to be fenced off and the cattle prevented from entering the habitat. There were payments towards the fencing and gates, but there was a time limit when this work had to be done, which was by the end of the first winter in the scheme. This was a lot of work for one man, and I left the final decision to Richard. Another requirement of the scheme, where I could be of more help, was in the production of a Waste Management and Minimisation Plan. I began to look into the paperwork on this, that Kirsty sent us, and then to work through where our system needed to be altered or adapted to make it environmentally sound.

In the end, Richard decided to go for it, and we contacted Kirsty again to tell her of this decision. She said she would come early in the new year and discuss the details of the scheme and produce our submission for us. This was called the Environmental Audit and it had to be handed in to SEERAD by March 31st. We would know if we had been successful, when they announced the points' threshold in the summer. The cost of producing this audit would be £500, of which half was recoverable, whether successful or not.

When the draft audit came, just before the due date for handing in, we had a total of 45 points, but when I looked through it, I saw that we could gain an extra two points if the farm operated a Nutrient Budget. I had been working my way through the Waste Management documents, and had recently come to the section dealing with fertiliser and Farmyard Manure. I had discovered that a Nutrient Budget was the balancing of these two products. By analysing the content of the soil to find out its strengths and deficiencies, adding in the useful content of any FYM that was available for application and applying these facts to the purchase of the right kind of fertiliser, it was possible to optimise the production of haylage. When this final product was also analysed, the inputs and outputs could be balanced for future reference. This was something that I would relish, sitting at a table in the warm, producing facts and figures, and I didn't hesitate to undertake this and gain us the extra two points. With forty-seven, we felt we must stand a chance of being accepted.

Once the audit had been handed in, there was nothing to do but forget about it until the points threshold came out, and we got on with the work of improving the farm and looking after the cattle. The financial year-end came and went, and we battled our way through the accounts and, in the end, we got it right between us. My poor broken brain is a large handicap, but I was able to sort out enough of it for Richard to be reasonably happy. Altogether, I think we worked the final balance sheet out three times, as the first twice he found gaping errors in my workings. I still get somewhat distressed at these times, but I need to keep persevering and trying to meet the challenge, otherwise I might as well give up altogether. Richard is very patient and doesn't hassle me at these times and, for that, I am very grateful.

The financial loss we made in this first accounting period was fairly substantial, and will continue to be so for at least a further year, as we get more of the equipment we need, but eventually we hope to move into the black and, meanwhile, we shall have enjoyed life.

We got home, one day near the end of June, to find a message on the answer phone from Kirsty to say that the SEERAD officials were beginning to visit the RSS applicants in this area. She couldn't tell me any details, what points were required, when they would be coming here, or even whether they would let us know they were coming. This is quite typical of SEERAD. They are not the most communicative government department I have ever known, but when they do send letters, they make us feel like criminals, trying to con as much money out of the system as we can. The fact is that the European Union rules are so very complicated that most farmers, who spend long hours at hard physical work, simply haven't the time to spend hours poring over the forms and mountains of paperwork involved. Every single process that we have to fulfil has a different set of rules, and each letter warns us that failure to comply with these rules will lead to loss of premium. Several times Richard has rung with queries of one sort or another, and they always tell him that they don't give advice, they only apply the rules. In twenty years in teaching, I never felt that the Education department officials were the enemy as I have begun to do with SEERAD, after one year in farming. However, I suspect that they don't give advice because the rules are so complicated that they can't understand them either!

And so we held ourselves in readiness for the visit, and felt that it must be a sign that we stood a chance of being accepted. Two, three and four weeks went by and nothing happened. I rang Kirsty again to see if she knew any more. Aside from the fact that SEERAD were informing some people of their visits, but not others, which was not very helpful, she didn't know any more. At the end of the sixth week, I was reading Farmer's Weekly and read that, in the whole of Scotland, only nine people had been unsuccessful and that the threshold had been lowered to a mere thirty points.

The visit eventually took place. We were given two days' notice, by telephone, that a Mr John Riddet would be coming to look at the farm and the RSS plans. We knew that he was the second in command at the SEERAD office in Dumfries, and we had had correspondence with him on several occasions, but had not met him before. He arrived promptly at the advised time and was duly invited in for tea and cake, of which he accepted the former and declined the latter. We sat in the kitchen and chatted whilst we drank, and, during the conversation, it transpired that Mr Riddet had been a student at Wye College, in Kent, back in the seventies, at the same time as Richard had been there doing post-graduate research. They hadn't known one another, but the fact formed a link between the two men. John is still 'the Man from the Ministry', a label which he hates, but he is someone that we can approach with our queries, with a little less trepidation than we used to feel. After the tea ritual was finished, he and Richard went off to view the areas of the farm that were to be in the scheme. By this time, although we had had no official notification, we knew that if John was able to verify the habitats and recipes that we had submitted, then acceptance into the scheme was assured. We were certain that he would be able to do this, and, indeed, it proved to be so.

Although this was to give us a fair amount of work over the next winter, getting the areas fenced off and the pond dug, it was nice to think that we would have some assured income over the next five years, to offset against the huge list of expenses that we were clocking up.

13

Water, water everywhere.......

We had been at Low Arvie for a few weeks and were getting used to the water system. On our arrival we had found, amongst the papers from Mr Kellie, a letter from Dumfries and Galloway Council referring to a report on the water in the well, from the testing laboratories at Scottish Water. The details of the analysis were also enclosed. They had apparently taken a sample on June 5th, just five days before the closing date, and had sent this analysis to the solicitors dealing with the sale. The report showed that our water was odourless, had 17.8130 mg per litre of nitrates, a turbidity of less than 0.2 FTU, whatever that means, a pH of 6.12 which is quite acidic, its conductivity is 268 uS per centimetre and there are 9 ugs per litre of lead. The page is stamped 'Satisfactory'. A second page tells us there are no Coliforms—apparently a good thing—and no Ecoli—definitely a good thing—and that although there are 231 cfu per millilitre of Heterotrophic bacteria at 22 degrees centigrade, this figure drops to only 3 cfus at 37 degrees centigrade. Since 37 degrees is body heat, I can only assume that this is also a good thing! I do not pretend to know what ugs, FTUs and uSs are, but since this second page is also stamped 'Satisfactory' and the bacteria counts were so hearteningly low, with negative Ecoli, we began to use the water freely and without any worries. Dumfries and Galloway Council state in the covering letter that the water will continue to be monitored at regular intervals.

The water came into the house by the corner of the small kitchen, where the pump was situated, and was sent from here to the two small tanks under the coomb in the west bedroom. A float switch in one of the tanks set the pump going, whenever the water level fell in the tanks. Apart from the pump noise when this happened, the system inside the house was, to all intents and purposes, the same as one where the house is connected to the mains. Apart, of course, from the third tap in the kitchen. Whenever the pump ran, this tap filled up with about five pints of water, which we used when it was there, and then the tap stood empty, until the pump ran again. It was several weeks before Richard suddenly realised its purpose. After investigating the route of the pipes around the kitchen one day, he discovered that this tap delivered water directly from the well, and not from the upstairs tanks, and was, therefore, intended for use as drinking water. The possibility of contamination along the delivery system to the tanks and thence to the sinks was eliminated. We began to keep a carafe of this water in the kitchen for drinking, and, also, filled the kettle from it and used it for cooking. If this tap was empty, I just used the water in the cold tap for these purposes, but when this third tap was full, I figured it was worth using.

One day soon after our arrival, Richard took a spade and began to dig around the concrete shape on top of the well. Soon, he had uncovered a heavy concrete lid, about four feet in diameter, placed on top of a square of concrete, under which we supposed we would find the well. Richard bent down to move the lid aside, but it resisted his casual approach with dignity, and it took considerable effort on his part to get it to move at all. However, slowly it slid aside to reveal a square aperture containing a spider's web of pipes and associated ironmongery. We had to peer hard beyond this network to see the dark, glistening liquid a long way below. The well was found to be a cylinder between ten and eleven feet deep. It was about thirty inches in diameter, and had been built using stone and cement. The water, measured with a very long wooden pole with the resultant wet part showing the depth, filled approximately the bottom metre of this. It was a very long time before I realised that the water returned to this level with time, after each running of the pump. We are in fact taking water from the water table, and the small amount we use can have little effect upon its overall level. We have now worked out—possibly the first time in my life I have used my Grammar School mathematics 'how to find the volume of a cylinder'!)—that there is usually around a hundred gallons of water in this private reservoir. In the early days, before I had taken all this into account, I worried about every drop I used, imagining that this would be used up in no time. I would go for a bath and sit shivering in a bare two inches, fearful that every egg cupful would be the last to splutter from the taps. Everyone that came to the farm—and we had quite a number of visits from the local community, curious to meet their new neighbours—would be quizzed on the history of the well at Low Arvie. I found out that it had only run dry when the farmers who had leased the buildings in the last five years, had tried to water ninety cattle from the well over the winter. Obviously, ninety cattle drink a huge amount of water, far more than two people can use, and gradually my panic began to subside. Always of the opinion that knowledge is better than ignorance, I have tried to become acquainted with the well and how it works. Unfortunately this has meant moving the heavy lid every time we want to measure the level, which I could not possibly do on my own, and so poor Richard is pressed into service.

The first spring that we were at Low Arvie was the driest that Dumfries and Galloway could remember and not even a drop of rain fell for three whole months from February to the end of April. We watched the level in the well very carefully, and I began to ration use of the dishwasher and washing machine. The lowest level we measured was around thirty-six inches, which still meant we had eighty gallons there. We agreed that if we used the dishwasher in the morning and the washing machine in the afternoon, then we could still enjoy our daily baths, in rather more than two inches, each evening. We did decide to leave the last bath water in the bath and use it to refill the toilet cistern for as long as it lasted, in order to limit the 'pull' on the well. I found by this means that the toilet uses a huge amount and often, the bath water ran out well before the next evening.

The crucial factor with a well is the time it takes to regain maximum depth and, with this careful usage, we came through the dry spell with no trouble.

One day when we returned from one of our trips to South Yorkshire, the pump ran as usual when we had used some water, but it sounded very different. I couldn't account for it and called Richard in to listen. For some reason, there was no water there for it to pump and, if it were left running very long in that condition, the motor would soon burn out. We turned the switch off and, before my panic had set in too strongly and visions of life without running water could impress themselves too deeply on my mind, Richard had opened the cupboard and unscrewed something on the pump. Quietly, he went to the tap and, drawing off a jugful of water, began to pour it into the little hole now revealed in the pump. This is known as 'priming the pump' and fills the pipe from the well to the pump with water so that, when it is turned on, the water flows again. All was restored to normality, and life carried on as usual. However, the next time we left the farm for a few days, the same thing occurred on our return, and it began to dawn on me that something was not right between the well and the pump. The pipes from the tanks upstairs, down through the house and out, through the pump, to the well should remain full of water at all times and, when the switch in the tank operates the pump, the water flows along the line. It was apparent now that this line of water had sprung a leak somewhere between the well and the pump, and this was allowing the water to seep back from the tanks. When we were not using the water for a few days, it was able to seep back past the pump, leaving it empty and, therefore, unable to pump anything. Refilling the system as far as the pump, through its little hole, enabled it to begin its job again.

Over the next few months the leak got worse and worse, and the priming had to be done more and more frequently. One day when we woke up, we found that the pump now needed priming after a night and, for quite a long time, Richard would leap out of bed on waking and rush downstairs to do the priming, before we used any water to set the pump going. Then we began to switch the pump off at night, so that it couldn't try to work before he had got it sorted out. When things got so bad that we couldn't go out of the house, even for two or three hours, without the water seeping back too far, we decided something had to be done. It wasn't totally our inertia that was the reason we had done nothing to mend the problem for such a long time, but we were so busy with other even more pressing matters and, whilst it was a nuisance, we were aware of the need to listen out for the pump's strangle-like noise when it needed priming, and it did not interfere too much with life. However, gradually Richard was finding it more and more difficult to fill the pump with enough water to set it going and, by now, had to fill it several times in succession before it 'got hold' of the water strongly enough to pull on the well. Also, we began to worry that it was having a deleterious effect on the motor. The plans for the extension were not moving at all quickly, and we didn't want to wear the old pump out before the new system was in place.

Our first line of attack was to ring a plumber. We had not found the tradesmen here to be very accessible and we usually had to ring to make an appointment for the plumber, electrician or whoever, to ring us and make an appointment to come. Our experience with the electrician and several of the agricultural traders, that Richard had had dealings with, had left us with little confidence in their punctuality and ability to deliver what they promised. I had dealt with the local plumber, when we wanted the dishwasher plumbing in, and had found him to be very expensive, and so I asked Hughie, who lived in one of the houses that we could see up the road, who he used. He got his wife, Gladys, to ring me with the number of a man in Dumfries, and I rang this number and explained the situation to the lady who answered the phone. Yes, she said, she would tell her husband when he came in and get him to ring me back. Three days went by before I decided that he was not going to ring back, and so we had another think. The previous day, we had had a visit from a builder who had been asked to quote for the extension work, and, during the course of his visit to 'suss' out the job, I had told him of our difficulties with local tradesmen. He had left me his card and told me that he had all manner of tradesmen working for him and, any time I wanted anything doing, "Just give me a call!" So I decided to do just that. "Leave it with me," he said, when I had explained the situation, "I'll get back to you!" These are the words that make my heart sink. There is absolutely no answer to them; you just have to accept them at face value and hope.

On this occasion, my hope was rewarded, when he did indeed 'get back to me' with the phone number of a man 'who was a wizard with wells'. This time I left it to Richard to ring him, as I sometimes think that, being a man, he gets slightly better service from these people, and he, at least, knew what he was talking about. I heard this end of the conversation, and there was a lot of discussion about models of pumps and the flow rate of water but, at the end of the conversation, the only tangible piece of information towards solving our problem was the phone number of another person who might be able to help. He proved to be yet another non-starter.

Thrown back to square one, we decided that our only option was to bite the bullet and ring the local chap. Once again, we went through the process of making an appointment to make an appointment. But just when I thought I had got the hang of this system, they threw me into confusion again by actually appearing in person instead. Two men drove up in a van and, jumping out, began to make preparations to replace the pump. Fortunately, Richard was in the yard at the time and enquired their purpose. "Hold on a minute, we do not need a new pump," I heard him say. Explanations followed and with a disappointed air, the two men tramped over to the well and, having removed the cover, lay down to disconnect the pipe that went down into the water. This was the only way that it was safe to reach in to the network of pipes, as it was almost an arm's length from ground level. "Have to be careful," said the man leaning over, "the last time our boss was here, his mobile phone fell out of his pocket and is still down there somewhere!" I idly wondered how long it was before mobile phone poisoning took effect and, also, what other artefacts of modern man may have found a watery grave in our well!

Unscrewing a few connections, the man was soon lifting a long piece of copper piping out of the hole. "There's your trouble," he said confidently, "yer foot valve is stuck open!" Sure enough there was a contraption on the end of the pipe, which was in the wrong position. It was a one way valve and, when the water stopped flowing, it was supposed to close and stop the water from flowing back into the well. He cleaned it out and promised to return in a day or two with a new one. The next morning the pump ran normally, and we breathed a sigh of relief. Short lived! On the second morning, we heard again the strangling noise that told us the pump had no water, and we had to rush to switch it off and prime again.

Three days later the man did return, unbidden, and fitted a new valve down the well and we relaxed once more. It was with mounting disappointment and a growing sense of defeat that we heard the strangling noise the next morning. I made another phone call to the plumber and explained that their action in changing the foot valve had had no beneficial effect on the problem. The lady answering the phone said she would report the matter to her boss. We are still awaiting his reaction to this message two months later. However, we did hear from him again, when, after six weeks of silence, I opened the morning post, one day, to find a bill for £125. The foot valve was priced at £18 and the remaining £107 was for the two visits, each of which had lasted less than twenty minutes and had taken place when the men were passing by the farm on their way to other jobs, which they often do. Enraged at this treatment, I sent him a cheque for half the amount and told him that I would not be requiring his services again. At the time of writing I am still awaiting a reply to this.

We were beginning to despair at this point and, as usual with me, panic began to set in. I became convinced that the pump would break down, and there would be no one to fix it, and we would have to live the rest of our lives without running water. Counsellors among you will recognise this as the 'awfulizing' syndrome, and I was subject to it very often. Richard on the other hand is far more practical and calmly sits and thinks things out. Although I have learnt to trust him to find solutions most of the time, this trust goes out of the window when I am 'awfulizing'. However, he did soon come up with another solution. It was April and the frosts had all but disappeared for the year, and so we would by-pass the underground pipe and connect the well to the pump over ground with new alkathene piping. Simple! Why didn't I think of that?

As soon as he had time, he began to disconnect the ironmongery at the pump, and then, digging down to the pipe where it left the well, he disconnected that also. Giving me a piece of pipe with the two end fittings fastened to it with a piece of wire, he bade me speed down to Castle Douglas to purchase the fittings to join a piece of new blue pipe to the pump and the well. Off I went with a light heart that the problem would soon be fixed, albeit temporarily, and that would last, until the new building work provided the entire solution by installing a new pump down the well, connected directly to new storage tanks in the roof space of the new part of the house.

I went first to the building supplies store and sailed in to the back part of the shop, where a young man served large items such as hardboard sheets, sand and cement and water pipes. I brandished my piece of pipe with its brassware still connected. "I would like a roll of pipe similar to this but the next size up," I said. He trotted off down the back of the hardboard sheets, only to return empty handed. "We only keep the size you have," he said. Snag number 1! "Not to worry," I answered, spirits still high, "I'll just take the connections required to fix this pipe to these fittings," showing him the elbows and thinking that the roll of new blue pipe we already had at home would manage ok and save a bit of money. "You get those in the shop," he said. Right, off I marched into the shop and up to the girl behind the counter. "I would like the fittings to connect these together, please," I told her, once more holding up the blue pipe with its dangling brasses. "Sorry," she said, shaking her head, "we don't do those. You could try Gordon's down the road."

Feeling slightly less confident and sensing the life without running water just beginning to creep back onto the horizon, I got back in the car and drove the half-mile to Gordon's.

With flagging optimism, I sallied into the shop and waved my 'pipe and fittings' contraption once more in the direction of a counter. I was only mildly surprised when the chap behind it shook his head and firmly declared, "It's impossible to fix those to each other—one's imperial and one's metric!" I did actually know this, but was confident enough in Richard's common sense to know that he would not have sent me off on a wild goose chase, and that it must be possible to connect them somehow. However, the man was adamant that he was right, and asked me why I wished to do it anyway. When I explained the problem, he drew his breath in sharply, and just as firmly declared that it would be a very expensive project and we would need a good plumber to achieve it. He was obliging enough to write down the names and numbers of two such men and, with my heart now considerably nearer my boots, I left the shop and got back in the car. It was by this time 12 o'clock midday and Saturday, so I was not hopeful of advancing the cause any further that day, but I decided to contact Richard, if I could, and see if he wanted to try and get one of the plumbers. For once he answered the phone, and I passed on the information I had gained, and then set off back home.

In the half-hour it took me to reach there, Richard had managed to get hold of one of the plumbers and explain the problem to him. He had said that he would send someone round 'at the beginning of the week' to make the connections for us. Whilst I prepared us a light lunch, Richard reconnected the fittings to the pipes and, priming the pump once more, allowed the tanks in the bedroom to re-fill.

After lunch, we took our tea outside to sit in the sunshine and gaze sadly at the concrete and earth covering the pipe. We sat and drank in silence, both thinking the same thoughts, but just hesitating to be the one to say it. Finally I cracked first. "There's only one answer to this problem, so let's get the tools and start digging!"

Richard went to the workshop and gathered together an assortment of picks, spades and other digging implements and, rolling up his sleeves, began to bray at the concrete close to the back door. He wanted to locate the pipe and then follow it until he came to the leak. We knew the pipe began at the corner of the 'wet kitchen' where it entered the house and ended at the well, but this was round the corner of the house some twenty metres away, and we had no idea of the route that it took in between.

By the end of the afternoon, he had exposed some ten metres of green copper piping, which was heading in a north-easterly direction. If it carried on in a straight line, it would mean that the pipe from the well had to head north-west, and the two would cross about five metres from the corner of the house, right in the path of any vehicles entering the farm yard. It also meant that there would be about twenty-five metres of pipe to unearth!

I can honestly say that I did my share of the work, but it only amounted to uncovering about three of the twenty five metres. I made up the difference by providing meals and tea at regular intervals, and digging in the spaces between, whilst Richard worked steadily away. I was spurred on by the fact that I wanted to be the one to hit water, which by now we had surmised was at the junction of the pipes. By laying out straight lines from the well and the pump, we found the likely place of this junction and only then did we notice the darker hue of the ground surrounding this spot. It had been plain to see for weeks, but we had just not recognised it for what it was. Eventually, I was the one to find water and gradually exposed the right-angled junction of the two pipes, and then we could see the slight but constant weep from the joint that was the cause of the problem. Richard finished off the line from the well and, by Sunday evening, we had the whole pipe exposed in the bottom of a trench, which varied in depth between eighteen inches and two feet. There were no other breaks in it, but it looked pretty battered and old. We hoped it would mend and last out until the new building work was done.

The end of the saga is very anticlimactic. Richard went down to Castle Douglas the next morning and, for £2.17, purchased a right angle elbow and olives in the correct size. In a very short time, he had sawn the ends off the pipe and reconnected them with the new joint. The problem had been caused by a very slight dent in the end of the pipe, which prevented a watertight seal from being made. We assumed that the heavy lorries and farm equipment, which had driven a bare two feet over it for so many years, had taken their toll. Richard placed an old oil drum over the spot, when he had filled the trench in, thus preventing a recurrence of the problem, and that's how it stayed for the remainder of its life.

The plumber finally rang the next Wednesday and said his lad would be round the next day, but I told him that the problem was solved and thanked him for his trouble.

14

Farm Sales

When we had been planning our future together and deciding to begin farming, I had confidently, but naively, suggested that a start-up capital of around £10000 would be adequate to buy all the capital items we would require. Richard had said nothing to this, which usually meant that I was wrong, but he rarely pointed this out to me, and this was one of the many good things about him. He always allowed me to find out for myself, and never gloated. However, this question of start-up money was important, and one which we came back to time and again, when looking at likely properties. We knew that there would be the likelihood of no income at all for at least two years, and we needed to live for this time, pay ordinary household bills and gather the machinery that Richard needed to run the farm. My mother always says that things happen for a purpose, and not getting the first farm we bid on was definitely one such example. We would have had a miserable time trying to balance the budget, whilst attempting to make the house even habitable and get the farm working. The much lower cost of Low Arvie and its already habitable state made the process much easier. My £10000 start-up capital allowance was spent in one afternoon on just one machine, and currently, after one year's work, we have just topped the £60000 spend mark. Everything to do with running a farm is just so expensive. The machine we bought for £10000 was a Matbro materials handler with a telescopic arm, upon the end of which several different implements can be fitted. This machine is so useful for a one man operation and makes impossible tasks, from lifting and moving heavy bales to carting and tipping road making stone, into a piece of cake. However, the tyres that were on the machine when we bought it had had a lot of use and were badly worn. On the wet and hilly land of Low Arvie, they slipped and skidded, and we decided to purchase new ones. The best price we could get them for was £215 each. When we replaced the tractor tyres, they were £280 each. Even the plastic tags that we have to clip into the cows' ears cost £4 each.

Our accounts' files currently bulge with over three hundred invoices, ranging from 99p to the Matbro at £10000, and all prices in between.

When we arrived at Low Arvie, Richard's library of farm implements comprised a 1953 Fordson Major tractor, currently still in Yorkshire, one cattle crush—a piece of equipment used for restraining cows whilst they are administered to—one wooden trailer, also still in Yorkshire with the tractor, and a small fertiliser spreader. He was 56 years of age and I am two years younger and, as we both come from long-lived stock, we reckoned that we would aim for fifteen years of active farming and would try to find equipment which would last us that time. I am not sure that we have been entirely successful, but we still have this in mind. It's a fine balance between what we can afford and what will last.

September saw the first of several farm sales taking place in the area, and we decided to buy what we could from these. We are now quite old 'hands' at the farm sale process but, in those early days, it was all new and slightly bewildering. There were two sales taking place on the same day, the first at eleven in the morning and the second at one-thirty in the afternoon some ten miles further away.

We drove to the first one and followed the FARM SALE signs, which led us into a field where a line of a dozen or so assorted Land rovers, pickups and vans marked the parking area. We pulled onto the end of this line, and I looked at the rest of the field. In the far corner, there was a flat bed lorry laden with all manner of what looked to me like rusty and broken junk. Stretching out from this, in long straight rows, were all manner of machines and equipment. In another corner, there stood a refreshment wagon advertising bacon rolls and cups of tea, and two or three green clad people were opening up the side to reveal a counter with milk jugs, sugar basins and red tomato sauce containers spaced along it. A little to the side of this was a large horsebox, with its backboard let down to make the dismounting steps. I looked around for horses but could see none, and idly wondered what they would be doing here anyway. Standing on its own along the hedge side, conspicuously proclaiming its purpose, was a bright blue portaloo with WC in FIELDS inscribed on its door. A few men, obviously farmers, were picking over the junk on the lorry and desultorily mooching along the lines of sale items, trying not to show any interest in anything, less their competitors for the chosen items should find out.

We joined the latter section and began to search for likely purchases, and to set our price limits. We had decided on this system as the best one to follow, as I was likely to get carried away and pay too much for things, if I wasn't careful. Richard marked down a square box with a few pipes attached to it—it turned out to be a welding machine—and a pressure washer amongst the smaller items. I wasn't really interested in these, to me, boring and useless things and wanted to hurry him along to the tractor and Matbro at the end of the rows. We had been thinking of buying a new tractor, as it is such a useful tool to the farmer, but Richard wanted a 100 horse power version and, after interviewing every make and model and frustrating many reps with requests for more discount, the cheapest we could find was still in the region of £20000, and we felt that this was too dear, when we had so much else to buy. Therefore, we hoped to get a decent second hand model at a farm sale, and there were two sitting at the end of the implements, obviously the last things to go under the hammer. However, Richard is not a man ever to be hurried and I had to 'possess my soul in patience' as I have to do so often, as we looked at everything in order. For once, there wasn't much else of interest to Richard until we came to the tractors, mainly because this had become a priority for us, now we were more than two months into our venture, and we looked at the two on offer with interest. They were not of the make that Richard would have preferred and they had seen many hours work, but he said we should go as high as £9000 for the bigger one. He said he would pay up to £8000 for the Matbro materials handler that was the last item in the sale.

Suddenly I realised that the field had filled up. The far side now had several dozen farm vehicles parked roughly in rows, and there were many people, mainly men with weather beaten faces and work worn hands, standing around in groups and greeting each other with all the diffidence of Galloway men, the usual and essential comments on the weather preceding the more interesting and relevant chat.

Gradually, the throng began to move towards the lorry containing the rusty junk, where several men wearing white coats and carrying gnarled sticks had now appeared. Punctually at eleven o'clock, one of them climbed onto the lorry and, aided by assistants, who held up the boxes of rusty nails and half-empty oilcans, began the sale. By this time, there must have been two hundred or more prospective purchasers, and each item was sold quickly and efficiently, almost before I knew what was happening. The auctioneer rattled away in his time worn fashion, "One-bid, one-bid, one-bid, two-bid, two-bid selling at two pounds," and, with a crash of his stick on the lorry floor, the lots were sold one by one. Each time he tried to start the bidding at a ridiculously high price, and the Galloway men stood steadfastly refusing to acknowledge his existence, until he had reduced his opening twenty pound, ten pound suggestion down to a fiver "to get me started." Then someone in the crowd would shout out, "One pound" and he would start his one-bidding all over again. It was fast and exciting, but I was too afraid to bid for anything at that first sale, until we got to the tractor. Richard was successful with the welder and the pressure washer at less than our set figure, but other things we had earmarked had gone too high. By the time we came to the two big machines at the end, I was feeling more confident, and, with Richard's set prices firmly fixed in my head, I decided to try and buy them for us. I waited until the bidding, which began at a quite low figure with many bidders, had slowed down at £8000 and then feeling nervous but determined, I joined in. The auctioneer was moving up in hundreds and I nodded to him to indicate a bid of £8100. Most of the others had fallen by the wayside now, and there was only one other opponent. He went up, so did I. We continued in this way until the bids reached £8900, which was me. I knew that if he went again that was me out, and he would get the tractor for our price. There was a long pause, and the auctioneer was shouting "eight nine, eight nine, at eight thousand nine hundred..." He raised his stick and was just about to crash it down on the mudguard of the tractor, when a voice from somewhere behind me shouted "Nine." This woke up my opponent, who then began again and eventually the tractor sold at £9600.

Precisely the same thing occurred with the Matbro and I dropped out at my £8000 limit, whilst two other people went on up to £10400.

Now the sale was over and people were beginning to make their way back to their vehicles. Purchasers were removing some of the items from the neat rows. "I'll just go and pay," Richard said and trotted off towards the horsebox, and, when I joined him there, I discovered that this was the mobile office, which housed the auctioneers. There was a table half way up the box and two girls were seated there, busily writing and handing out receipts to the line of farmers, who shuffled along taking their turn to pay. Each had their chequebook in their hand, with the top cheque signed and the remainder left blank. They handed them over to the girls, who calculated the sum total of the purchases and filled in the amounts on the cheques, before tearing them out and returning the book to the farmer, with his receipt. When Richard had paid, we came out of the horsebox and walked over the field towards the welder and pressure washer. Only then did it dawn on me that we had a problem. For some unknown reason, we had gone to the sale in my small car, not thinking that we may need to transport things home, *and* there was another sale to go to. We were standing contemplating the problem and deciding that, either we went home and got the van and missed the second sale, or we left the two items there until the next day, when we spotted David, whose cattle were currently eating the grass on Low Arvie. "Have you come in your pickup?" Richard asked him. He had come with Peter Black, who farmed next to him in *his* pickup and, with no more ado, he went and found him and asked if he could take our things for us. In a short time, the red pickup came bouncing along, and we were introduced to Peter. His pickup had a fixed roof, and the men began to discuss the best way of fitting our two items in it. They were both heavy and unwieldy objects, and it took all of the men to lift the welder into the truck and push it to the back, but eventually it was installed. This left the pressure washer. This was large and very heavy and had two handles at the back and a wheel at the front, so that it could be trundled around wheelbarrow fashion. It was universally agreed that it was too high to fit in Peter's van in its present state and discussion ensued again as to the best way to proceed. I left the men to it and wandered off to investigate the bright blue edifice by the hedge, now that many men had left and those that remained were mostly occupied, like Richard, with removing their purchases. When I exited the loo, I could see that the wheel had been removed from the front of the pressure washer and the body of the machine was being eased over the backboard and into the vehicle. With our things safely stowed in Peter's van, we were free to go with them to the second sale, and this we duly did.

The afternoon was warm and sultry, as we drove through Dumfries, and I looked forward to a refreshing cup of tea from the green wagon, when we arrived. I was disappointed, therefore, to find that this was the only vehicle that hadn't made the journey to Nether Dargavel farm, and there was no replacement. I left Richard to look around and drove back to the garage we had just passed and armed myself with enough snacks and drinks to see us through till we got home. When I returned, the sale had begun. This time the rusty nails and half empty oil drums were laid out, with the other small lots, in the cow shed, and the farmers were all surging from one end to the other following the auctioneer, who was one-bidding like mad again. I eventually found Richard outside on the field, where the now familiar lines of machinery and equipment were situated. He was looking at a line of blue tractors, examining each one in his careful way. There was one in particular that held his attention, and it had the numbers 7740 marked on its side in white writing. I hurried over to him and found him discussing horse powers with a stocky, dark haired man. There were several others around also looking at the tractor, and I heard the man say, "This is the chap to tell you about Ford tractors, for he has them," and he indicated a slight, but neatly dressed man close by. Nobody introduced themselves by name, but all were very pleasant and helpful, and soon we moved on to examine the other things that Richard was interested in.

The thing about moving into a close knit community, like the farming one we have entered, is that everyone knows everyone else, and you stick out like a sore thumb. The effect of this is that everyone knows who you are, but you meet so many new faces that it is a while before these people begin to fit into context. The two men that we talked to that day have become good friends since but, of course, we weren't to know that then and, I am ashamed to admit that, the next time we met both of them, they had to explain that we had spoken before.

We enjoyed the snack I had brought from the garage, whilst sitting in the sunshine and discussing our pricing strategy. The main item was the 7740 tractor, which Richard thought would be a good buy at the right price, and, based on our knowledge from the morning sale, we wrote down £9000 as the price we would go to.

The crowd suddenly emerged from the cowsheds and made its way towards the far line of artefacts. The usual array of bent gates, ring feeders in various states of repair, sheep hecks and cattle troughs made up this first row, and we joined the throng about half way down it. We weren't interested in the sheep equipment, as Richard didn't intend to have any sheep, and it was all too small for use with cattle. When the auctioneer came to the first of several lots of fencing posts, or stobs as they are called here, Richard put in a bid and set the one-bidding off. Eventually, one of the piles containing around twenty-five stobs was knocked down to us at a net cost of around fifty pence per stob, and they were to come in useful in due course. I felt particularly proud when the auctioneer announced "Walton, Low Arvie" to the assistant who was writing down price and purchaser for each lot. I was to hear it again when we successfully bid for a topping machine to control the thistles, nettles and docks, which had been allowed to flourish unchecked on Low Arvie's land for several years.

Within a short time, the auctioneer was describing the 7740 Tractor and inviting bids from the crowd. I insinuated my way to the front, so that I should be seen, if the price enabled me to join in the bidding. After the auctioneer had done his usual stuff of starting with a sky high £10000 and reducing gradually to try and attract a starter bid, someone whispered "£7000." I have realised that an auctioneer needs very good hearing, as he could easily miss these self-effacing murmurings. It seems that farmers are very bashful and bid almost shamefacedly at these auctions, as though they don't wish anyone to know what they are up to. I looked around, and could see no one who even looked as though they might be bidding, but the auctioneer was going up rapidly in hundreds. When I looked back and began to concentrate again, he had gone up to £8000. The pace then slowed a little, and I was able to get in with £8100. I had decided that the way to work these auctions was to look straight at the auctioneer's face and bid clearly and firmly and, most of all unhesitatingly, until my limit was reached. That way any opposition might be induced to think that I would keep going, whatever they bid, and drop out early. I decided to build up this reputation, if I could and hoped it would pay off in the future. Accordingly, when a bid came for £8200, I immediately and confidently attacked with £8300. I was feeling quite relaxed, as our limit figure of £9000 was still someway off and I could enjoy the next few minutes without worrying, knowing that Richard would be happy whatever happened. The opposition was hesitating, and I felt I had him on the ropes. I just hoped there was no one else waiting to pounce, when I had finished him off. By this time, I had him identified and I gave him what I hoped was a long hard stare as much as to say "Come on then, matey, I'm ready to go on!" I hoped he would say nothing and willed the auctioneer to crash his stick down and say the magic "Walton, Low Arvie," once again, but just before he managed to do this, the opposition came back again with £8400. I was conscious of a slight disappointment, but countered immediately with £8500, loudly and clearly. This was the knockout punch, and the man was counted out, as I heard the auctioneer put Richard's name on the tractor. We felt we had done well to get it at £500 below our limit price and, after paying once again in the horsebox, we set off home with our purchases. Richard drove the tractor with the topper connected to it, and I had loaded the stobs in the back of my little car. It had taken a while to load and connect and, as we drove home slowly in convoy, we didn't arrive until after six o'clock. I was quite surprised when Richard stopped the tractor at the head of the drive, instead of going on into the yard, and I had to drive around it to get in. He said later that he daren't go another turn of the wheel further, as the gauge had been showing empty of diesel all the way home, and he had stopped there, right by the diesel tank, to fill it up.

When we got into the house, I remembered about the two items we had bought in the morning, and went to the phone to ring David to ask him when it would be convenient to come and get them. David's son Colin answered the phone and I explained my mission. He sounded surprised, but not nearly as much as I was, when he said, "We brought them up and put them in the barn on our way home!" It hadn't even occurred to us that their kindness would extend that far, and we were choked to find that, not only were the two machines in the barn, put tidily out of sight, but the wheel had been remounted on the pressure washer.

It was some days later when we became aware of the true extent of the nature of these people, whom we had come to live amongst, when David called in for a cup of tea after checking his cattle in Eastside. Peter had purchased a lot of sheep hecks, the long wooden troughs used to feed the sheep in the fields, at the second sale and, after coming all the way back to Low Arvie and putting our things in the barn, he had had to go back the twenty or so miles to get his own purchases. It was a humbling, but nonetheless heart-warming, experience, and we felt our attempt at showing our appreciation with a bottle of wine at Christmas to be wholly inadequate. We hope to be able to repay them, in an altogether more suitable way one day.

All of the people mentioned by name so far have now become our friends and, when we went to the last farm sale of the year, we felt an integrated part of this community, as we were greeted by all of them, and we were the ones standing around in groups discussing the weather, the haylage and the machinery on offer. I am quite sure that we have provided them with much conversation and quite a lot of amusement, as they have watched our bumbling efforts to set up our farm and our new way of life, but I know that it has all been good natured, and they have all been there to help and advise, as we have needed it. It is said that it takes twenty-five years to become accepted as a Yorkshire man when you move to that county, and I don't know how long it takes in Galloway, but, after one year, we feel more truly at home here than anywhere we have ever been, and this is in no small part due to these reserved but genuine people.

15

Mother Settled

Mother continued to settle into life at Strathdee, the Kirkcudbright Abbeyfield house, and, each time I visited her, she was more relaxed. The weather continued to be fine and warm, and she was able to get out for her walk each day. She had managed to find a pleasant route around the back of the house, where a group of pensioners had their bungalows and seemed to vie with one another to produce the prettiest garden. At this time of year they were all filled with the most colourful array of bedding plants and added greatly to Mother's pleasure in her daily walk. The church community organised lifts for her to go to church on Sundays, and I visited several times a week. Her life was taking on an ordered routine, with Willie continuing to deliver her paper from the front door to her room door each morning and pleasant regular mealtimes twice each day with fresh cooked and well-presented food. One day, she had a visit from Bill and Sue Erskine, a couple from our home village in Yorkshire, who were visiting relatives in the area, and she was able to show them her new home and tell them of her new life, which they, in their turn, relayed back to the church community she had left.

The only snag to all of this was the length of my journey to see her. It was a good forty mile round trip, but I made a point of going a different way each time and this helped me to get to know the surrounding countryside, and how the villages were connected to each other. At that time of year, with summer at its height, I enjoyed my excursions down narrow country lanes, with their verges full of wild flowers. There were long stretches where the black ribbon of the road was edged with the frilly lace of cow parsley, and then others where the lace changed to the bright pink of red campion or the frothy green of ferns. Even getting lost was no hardship, as I always found my way back to the main roads eventually. These excursions served to confirm to me the natural beauty and splendour of the region, and gave me cause, over and over again, to rejoice at the happy chance that had brought us here. No wonder the roads were full of cars, some towing caravans, and others with foreign number plates, all summer long, as people came to share the glories of the Galloway countryside.

We seemed all set to continue in this way, and I was, therefore, surprised, when I answered the phone, one day, and found Ivy Stanley calling me. They had finished the work at Bothwell House in Castle Douglas, and the new rooms were in operation. The two people who were above Mother on the waiting list had both decided that their time to move into this sheltered form of housing had not quite arrived and, therefore, she could not only offer Mother a place there, but she could also have the choice of two rooms. This came as quite a shock to us, as she had only been in Kirkcudbright for two and a half weeks, and had we known that this would have come so soon, she would have waited in Yorkshire and then moved straight to Castle Douglas. However, Ivy had obviously been unable to say how long a room might be, and one can only make a decision based on information available at the time. The other thing that Ivy said was that, although Mother had only been with them a short time, they had known her long enough to be sure that she would fit into their system and, therefore, her four week term of probation could be carried over to Castle Douglas. She would only need one more week there, before we could finalise the arrangements, and she would become a fully-fledged resident.

I drove over to Strathdee as soon as I could and spoke to Mother about the situation. Ivy had suggested that I bring her over to look at the two rooms and meet the housekeeper, and then we could discuss what she wanted to do. We arranged to go over the following Monday.

Richard and I were committed to a trip to Yorkshire for the next three days, and this seemed like a good time to bring Mother's own furniture back with us, and then she could move to Bothwell House and have her own things with her from the beginning. Mother and I worked out together what she would need. She is a singularly unsentimental woman, and it was very easy to agree with her what we should bring. Before she left, we had gone through all her things and she had decided that she wanted very little in the way of mementoes. There were, of course, essentials—TV, video player, bookcase, reclining chair and bed—these were easy decisions, but where Mother made it very simple was in the non-essential items such as ornaments and photographs. She packed several photos of Father into her case and requested that we bring the graduation photographs of the four grandchildren who had gone through that process, and which had adorned the chimney breast, increasing in number as each one achieved their degree (now five—just one more to go!) Mother was very proud of these. She had a collection of more than three hundred china and porcelain birds and I wondered what she would want to do about these, but again it was simple. "I'll just take Olly," she said pointing to the large Eagle Owl, "He's always been my favourite!" On the trip down with Richard, in which we packed up these thing to bring, I tucked in a few more things, such as pictures that had always been a part of the home and vases, which would be useful for any flowers she was sent, but really, Mother was able to walk away and leave ninety years behind, her eyes firmly set on a new and, I think, exciting future.

I picked her up at 3 p.m. the next Monday afternoon and drove her the nine or so miles to Castle Douglas. We were met by Janet Scott, the Bothwell House Chairperson, as Ivy was unable to be present, and Norma the housekeeper was off duty. We drank tea and chatted in the beautiful dining/sitting room but, as on our first day at Kirkcudbright, I could feel the impatience that I knew so well in my Mother. She had no time for social chitchat and was anxious to get on and see the rooms. After what seemed like forever, Mrs Scott asked if we would like to do this, and she led us down the fourteen stairs to the basement of the house. There were four steps, and then a one hundred and eighty degree turn to the last ten. At this turn there was a huge picture window, which looked out onto the back garden and over the wall to the loch, showering light into the stairwell and the entrance hall above. At the bottom of the stairs we found a rectangular hallway, with four doors opening off it. They all contained square brackets for name labels. The first contained the name of a resident, the next two were labelled Store 1 and Store 2 and the fourth was empty. Mrs Scott led us to this one and opened it. We passed through into an entrance hall with two further doors opening into it, which were both open. Through the first, which was on the right, we saw a large shower room some three metres by about two metres in dimension. It contained shower, toilet, hand basin with cupboard beneath and mirror above, a large radiator and a cork topped bathroom stool. Besides these, there was plenty of room for further drawers or cupboards to create more storage. The shower and toilet were both provided with grab handrails. This was the room's private shower room, and we marvelled at the space and appointments. Moving back into the passage, we walked through the second door and found this led into a very large room, which must be about five metres square, carpeted in green. Opposite this door was a long window looking out the same way as the stair window, where matching green curtains were billowing gently in the breeze from a door in the left hand wall, which stood ajar. We could see that this led out into the garden, but that the level was half a storey below the garden, and a path led from the door to some steps up onto the main level. On our right was a small

kitchen unit, with sink, worktop, cupboard and tiny refrigerator. This unit projected out into the room and, behind it, was an empty space reaching to the right
hand wall, just long enough and wide enough to take a single bed. The remaining
three and a half metres was a large open space containing a wardrobe at one side
and a matching chest of drawers at the other. It was easy to see how Mother could
be made extremely comfortable in this large, attractive room. She had settled
happily in one half the size in Kirkcudbright, but this was the icing on the cake.
Mrs Scott told us that the wardrobe and chest of drawers belonged to the room
and had to stay, but Mother could furnish the rest with her own things. She said
this with an apologetic air, as though we might be disappointed, but little did she
know that these were the very things we would have had to buy, as Mother had
had fitted furniture in Yorkshire.

To be polite, we then followed Mrs Scott back up the stairs to view the second
room on offer, but I knew that Mother was already sold on the one downstairs.
So was I. It was absolutely perfect. The downside to it was that Abbeyfield had
been unable to fit a stair lift on the staircase, as it turned so sharply, and many of
the residents were no longer able to manage stairs on a regular basis. I could see
this perhaps becoming a problem for Mother too, at some stage in the future,
but, at the moment, three or four trips up and down each day would be beneficial
in helping to keep her legs going as long as possible.

The room upstairs, though perfectly pleasant, had none of the advantages of
the one downstairs, and we told Mrs Scott that Mother would like to come as
soon as possible. She had moved to Kirkcudbright only three weeks previously,
and I could see no point in delaying this second move any longer than necessary.
She would, I felt sure, soon adjust and settle in here just as well. There were several other bonuses to this house also. Some of the residents were English so there
would be no difficulty in communication as there was in Kirkcudbright. The
church was right next door and no arrangements would have to be made to get
Mother there on Sunday mornings, for the first time in several years, she would
be able to go under her own steam. The park with its many pathways leading to
the loch was next to the church and would provide variety and interest for her
daily walks.

We arranged with Mrs Scott for Richard and me to take down Mother's furniture, which, at present, was still in the van after its trip up from Yorkshire, and
install it into her new room the next day, and that Mother would move from
Kirkcudbright on the Thursday.

We drove down to Kirkcudbright early on the Thursday morning and packed up the things I had unpacked just three weeks before. This time Richard was there to do all the heavy carrying, for which I was very grateful, and, in no time at all, it was time to say goodbye to Strathdee and its inhabitants. They all wished Mother well in her new, new home.

At the time of writing she has been at Bothwell House for ten months, and, at my every visit, enumerates the pleasures and benefits she has found since moving in. She has worked out for herself a very nice routine, which she follows most days. Up by seven and breakfast with the crossword, then read the paper, which takes most of the morning. Lunch is followed by afternoon television programmes till around 3.30, leaving just enough time for a stroll in the park before tea time, and then more television and reading time before bed around 10.30 p.m. With church on Sunday morning, my two or three visits each week, Mother's Union every fortnight, social contact with the other residents at mealtimes and the occasional trip organised by the Abbeyfield committee, providing just enough variety, she is very happy with her lot and is now well into her ninety-second year and looking fit to make at least the century.

16

Ethel's Story

With Mother finally settled and happy, I turned my attention to my promise to see what I could do about Ethel. Before discussing the situation with Ethel herself, I called in to see the manager of her care home on one of my visits to Yorkshire. She was called Mechele and I knew her quite well. I wanted to get her opinion on whether she thought Ethel would settle in to a place so far away, even though it would mean that my Mother's visits could still continue. We talked about it, and Mechele said she thought that it would be the best thing to do, and that Ethel would move almost as easily as Mother. She called one of the other carers in for a second opinion, and she agreed that there shouldn't be any problem.

My next move was to try and find a place up here in Dumfries, so that, when I went and spoke to Ethel herself, I would be able to describe the place that she might go to. Accordingly Richard and I took Mother on several visits to interview homes up here. I was in touch with Ivy Stanley too, and one day she called and said there was a room coming available in the Abbeyfield home at Dalbeattie. I couldn't believe our luck because this was the place I would really like to get her into. We had looked round it a few days previously and had found it to be a caring and happy home. Indeed, there is no doubt that Mother will go there, if Bothwell House becomes no longer suitable for her, and neither she nor I have any worries about it whatsoever. The problem with moving Ethel up to Scotland was now only a matter of finance. Her income was insufficient to pay the whole of her care fees, and Doncaster Council made up the difference. The total weekly cost of the home in Yorkshire where she lived was £244, as she only requires residential care and not nursing care, which has a much higher cost. I got in touch with the Social Services manager in Doncaster, Mr Ken Askew, and enquired as to the procedure for moving Ethel. What he told me was disturbing, but understandable. A person can choose wherever they want to live in the country and Doncaster is obliged to continue funding them, *but* they will only fund them to the same level as the Doncaster charge, i.e. £244 per week.

The system in Scotland is different, and the charges in residential homes include a charge for personal care of £145, which is paid for by the Scottish government for all their residents. Coming from England, Ethel would not qualify for this funding and, therefore, this charge would have to be paid for independently. The total cost for a place in the home in Dalbeattie was £325, and was set to increase the next April. This left a shortfall of some £81 currently, and the prospect of a greater one in the near future. Ethel had a little money of her own but this would soon be used up at the rate of £81 per week.

I did my best to explain all this to Mother, and she was disappointed but understanding. I couldn't possibly undertake to finance Ethel for an unknown number of years at a minimum rate of £81 per week. It was very frustrating that the place was there, and Ivy guaranteed to hold it for a little while, until I tried to sort out the funding. Indeed, she was helpful in suggesting places I could try. She even used her acquaintanceship with the local M.P., Peter Duncan, and sent him the details to see if he could help, but disappointingly I got no response whatsoever from him—not even an acknowledgement of Ivy's email. I spent a week or more emailing anyone I could think of. Ethel had spent all her working years in the Doncaster Co-operative stores, where my grandfather had been a manager. She had worked there continuously from the age of fourteen until she retired at sixty, having had no family to cause the usual breaks in a woman's working life, and I wrote to ask if they had any kind of hardship fund for ex-employees, but they were unable or unwilling to help in anyway. Even a small contribution would have been welcome, but I found nothing at all.

At this time my brother came up from Birmingham to see Mother and her new home and, as we discussed together the situation about Ethel, he came up with the suggestion that, as a family, we might be able to make up the difference. We have another brother in Canada and, with Mother making a fourth, we felt that £20 per week each might just be possible. I told him that Ethel had a little money of her own—perhaps enough to make up the difference for a couple of years—and so we said that, if we used this first and then guaranteed to make up the shortfall when this ran out, it wouldn't be too bad. He also said that he would contact Canada and see what the reaction was from there. We felt that we were doing it for Mother, as much as, or perhaps even more, than for Ethel. Of course, we had no idea how long it might be for, but we would just have to stick with it. If we started, we would have to see it through, but as Ethel was already almost ninety-eight, although granted with no ailments, we still felt it wasn't too great a commitment. We went over to visit the home in Dalbeattie whilst Philip was here, and he was as pleased with it as I was.

The reaction from our brother in Canada was favourable, and he said he would join us in the scheme.

Feeling altogether happier that things were once again working out well for us, I contacted Mr Askew and told him that the family was willing to make up the shortfall, when Ethel's money ran out. Then came another blow. We weren't, he said, allowed by law to use any of her own money to make the top up. It all had to come, right from the beginning, from a third party. This seemed to me to be particularly unfair that she couldn't contribute to her own fees. However, he was adamant that this was the law, and he could do nothing about it.

I went back with this to my brother and we decided that we would just have to start topping up straightaway, and hope it didn't go on too long, which is quite a terrible position to be in, really, but we knew what we meant. Mr Askew had told me that one person had to make the contract with the Social Services, and it all had to be drawn up legally and properly.

I contacted Mandy, the manager at Dalbeattie, who was holding the room for us, whilst I was getting all this sorted out, and told her that I was going down to talk to Ethel, now that I could see the way clear to her coming, and see what her reaction was.

I went to see her and explained as carefully as I could what had happened, that I had moved up to Scotland and Mother had come up to be near me, that we had found Mother a very nice home and there was a place for her to come and be near us, too, if she wanted to. I was not surprised, when her reaction was as instant and as positive as Mother's had been. "Oh yes," she said, "I want to come." I spoke to her about it for a while, and then I left, asking Mechele to talk to her about it another day, and see what reaction she got and let me know what her opinion was, about the whole issue. She promised to do this.

She was as good as her word and, the next day, she phoned me and said that she had spoken at length with Ethel and that she had remained adamant that she wanted to go to be near to Mother and me. I arranged with Mechele that I would come back down to Doncaster on October 19th and take her back with me. I then rang Mandy and told her that Ethel would be arriving on that date. All I had to do now was write to Mr Askew with the wording that he had already given to me about the funding, confirming that I would be responsible for the fees and asking him to organise things with Dumfries and Galloway Council, ready for the move on October 19th. Exhausted, but satisfied with all my efforts, I drove back up to Low Arvie and tried to relax a little for the ten days, before I had to go and fetch her.

On the Monday before we were due to take Ethel to Dalbeattie, I rang my contact in the Dumfries Council Office to check everything was in order and, to my consternation, she replied that they had had no word whatsoever from Doncaster. She said that Ethel wouldn't be able to come without certain paperwork between the two councils being completed. She was very good and told me exactly what she required Doncaster to do, and even said she would accept the paperwork faxed up there to speed things up. I rang and left a message for Mr Askew to contact me, but he failed to do so that day. The next morning we put my little car onto the trailer—as a more comfortable vehicle for old ladies to travel in—and, pulling it with the van, which would be loaded with more goods and chattels, we drove once again to Yorkshire. We set off later than we intended, and I was concerned that I wouldn't be home in time to phone Mr Askew before he left the office for the day, and so I decided to phone him from the public phone at our usual stopping place at Scotch Corner. To my consternation, I was informed that he was not in the office that day—he was off ill and no one knew when he would be back. I asked for the person who was doing his work and was told that no one was, and there was no body there who could help me.

I spent an anxious night, and first thing next morning I phoned again and, explaining the situation and its urgency, asked again for someone who could act. Eventually I was put through to an extremely helpful man, with some authority about him, who admitted that, from the file, it seemed that nothing had been done about Ethel's move. He found my letter of some weeks earlier asking for the paperwork to be completed and the projected date of the move. To his credit, this man, whose name I unfortunately cannot remember, did everything I asked and got things moving. He just had to send someone out to see Ethel and make sure that the move was what she wanted, and then he would get things sorted out in time for the Saturday journey. He organised to send one of his officers out to the home the next morning at 9 a.m. He couldn't have done more.

I went down to see Ethel the next morning just before nine, and again talked to her about the move she was going to make. Once again, there was no hesitation in her answer that it was what she wanted. Mechele also said that she had spoken with her about it again.

When the officer came, her attitude to me was quite hostile, as though she suspected me of carrying off this little old lady against her will, and, abruptly, she asked me to leave the room while she spoke to Ethel. Mechele was also there and, as I left, I turned round to see the frail figure of my aunt sitting in a low chair with Mechele on one side of her and the Social Services person towering above them both from her position perched on the end of the bed. Reluctantly, I continued out of the room and waited in the corridor. I would dearly love to know what was said in that room. They stayed in there for a very long time, and the clock was moving rapidly towards ten o' clock when I had a second appointment. At ten minutes to, I knocked on the door and went back in saying that I must leave very soon. Even then, I was not prepared for what came next. "There is a problem", said the Social Services lady, "your aunt isn't sure that she wants to go!" To say I was flabbergasted is an understatement. However, the very last thing I wanted to do was to move her against her will and, if she was happy to stay here, then that was fine by me, and I knew it would be by my Mother too. We were only concerned that she should have a free choice, and I had acted on her wishes as expressed to me and Mechele, up to that point.

Ethel then said something that made me sure that she understood the situation. She said, "Mary can always write to me." This showed me that she was aware that Mother would no longer be making her weekly visit and, re-assuring her that I would go and see her as often as I could, I left, feeling shell-shocked to say the least, to go to my other appointment.

When I got back, I phoned my brother and my mother and told them what had happened. Their attitudes were the same as mine. We had made it possible for Ethel to have a free choice, and she seemed to have made it in the way we least expected. We respected her choice, and my brother said he would play his part in visiting her as often as he could and we left it at that. It would certainly make my life much easier as I wouldn't now need to take Mother to see her, to say nothing of the money that we weren't now going to have to find. I rang Mechele and between us we agreed that if it was what she wanted, then that was all that mattered. I knew she would be well cared for.

The worst thing was that I had to tell Mandy and Ivy what had happened but, fortunately, they were both very understanding and begged me not to worry, but I did. They had been so kind in keeping the room free, for the weeks that it took me to sort things out, and then we didn't use it after all.

Looking back now, I think it was probably the best outcome for Ethel. She had been in the home for five years and, at that stage, it was the only home she could really remember. She was well used to the staff and the other residents, and she continues to thrive in that environment. I call in whenever I am down there, which has worked out to be approximately once a month. I took Mother to see her once, when we were down in Yorkshire for my nephew's wedding, and she was reassured that all was well. Ethel will be ninety-nine years old in five months time and, like Mother, seems fit to carry on for a few more yet.

17

Cattle Sale

All the time we were dealing with these issues, we were very aware that the dead-line date of December 6th, when we had to have fifteen cows on our land, was not too far away. There is an annual sale of Black and Belted Galloways every autumn towards the end of October, and it was at this sale that we hoped to buy ours. But, back in August, there had been a special sale of Galloways at Wallets Mart, as one farmer in the area had decided to go out of Galloways and concentrate on another area of farming. We decided to go along to this sale and try and learn the ropes. I had never been to a sale before and I wasn't sure that I would enjoy it too much. I had seen them on television, and they had seemed to be noisy affairs, with the poor cattle being poked and prodded around, as they circled the ring, trying to find the way out. However, I decided to go and see for myself what went on at our local mart.

The sale was to be held in the Number two Sale ring, beginning at 11 a m. Richard and I got there about 10.30, and there was a fair number of farmers assembled. They stood around in groups, talking farming and calling out greetings to others as they passed. We felt quite conspicuous, as people turned around ready to greet a friend or acquaintance and then turned hurriedly away again, when they saw two strangers in their company. One or two nodded, but few actually spoke to us. I looked around taking in the atmosphere. The selling ring was a circle about fifteen metres in diameter, and the floor was covered with a fair depth of clean sawdust. Around the edge of this, was a solid barrier, perhaps four feet high, and suspended a foot above this, was a steel bar. Some of the farmers were already leaning on this barrier, securing for themselves a good place to see the cattle, when they entered the ring. Around the edge of this ring, was a passage way, some two metres in width, and then ranks of steps rose up around this, almost to the full height of the roof. People were also beginning to sit around the topmost of these steps, again securing a vantage point from which to view the proceedings. We decided to join these and climbed up to the next to the top layer and sat down. Opposite us, at the far side of the ring, there were two sets of metal doors, both obviously securely closed, with heavy chains threaded through holes near the handles. Beyond each of them, we could see a pair of wide passageways, one up which the cattle would enter the ring, and the other where they would leave. Above these doors, there was a huge screen with letters picked out in small red round lights, which read 'Dispersal Sale of the Corrie and Castlemilk Gallo- way Herds' and underneath 'Starting time 11 a.m.' I looked around and saw only two faces I recognised, one was Robin Anderson, who was the Managing Direc- tor of Wallets and the auctioneer for the day, and the other was Drew Brown, the farmer who had mown our grass and whose cattle were currently eating the grass at the west end of Low Arvie. He was one of the men leaning against the ringside barrier. In the far corner of the room, to one side of the ring, there was a pulpit like construction, with microphones attached to its rim. This was obviously the auctioneer's corner, from where he could preside over the sale and see the whole of the room, where the bids would come from.

As 11 o'clock drew nearer, more and more people poured in through the doors. There were a few women amongst them, but they were predominantly men and obviously all farmers. Sales are important occasions for the farming community, and it is here at the mart that the main social contact takes place. Farmers are busy people who don't keep working hours separate from leisure time very often, and they take these opportunities to meet and mix and enjoy a chat. The sense of community is very strong, and the bond that exists between the farmers of a district is forged and tempered at these times of gathering. We sat quietly, enjoying the obvious camaraderie that was played out before us and, although we weren't a part of it, we didn't feel pariahs, and I hoped that one day we might be included in the warmth that was apparent in the room.

Exactly at 11, Robin Anderson appeared with one or two other men in the 'pulpit' and began to welcome everyone to the sale. A tall man came and stood in the ring below Robin's pulpit, and we gathered that he was the stockman or farm manager, who had cared for these animals for many years. He looked very unhappy at the dispersal of his stock, and I felt very sad for him. Robin explained the nature of the sale and praised the quality of the cattle he was selling. It wasn't a long speech, and, very soon, the right hand pair of metal doors, at the far side of the ring, opened to admit the first cattle to be sold. This was a Black Galloway cow, twelve years old, with her calf. Robin told us that she was three and a half months in calf again. Her name was Silverbell of Corrie and her calf was Silver- bell 13th. They both had black shaggy coats and, with their fairly short legs, seemed quite small. They trotted around the ring, whilst Robin took bids from the room. The calf looked a little bewildered, but old Silverbell just looked as though she had seen it all before and, on her third or fourth revolution, she spotted that the second pair of doors had opened and she led her calf through and away down the passage way to the pens at the back of the building. They had been bought for seven hundred guineas. Her purchaser had got a good cow, a good calf and the prospect of a new calf in six months time—three for the price of one, but, of course, this had been taken into account by the bidders. The sale continued, and the cows with calves at foot followed, one after the other into the ring. The catalogue gave the pedigrees of each one, and I read the unfamiliar names and wondered where they all came from. Sovereign of High Creoch, Barlaes Brownie, Blackcraig Moss Rose. A year further on I have become more familiar with these names and know that any animal with the prefix Blackcraig was born and bred on the Finlays' Blackcraig farm, five miles up the road from Low Arvie. Barlaes is the farm owned by the Fergusson family and High Creoch belongs to Gordon Gilligan at Gatehouse of Fleet. They are all well known and highly respected breeders of Galloway cattle and have won many prizes between them.

The cows with calves were followed into the ring by bulling heifers, female cattle that have not had a calf but who, at two years of age or a little more, are ready to go to the bull for the first time. From time to time, the tall, sad faced man leaned over and whispered something of the history of the animals to Robin, who relayed the information to us. Some of these youngsters fetched really high prices, and I looked at them, trying to decide what it was that the farmers could see to make them so desirable. Those that fetched the very highest prices—well on towards the two thousand guinea mark—seemed to have a sturdiness and a symmetry of shape not possessed by the cheaper ones, and I supposed that all this played a part in determining the level of value, along with breeding.

After the heifers came one bull, not quite two years old, and, therefore, barely tested in the line of duty. His price was lower at only five hundred guineas, for this reason. We noted that his purchaser lived in the very North of Scotland, so he would have a long journey, before he got to his new home. This ended the sale of the Black Galloways, and we moved on to the Dun herd. The Duns are a beautiful, soft coffee colour but exactly the same conformation as the Blacks, and these seemed to be good examples, from what Robin said about them. However, only the bulls fetched prices over one thousand guineas, and I wondered why they were less popular than the Blacks. We were pleased to see that the sad stockman was able to buy one or two of the animals himself, and we thought that perhaps he was going to start up a small herd for himself. We did not know if he had been put out of work by the sale of the stock, but we have known this happen to two other people, in the time we have been here.

Altogether the sale lasted two hours, and I was unsure whether I had enjoyed it or not. Nobody had poked or prodded the animals, who had all seemed fairly ambivalent towards the proceedings, and I had certainly begun to learn something about Galloway cattle and, also, the farming community around us.

Richard and Linda, warm at last by the new Aga

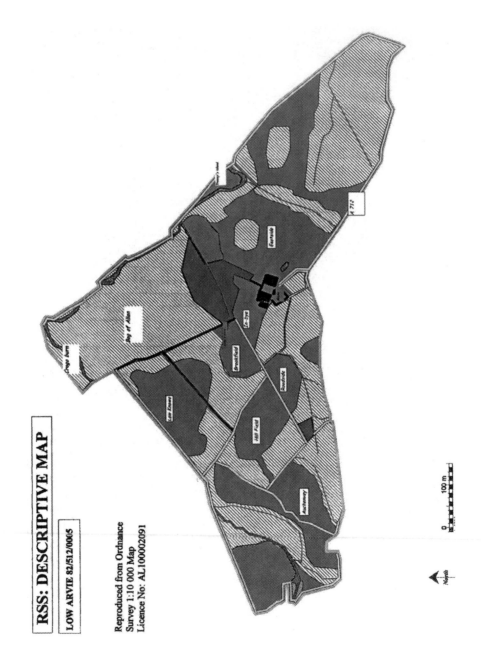

RSS: DESCRIPTIVE MAP

LOW ARVIE 82/512/0005

Reproduced from Ordnance
Survey 1:10 000 Map
Licence No: AL100002091

100 m

Craigie Barns

Bay of Allan

Eastfield

Low Barns

Hill Field

A 716

Crogo Burn

... the view, which always bring balm to
my spirit ...

Clearing away the Rubbish heap

The Matbro handler and the Ford 7740

Mother and Ethel

The Ladies of Low Arvie

Graham McQuaker brings another load of stone

Making a new road from In-bye to
Roadside

The noble Zeppelin of High Creoch

Susan, Number 47

Susan with Eddy of Low Arvie

Divining over the well

...two rodent operatives now patrol the shed...

Wodan in his worst moments

Wodan six weeks later

Lucky, with Gladeye, keeping her 'glad eye' on him.

Beauty with Lady Olga of Low Arvie

Mum watching over new born Quincy

3 cows graze on
Tracey's Island

Lady Rebecca, Lady Freya and Lady Ann down
in the rushes.

Lady Jade with Lady Jayne, just one week old, born 19th May 2005

Richard enjoying a conversation with Charlie

The New Conservatory

Rear of Low Arvie Farmhouse 2002

The rear of Low Arvie Farmhouse 2005

Low Arvie Farmhouse 2005

18

Buying the cattle

In the end, buying the cattle proved to be easier and less stressful than we had anticipated. We learned, towards the end of September, that there were few, if any, Belted Galloways to be bought, either at the October sale or privately. The Foot and Mouth outbreak of the previous year had wiped out many herds, and those breeders who still had their cattle, had been inundated with requests to buy, which had pushed the price up and had left the annual sale bereft of animals. This was a blow to our plans, and it meant we would have to think again about what breed to buy. We decided to wait and see what was available at the sale, but thought that we would probably have to settle for Black Galloways.

A few days after we had bought the tractor at the farm sale, I was preparing to go down to Castle Douglas to do my shopping and visit my mother. As usual, I asked if there was anything that Richard required, as we always tried to minimise the twenty-mile round trips by combining shopping and visiting with bill paying and buying farm equipment. We had a good system, where Richard rang up the machinery dealers and discussed with them what he wanted, and I picked it up for him. This saved him the time and trouble of leaving the farm to collect them, and me from bringing the wrong things. On this particular day, he asked me to call at Wallets Mart and ask Robin Anderson if he had the operator's manual for the tractor.

On my way home, I called into the Mart offices and found Robin at work behind his desk. He told me that they usually had the manuals for the machines they sold, but, on this occasion, they didn't appear to have ours. He wrote down the telephone number of the previous owner and gave it to me, so that we could ring and ask him if he still had it. During the course of our conversation, I mentioned to him that we had leased in quota for fifteen cows and were hoping to buy them at the October sale. I said that we had been hoping for Belties, but that we had discovered there were none. He verified this and told me that they only had one entry for the Belties sale, which was a young bull.

Almost as an after thought, Robin mentioned that he had heard of a complete herd of cattle for sale. "In fact," he said, "it is the same man who had your tractor. He is the farm manager of Cairnsmore farms at Cairsphairn, and they have decided to sell up. He is trying to sell the herd as a complete lot, rather than selling them off at the Mart, as he would like them to stay together, but there are more than fifteen, and they are Black Galloways not Belties. They have lived up on Bardennoch Hill and are used to the conditions up there, which are harder than at Low Arvie, so they would be all right on your land." I said I would tell Richard so that he could decide whether to mention it, when he rang the man about the tractor manual.

Later that day, Richard did ring the man, who was called Marcus Adamson, and spoke to him about the tractor manual, which Marcus said he had given to Wallets at the sale. Before he rang off, Richard mentioned the cattle. Marcus told him that there were twenty-four cows and eighteen calves. The cows were between five years old, having had two calves, and eleven years old with their eighth, but they weren't in calf at the moment. The present crop of calves had been born over such a wide period that he had decided to wait, before putting the bull in again, until the last one to calve was ready. This would give a tighter calving period the next year. However, before he could do this, the farm's owners had decided to sell up. Marcus didn't seem too sure about the sex of the calves, but thought there were only two bull calves and the rest heifers. He arranged get in touch with Richard in two or three weeks' time, for us to go and see them. They had spent the summer out on the hill, and he had only just begun to feed them every morning to get them tame enough to be viewed. This sounded a bit worrying, but Richard agreed to talk to Marcus again in due course.

The Galloway sale at the Mart was only two weeks away, and we had to decide before then, as it was imperative for us to get at least fifteen cattle soon, in order to claim the subsidy and retrieve the money we had spent leasing the quota. Two days before the sale, Marcus called at Low Arvie, and we spoke again about buying the cattle from Cairsphairn. He brought a bit more information, saying that there were, in fact, six bull calves and twelve heifers, and the oldest ones were seven months old and the three youngest being five, four and three months old. It was more or less agreed at this meeting that we would buy the whole herd, and that we would all go to the sale at the Mart to get some kind of guidance as to the price we should pay for them. Marcus said that he would be happy to keep them on the hill for a few more weeks and go and feed them every day, so that they would be more manageable. He said they were beginning to come down when they saw him coming, but they were still pretty wild. The fact that we wouldn't have to have them until late November would be a great benefit to us, as it would give us time to make several more trips down to Yorkshire to get more of our possessions. There were still quite a lot of things to bring up. We arranged to see Marcus at the sale, and then go the following day to see the cattle and finally agree to buy them, if we liked them, and talk after that about the price.

This way round of doing things was quite stressful to me, as there were too many what ifs and buts attached. If something went wrong and we couldn't buy the Cairnsmore cattle, where would we get more from? What if we couldn't agree a price? What if they were skinny and ill? However, Richard carried on in his usual calm way and refused to listen to my qualms!

Sale day came, and we drove down to the Mart at Castle Douglas once again. When we arrived in the saleroom, the atmosphere and anticipation were already starting to build. Farmers were once again standing around in groups, discussing topics of interest, and this time, we were able to recognise a few of the faces, and several of them nodded a greeting to us. By the time 11 o'clock came and the auctioneer entered his pulpit to start the sale, the room was full. Once more, it was mainly the men who gathered for the sale, but there were enough ladies for me not to feel conspicuous. After a short introduction from Allan Patterson, who was today's auctioneer, the metal doors opened and the first cow to be sold trotted into the ring. The only difference between this sale and the previous one was that, instead of the same sad man standing by the auctioneer watching his stock sold, each animal was accompanied into the ring by its owner.

The sale progressed and, once again, I studied the animals and tried to decide what it was that made some of them worth so much more than others. There was symmetry of shape and sturdiness of gait about the dearer ones which, accompanied by a proud carriage of the head and blackness of coat, seemed to contribute towards the higher prices. By this time the pedigree names were becoming more familiar and, with the owners accompanying the animals into the ring, I began to put names to faces.

When the sale was over, we ran across Marcus, and he said that he would be up at the cattle by about 8.30 the next morning. He would try and gather them into the pens, so that we could see them. We arranged to get there about 9 o'clock, to give him time to do this. We were to go on from there to another farm sale, which began at 11, so the schedule would be pretty tight.

It was drizzling as we left Low Arvie and drove along the road to Balmaclellan and, from there, up the Ayr road towards Cairsphairn. The cattle pens were this side of Cairsphairn, at the foot of Bardennoch Hill, where the cows had spent a lot of their life. The calves were born there and stayed with their mothers on the hill until it was time to wean them, at around seven months of age. This gave their mothers time to build up their reserves before the next calf came along, and the process began all over again. At the age of seven months, the calves were removed from the hill and taken onto the farm near Dumfries to be fed and watered and allowed to grow on, until they were mature enough to be sold, either as beef or as breeding stock, or taken back to the hill to join the herd there.

We had not been along this road before, but it was easy enough to find the place from Marcus' directions and, in any case, we spotted his Land rover Discovery parked just off the road. Richard drew up behind it. I looked to my left just as Richard said, "There they are!" and I had my first glimpse of 'The Ladies of Low Arvie.' They stood around in a shaggy group, their black coats gleaming with the early morning rain and, as we got out of the car, they began to move around restlessly, wary of the strangers. By Marcus' attitude, I could tell that he was nervous and worried that the cattle would not like us, and so I stayed by the gate and let Richard walk slowly and quietly up to the group. Although they were obviously on their guard, the cows allowed him to walk amongst them, and the calves hid themselves from my view amongst their larger mothers. I could see that the cows looked sturdy and strong, and I felt the first flood of relief that they were not scrawny and thin. The cows all appeared to have orange tags in their ears and, in the few glimpses I had of the calves, I noticed that theirs were yellow. I stood very still and looked at the milling throng of black bodies, with Richard moving through them, and wondered what his reaction to them would be. He had had a fair bit of experience with cattle, although mostly with beef animals, and, when I asked him later what he thought, he said that he, also, had had a pleasant surprise at their appearance and condition, and he had agreed with Marcus that we should buy them.

All that was left now was to set the price that we would pay. All the cows were full pedigree Galloways except one, which was a Black Galloway cross Blonde d'Aquitaine. There were twenty-four cows, but Marcus said he would only sell twenty-three, as one was no longer any good as a breeding cow. Also, there was one other that had a permanently snotty nose and looked as though she wouldn't go much longer. Richard decided to wait and see the prices, before deciding finally on this one. Of the others, three of them had borne no calf that year, and three had lost their calves. This was not a good sign, and cows that did not get pregnant were usually culled and replaced with new stock. Farmers cannot afford to feed animals that are not producing, and cows eat an enormous amount of food every day. In general, as with every other business, profit margins govern policy, and, where the cast-offs are old worn-out machines that do not work properly any longer, nobody has any problem with replacement, but, when it is a living animal which is the production unit, then its destruction and replacement becomes a highly emotive subject. Marcus had to send the old cow to the abattoir and incinerator in Kilmarnock. Government policy in force at any one time decrees what happens to 'fallen stock' as dead animals are called. Any that were just too old to produce any longer used to go into the food chain as pie meat, and the very worst ones that were sick and ill were sent to be made into glue, fertiliser and others things Since the 'Mad Cow' outbreak of the early nineties, the policy had been changed and, at the time we bought the Ladies, no animal over the age of thirty months was allowed enter the food chain, but had to be slaughtered and incinerated. We had heard of farmers mistaking the date and forgetting to send good beef animals to the Mart in time for them to be slaughtered before they were thirty months old. They had to send them to be incinerated, instead. Even one day too late made this necessary. This policy seems to be about to be reversed in 2003 with the reduction in the number of cases of vCJD.

Richard decided to take all the other twenty-three cows and, with the possible exception of Snotty Nose, who would remain on death row for a while, give them all another attempt at calving. A Slaughter Premium is paid to farmers who have to have animals destroyed, and, in order for us to qualify for this on Snotty Nose, she would have to remain on Low Arvie for sixty days before slaughter. So she had that amount of time left to either recover or get worse. With Low Arvie being at a lower altitude and having much kinder conditions than Bardennoch Hill, we thought it would be worth giving her the chance.

When Marcus came to the price fixing, he brought with him the pedigrees of the cows We found out that of the twenty-three cows, seventeen of them had been born on Bardennoch Hill and had presumably lived most of their lives there. When they were weaned at seven months, they would have been taken back to the farm to grow, and then returned to the hill as herd replacements, when they were old enough. The oldest two had been born in 1991 and were thus eleven years old, Snotty Nose and two others were from 1992 and six were from 1993. These all had the same father; a bull called Glenapp Trooper. The remaining five cows from the hill were born on Bardennoch in 1994 and their sire was Penninghame Xanthin. Amongst these home bred cattle, there was a mother and daughter, three sets of full sisters and two half sisters. Marcus had bought the remaining eight cows from another breeder at Dalswinton and they were younger, having been born in 1995, 1996 and 1997. They were the daughters of three different bulls.

Over two pots of tea and most of a cake, we fixed a price for the cows and calves to everybody's satisfaction. We paid a lot less for Snotty Nose, and she would turn out to be either a bargain or a break even, depending on whether she bore another calf or not. Until now Richard had paid for everything to do with the farm from his capital, and I paid for the domestic expenses, and, although we regarded everything as ours, I felt that I wanted to make a contribution towards the farm as well. I, therefore, decided to buy the cattle, as a present for Richard, because the business was entirely his, although we jointly owned the land and buildings. To do this, I had cashed in the Premium Bonds, which I had bought with high hopes some time before, but which had never fulfilled those hopes, and I enjoyed the thought that the money had now been put to this much more exciting use.

We also agreed with Marcus that we should get the cows from Bardennoch on November 20th, and he told me what I needed to do before this, to fulfil the many rules and regulations that exist in twenty-first century Britain, concerning the keeping of cattle.

19

Red Tape

This area was where I felt I could be of most use to Richard. He, like most men, had little patience when it came to paperwork, and preferred to be outside, whereas there were so many things about being outside that I didn't like—cold, rain and insects to name but three. I was far happier sitting at a table or the computer, using my brain, rather than exercising my muscles.

I set to with a will, therefore to work my way through the maze of regulations concerning the legalities of cattle keeping. Marcus put me on the path by telling me that I had to ring something called BCMS to let them know that we were getting some cows, and get them to send me some 'stickers'. Apparently I had to get these before the cattle came. BCMS, I discovered, was the British Cattle Movement Service, and they operate something called the Cattle Tracing System. Every bovine animal in the UK has to be registered with this system from its birth, right through every change of location to its death. By far the simplest and best way to record all these movements, is through the Internet, and I had purchased my new computer just for this very moment. As soon as Marcus had left that afternoon, I logged on to www.bcms.gov.uk and sent them an email entitled 'First Steps', asking them to tell me how to get up and running. Within an hour, I received a reply, "Crikey," I thought, "these people are really efficient!" and I clicked on the open button. However, I was slightly disappointed to read:

Sent: Monday, November 04, 2002 5:15 PM
Subject: RE: First steps

Dear Sir/Madam,

Thank you for your e-mail to CTS Online.

It has been forwarded to the Customer Service team at the British Cattle Movement Service.

Please allow 5 working days for a reply to be sent to you.

BCMS wishes to communicate with our customers in an efficient and effective way, whether it be over the telephone, by letter or by e-mail. Whenever we receive e-mails, or are advised by a keeper of their e-mail address, we intend to keep a note of the address so that we can contact you by e-mail where it is appropriate to do so.

Still, I figured that five days was not too long to wait, there was plenty more to be getting on with and there was still sixteen more days to go, before we were actually to take delivery of the animals.

The next morning I rang SEERAD in Dumfries to enquire what we should do about using the quota we had leased. They told me that we had to fill in an application form, telling them that we had the cattle on the farm and giving the ear tag numbers of those we were claiming the subsidy on. This form had to be received by them before December 6th, or we would lose the premium payment. The best way to get this form to them was to take it in person and get a receipt, because the post was not totally reliable, and proof of postage was not proof of delivery. The cattle then had to be retained on the farm for a minimum of six months from the date of application, so, although we didn't intend to get rid of any of them, except perhaps Snotty Nose, I thought we should send in the application form as soon as we were eligible. It was a good job that I made this phone call, as I spoke with a man who was very helpful, and he explained quite a lot of things to me. This, roughly speaking, is what I learnt:

- All cattle have to be fitted with an ear tag in each ear within, in our case, 20 days of birth.

- The ear tags have to be specially created for each farm and have printed on them the birth farm code number and the individual number of the animal.

- The ordering of these ear tags must be done through registered orderers, who are the only ones who can deal with the ear tag manufacturers.

- The ordering of these ear tags generates the British Cattle Movement System headquarters in Workington to send out the corresponding passport applications, to go with the numbered ear tags.

- When a calf is born, his ear is tagged and the number is registered on the Cattle Tracing System at Workington, and he is issued with a passport.

- His passport goes with him wherever he goes, from birth to death.

- This passport is like a chequebook, where the 'cheques' are movement documents

- Every time the animal changes location or ownership, one of these 'cheques' has to be removed and sent to the British Cattle Movement System headquarters at Workington, *unless* one is connected to this system via the internet, when the movement has to be registered on the website, and *on no account* in these circumstances must a 'cheque' be sent to Workington. In either case, the movement must be registered at Workington within seven days of the movement's taking place.

- Workington issue sheets of small stickers, containing the name, address and farm code number to every livestock farmer, and, when the animal arrives on his farm, he must place one of these stickers on the 'cheque' in the passport containing that of the seller, and this cheque must be sent to Workington *unless* he is connected to this system via the internet, when the movement has to be registered on the website and *on no account* in these circumstances must a 'cheque' be sent to Workington. He then puts one of his stickers on the new topmost 'cheque' and keeps the passport safer than Fort Knox keep the USA's gold reserves. When he sells the animal, the new owner must put one of his stickers below this one, remove the cheque from the passport and send it to Workington, *unless* he is connected to the system via the internet, when the movement must be registered in that way, and, *on no account...*

- When Workington receive these movement cards or when they get round to looking at your entry of movements on the website, they check the animal's numbers in their records and, in the case of movement cards, enter the movements into the relevant farm records, or, in the case of website entries, allow them to pass into the system as verified.

- If the number of the passport cheque or the number entered on the website does not tally with their records, then the entry goes into a section called Queried movements.

- It is the farmer's responsibility to check that the people at Workington have made these entries correctly, and up to him to contact Workington if there is a problem. Even if the farmer sent in the correct records at the correct time and

Workington make the mistake, it is still deemed to be the farmer's fault, if the records are wrong. If the farmer does not do this checking and he subsequently applies for subsidy on an animal that is in the Queried section, then the payment will be withheld. Every time a payment is claimed on an animal, Workington check to make sure that it is where it is supposed to be, according to their records.

I felt really pleased at this point that Richard had decided to spend his declining years rearing beef cattle, and not sitting by the fire reading! However, I plodded on and found out that we got a farm code number from yet a different organisation called Animal Health, and, for us, the local office was in Ayr. When I phoned them, I spoke to a very nice, helpful lady called Jean, who said that she could fill in the necessary form, whilst speaking to me on the telephone, and she began to ask me the relevant questions, name, address and so on. She said that we had to nominate a Veterinary Surgeon to be placed on our record and, since I had no idea of who or where the local vets were located, I got out the Yellow pages and picked the first one on the list in Castle Douglas. I gave her the name of Dunmuir Veterinary Group. She gave me some further information about their rules for keeping cattle:

If a cow calved prematurely, the vet had to be called to take samples to be tested for Brucellosis, or Contagious Abortion, a nasty disease that is thought to be spread by badgers. Also, they require medical records of treatment given to cattle to be kept, and these must be available for inspection at any time.

She then said she would issue us a Holding Registration Document and Herd Mark, which would be put on the ear tags and passports of all cattle born on Low Arvie.

We now had a Farm Code Number 82/512/005, denoting our County, the parish within the county and the holding within the parish, respectively, and a Herd Mark, which turned out to be 585065.

Everyday I checked my emails for the answer from Workington, but five days came and went, then six and seven and still there was no reply, and so, in frustration, on the eighth day I rang them. After several lists of options, pressing different buttons and holding on for a while, I eventually spoke to a real human being by the name of Michael O'Donnell. He was extremely helpful, and I explained to him what I required. He talked me through the Cattle Tracing System and what I was required to do. As with the Animal Health lady, he filled the form in over the telephone and said he would send me my Internet user ID and password, our farm stickers and a file of information the next day. The stickers are printed with the farmer's name and address and the farm code number. This is also on the sticker in barcode form, so that it can be scanned by machine when necessary. Michael told me that I would need to enter the website and log in with my user ID and password, and then I would be able to enter all cattle movements, both on and off the farm. He told me that all cattle now have to have two ear tags and, if they lose one of these, then a new one must be ordered and the replacement made as soon as possible. This system has only been introduced since the BSE crisis of the mid-eighties and, prior to that, cattle only had one ear tag, therefore our older cows born before the crisis may only have one. The new yellow ear tags are made with the animal's 12-digit number, which consists of the farm of birth's 6-digit herd mark, followed by an individual number of a further six digits. This number is stamped on the accompanying passport and must be entered on the Cattle Tracing System within twenty days of birth, in the case of beef animals, or three days in the case of dairy animals. This is presumably because beef animals stay with their mothers on the farm, whereas dairymen take the calves from the mothers after 24 hours and, often, the calves are sold soon after. Michael also said that when the time came for calves to be born on the farm, we must order ear tags through the usual supplier, and passport application forms would be generated automatically. However, if we were entering information on line then, *on no account*. All this was very new and somewhat confusing to me, at this point in time, but I have realised that the thing to do is to take one process at a time, as it arrives, and work through it. Each time, the procedure becomes more familiar and less worrying.

Michael was as good as his word and, two days later, we received a large brown envelope containing BCMS Information Leaflets 3 to 10, a letter explaining that BCMS Information Leaflets 1 and 2 are now obsolete, as all the information is now contained in leaflets 3 to 9, and a list entitled 'Ear tag Manufacturers Supplying Currently Approved Cattle Ear tags'. The title of the leaflets and the number of pages in each one might help to explain the complicated machinations that farmers have to be aware of at the present time:

No.3 Guidance Notes on Cattle Passports—19 pages
No.4 Completion of the Cattle Passport application form—10 pages
No.5 How you can help us to give you the best possible service—2 pages
No.6 Cattle Identification Inspections explained—3 pages
No.7 BCMS: Progress and New Developments—6 pages
No.8 The Certificate of CTS Registration (CHR3) Guidance notes—11 pages

No.9 Application for Certificate of CTS Registration (CHR3) Guidance notes—10 pages
No. 10 BCMS: Changing to meet your needs—9 pages

On the last page of this last leaflet I read the following familiar paragraph:

Communication by e-mail

We want to communicate with our customers in an efficient and effective way, whether it is over the phone, by letter or by e-mail. To help us to do this, we would like to collect customer e-mail addresses. We will add your e-mail address to the information we already hold, such as your holding number and address, on the Cattle Tracing System (CTS) database and on our internal system for logging calls and correspondence….

By separate letter we received our user ID and password to enable us to log on to the system's website and we were ready to enter in our 'Movements On' when the great day came!

Oh yes, remember the email I sent on November 4th and the 5-day reply? This was November 14th and still no answer! I did eventually get one, or to be more precise six answers, on the 23rd, 26th, 27th and three on the 28th of November. All of them said

Dear Sir/ Madam
Thank you for your email to CTS on line.

It has been forwarded to the customer Services Team.
Please allow 5 Days for a reply to be sent to you.

BCMS wished to communicate with our customers in an efficient and effective way….

Sometime later, long after we had got the cattle, I received a phone call from someone at BCMS wanting to help me set up my system!

20

The Ladies arrive

As well as trying to learn the ropes with BCMS and SEERAD and preparing the fields and fences to contain forty-one Galloways, we had decided to make two more trips down to Yorkshire before the cattle came, to bring up more of our things. Although the journey could be done in three and a half hours in a car, it was nearer to five and a half in the van towing the trailer, and, on a three day trip, this didn't leave too much time for packing and loading at the Yorkshire end. We also tried to see family and friends whilst we were down there, as it would be a good while before we could welcome them to Low Arvie, and so life during these few weeks was extremely busy and tiring. I was thankful that I had got Mother settled into Bothwell House and I didn't have to worry any longer about her. Norma, the housekeeper, proved to be wonderfully supportive during this time, and indeed, has continued to be so.

Whilst Richard was out on the farm repairing one of the fences, he stubbed his finger on a fence post, and a splinter of wood had gone down his right hand index finger nail and penetrated the nail bed. Over the course of a few days, this became infected and created a large and very painful abscess under the nail. It was another problem to add to our difficulties at this time, and, not only caused him sleepless nights, but considerably hindered his ability to work. It became clear that it was not going to cure itself, and several hours on one of our trips south was taken up sitting in the casualty department of Doncaster Royal Infirmary. This was precious time that we could hardly spare and, when one of the nurses told us that, as a non-emergency, we would be several more hours, he reluctantly decided to go home unattended to and continue taking the painkillers, whist trying to get on with the loading of our goods.

On our return journey to Dumfriesshire the next day, we called into the hospital in Dumfries to see if that would be any more helpful. In stark contrast to the emergency department in Doncaster, the waiting room in Dumfries only contained three people sitting on the rows of chairs, and I had barely opened the

Reader's Digest I picked up from the table, when a nurse came and called Richard's name and led him away. When I had perused not just this magazine, but three or four more that I found, I was astonished to realise that almost an hour had passed, and Richard was still missing. I tried to exercise my newfound patience and flicked idly through three or four more women's magazines, having exhausted the Reader's Digests. After a further half-hour, my patience was still intact, but worry began to insinuate itself into my brain and, as nonchalantly as I could, I got up and began wandering over in the general direction of where Richard had disappeared. Encountering a nurse, I asked her if she knew where he was. She very kindly went to find him and soon returned to say he was still being attended to. I decided he must have been taken away from the general waiting area and left in another area for a while, as he couldn't possibly have been under treatment for all this time! After a further quarter of an hour, during which time I tried to divert my attention by reading the posters and notices around the room, and deciding that I most definitely was in the early stages of diabetes, pregnancy and all the other conditions featured on them, I could wait no longer. Quietly I began to make my way down the corridor that the nurse had gone down, to see if I could find out what exactly was happening for myself. There were very few people about, and no one challenged me as I walked slowly past a few doors trying to listen if anything was happening inside. Eventually a nurse, clad from head to toe in hospital green, emerged from a room further down the corridor and, when she had disappeared into another room, I moved swiftly to the door. It was a swing door with no actual fastening, and I leant gently on it and peered inside. In the middle of the room was a bed and lying full length on this bed was Richard, with his right arm stretched out along a kind of small ironing board. He was talking to a young man dressed in white, who was in the process of wrapping the offending finger in a large white bandage. Neither of them saw me, and, reassured that Richard was still with us and apparently happy and healthy, I slipped away back to the waiting room to continue my vigil.

Altogether he was gone just over two hours, and all of the time was spent in that room, being treated. The abscess was in a very nasty place under the nail, and he had undergone almost an operation to have it lanced and the resultant, gaping wound packed and dressed. With all that we had to do in a short space of time, such a wound was a great handicap. Apart from the restrictions it placed on Richard's abilities to use his hands, we had to take time to go to the surgery in Castle Douglas three times a week to have the dressings changed, and it was a great relief, in more ways than one, when it eventually began to heal.

We made one further trip to Yorkshire the weekend before the cattle were due to arrive, leaving on the Friday and returning on the Sunday night. We tried to think of everything that we would need over the winter and include it in the equipage for the return journey. Any spare space was taken up with furniture and effects that we wanted to keep, but for which there was no room in the house as it was at present. The alterations would be expensive enough, and we wanted to prevent the need for purchasing items of furniture that we already possessed. The problem with this policy was not just the transportation of them, but the storage for the foreseeable future at Low Arvie. The house was already at bursting point and very difficult to keep dust free, and many of the outside buildings were full of farm equipment and vehicles and, in any case, were not weatherproof or secure enough to house household furniture and effects, without risk of spoiling. The only area available for this was a part of Richard's workshop, and the floor space in this gradually became smaller and smaller as tables, cupboards and boxes of pots and pans were piled up in one corner.

There was a second floor room in the large shed across the yard from the farmhouse that was empty, but it was the home of Barney the Owl, and he wasn't the most house proud of creatures, to say the least! Also, the entrance to it was up a very rickety flight of wooden steps and, as it had once been the meal house for the farm, there was just a small landing at the top of the steps and then a barrier of two or three feet to climb over, before you could get into the room. This had been to prevent the meal from cascading down the steps, as it piled up on the floor of the room. There was no way that furniture could be taken up that way. There was, however, a door in the farmyard face of the room, overlooking the yard below, where the meal had been put in, and Richard decided that, with the help of the Matbro telescopic handler, which we had bought in Carlisle on one of our trips South, he could access the space through this. Accordingly, he spent a day rectifying years of Barney's neglectful housekeeping, and painting out the room with white emulsion. Poor Barney was not a happy owl and, for a while, we missed his nightly flights around the buildings. However, he is not an owl to bear a grudge for long, and he soon found other more suitable accommodation in the cattle shed and now resides peacefully behind the water tanks at the far end. This has brought us an added benefit, too, as his presence in there has helped to keep away the forty or so crows and jackdaws, which were using the shed as a night roost for the first few months of our occupation. We hope he realises that his move was in a good cause, and he soon finds a Mrs Barney to share his new quarters with him!

We eventually got our goods and chattels stored and Richard's finger healed, and at last the great day came. We were up early and breakfasted quickly, then Richard went off outside to make the final preparations for our new 'family'. Straw was spread on the floor of the building, and the sacks of suckler cow rolls were piled up on the far side of the trough. The cattle shed is old, but still service-able, and consists of two sections separated by a low wall that is topped with a feeding trough about eight inches deep. The animals have access to one side, and the other side is used for feed storage and for putting the food into the trough. At three or four points above the trough there are drinking bowls connected to the water tanks in the other building. They have a valve in them that is operated by a large back plate and, as the cow drinks, her nose presses on this back plate and opens the valve, thus allowing more water to seep in to the bowl. This was to be the feeding place for the cows for the first week, as we needed to get them used to us and to tame them as much as possible, because they were soon due to have their annual vaccination against liver fluke and the insertion of a copper tablet into their stomachs to keep them healthy. Cows are very friendly animals and respond, as we all do, to kindness, if they are brought up near to people. The cows that we bought were now quite old and had lived most of their lives away from people, so we knew that it would be a hard task to 'tame' them very quickly. Also, after living on the same hill for years and years, they would be disorientated and wary at being snatched away from it and dumped in a strange environment. Someone said to me recently that vets have to be so much more skilled than doc-tors, because their patients cannot tell them where they hurt and the vet has to find that out before he can begin to help. How often I have wished that the cows **could** understand, when we try to offer them reassurance that all is well. It has been a long slow process of example and experience on the part of the animals, and patience on our part, but I think we are getting there slowly.

That day, November 20th 2002, was the day we began. It was about 10 a.m. when the McWilliams cattle wagon rattled into the yard and backed up to the gate in the middle of the cattle shed wall. The driver jumped out and opened the back doors, and the cows had their first glimpse of their new home. Gradually, they backed out of the truck and into the shed. They were hot and steaming, after being in an enclosed space for the half-hour or so of the journey, and stood look-ing around in a bewildered fashion. We had opened a bale of haylage and put some into the trough to try and reassure them that we were friendly, but they didn't show any interest at first, and just continued to stare balefully around them. This first load was just twelve cows, and they had left their calves behind on the hill, so that was a further stress factor for them, and I hoped the next load would not be long. They were bringing the cows in two trucks, and the first one was to go back for the eighteen calves. The driver said that the second batch would not be long, and he left to fetch the calves.

I stood on the far side of the feeding trough and watched Richard move quietly amongst the new arrivals, speaking to them soothingly in a quiet voice. We tried to tempt them to the trough to try our haylage, and, as the steam rising from their backs lessened and their breathing became quieter, one or two of them began to amble slowly towards the proffered fare. I have no idea which one it was that took the first mouthful, but I would like to place a bet that it was the one with number 31 on a red tag dangling from her ear. This is Bardennoch Hill Brownie, daughter of Glenapp Trooper and Brownie Voracious of Mosscroft, with ancestors bearing such noble names as Ulysses 2nd of Lochurr and Prince of Glenturk, but more affectionately known to us as Spot, owing to a round white mark at the point of her left jaw bone, about the size of a ten pence piece. She is one of the older cows and has proved to be a great character. She is very much her own cow and can often be found lying down, chewing a peaceful cud on her own, with no thought or worry as to where the rest of the herd are.

After this first move, the others slowly began to make their way over to the trough, and soon there were twelve heads moving up and down rhythmically as they pulled at the grass and chewed thoughtfully away.

Eventually, I realised that an hour had passed since this first truckload of cows had arrived, and the driver had said that the second load would not be long. Every time I heard a diesel engine passing, I looked anxiously towards the road in the hope of seeing it coming along, but the only things that passed were the lorries loaded with logs from the forest and tractors. I looked at my watch and saw that it would soon be lunchtime. But, just then, the diesel engine I could hear **did** belong to the cattle truck, and the next batch arrived. The driver said they had had trouble separating the cows and calves and had had to wait for help from the first driver, but I did not want to enquire too closely into the reason, imagining animals in distress chasing round and round the pens. As the back door was opened, I could see that one of the cows was lying down, and it appeared that the others were trampling on her. For a while, I was concerned that she had died on the journey, but after a minute or two she began to struggle to her feet. Before she had achieved this, the cows behind her started to move towards the light, and she was pushed out of the lorry, slithering and sliding down the aluminium ramp into the shed. Half standing and half lying she blinked her eyes and looked round her, as her sisters rushed past her to join the first batch in the shed. Only when the rush was over, did she manage to stand up and, appearing to be little the worse for her experience, she ambled over to the trough and picked at the hay-lage. It wasn't many minutes before the other truck pulled up, and the calves were let out to be reunited with their mothers.

Although most of the calves were seven months old, they seemed tiny at the side of their mothers, as they quickly sorted themselves out into family units again. As with all young animals, they had a cuteness and appeal not shared by the cows, and I felt pleased and proud to share the ownership of these small, black creatures and their mothers with Richard. They were a much more enjoyable asset than dusty old Premium Bonds that sat in a filing cabinet, and, although they might not have the potential to win us a million pounds, I felt sure that we would gain much more than a million pounds worth of pleasure from them.

The Ladies of Low Arvie had arrived!

21

Tragedy strikes

The cattle were to stay on the fields closest to the farm buildings for the week following their arrival, in order for them to have time to get used to us and their new home. Drew had taken his cattle home when they got near to calving some weeks before, and this had given the grass time to put on some more growth before the season ended and the winter came, so there was plenty for them to eat. This was also supplemented with the pellets that they were fed every morning in the shed to help them into condition for the coming of the bull. Marcus had arranged with a local Galloway breeder for us to hire one of his bulls, and he was due to arrive on December 2nd. We felt we should lose no time getting the cows in calf again, as they were already well overdue in the normal scheme of things. Usually they will go to the bull when the new calf is about two months old, and the calf will suckle until the cow is about seven months pregnant and will then be taken away from her to allow her to 'dry off' and prepare for giving new life to another calf.

When the cows came to us from Bardennoch Hill, they were not used to human beings. Marcus had gone up to check on them every day, but he had other duties in Dumfries, and so was only with them a short time. Because our duties were only concerned with looking after the cattle—and ourselves—and we were altogether on the farm, it was easier for Richard to give them more attention. He spent spare moments walking amongst them, both in the daylight and the dark, talking to them and, gradually, they lost their wildness and became much calmer. Before long he was able to approach them without causing any uneasiness in the herd. However, it was sometime before they were as easy about the approach of two people together and, for the first few months, it took very little to 'spook' them into stampeding off in the opposite direction. Because of this stampeding, which is very frightening to experience, as cows are large animals and can move very fast when they wish to, I did not very often venture near them with Richard during this period. This practice of Richard's of calmly moving

123

amongst them has paid off now. When they need any treatment, he can get them into the crush by himself, and we do not have to trouble other people for help. He has a system of gates which swing round 180 degrees and, by clever manipulation of these, he can 'persuade' the cows to go where he wants them to in the shed. It still is impossible to drive the cows forward as a herd, but he can sometimes lead them, carrying a feed sack, to the desired destination.

The vet had been booked to visit us on Wednesday 27th November to castrate the six bull calves and inject the whole herd with anti-liver fluke vaccine, and Richard decided to take the calves away from the mothers at the same time and house them in the large cattle building across the yard. They would remain in this building for the winter months and be weaned onto protein rich 'muesli' and the haylage Drew had made in our fields on our arrival. It was unfortunate that we had sold off half of the haylage, thinking that we were only going to buy fifteen cows, as we would only have enough for the calves and would have to buy in food for the cows. There would be enough grass for the first few weeks, but when that was gone and had stopped growing, they would need something else besides their daily ration of pellets. Richard had already bought some bales of barley straw and transported them up from Yorkshire, and this would be the diet of the cows along with the pickings off the land and their daily ration of pellets until the grass began to grow again next spring. There would be plenty of rushes if they got desperate! (They never did get *that* desperate, unfortunately.)

Farmers must minimise the amount they spend on animal feed, as the profit margin on selling their products is very low. The one good thing is that the cattle are saleable propositions at every stage of their development, and it is up to the individual farmer to decide the time that he can make the best profit on his animals. There are suckler herd farmers who keep their offspring until they are 'finished' and ready for slaughter, and there are others who sell the young animals at weaning, to others to finish. We had made no decisions about our six bull calves and were going to wait and see how things developed. Galloways are, by nature, slow growing and, whereas some breeds can be finished in a year or less, they need between two and three years to grow. Richard had made enquiries of the local feed merchant 'Tarff Valley Ltd.' as to the prices of various ingredients and sat with pencil and paper working out percentages of protein and other necessary constituents to give the best feed value at the lowest price. The calves would need to be started on special calf mixtures that were quite expensive, and then once established, like babies on solid food, they could be moved onto mixtures that cost a bit less. It is illegal now to feed herbivore animals on animal protein—a practice that gave rise to the BSE outbreak in the eighties—and the protein content of their feed now comes from plants like peas and Soya beans. The other ingredients include wheat, barley, sugar beet and their by-products.

The first week that the cows were at Low Arvie was one of the wettest we had known, and the rain poured down unceasingly in torrents. The building that the cattle came into every morning for their pellets was one of the central buildings, and they had to pass by the end of the workshop to get into it. The gutters on this large edifice drained directly onto the land, in the path of this daily journey and, after two days, there was a muddy quagmire, where previously there had been lush green grass. As the days passed and the rain continued, this area of land became wetter and wetter, until the animals were squelching through it up to their knees, and it was impossible for humans in wellies to walk on the slimy morass. We had given them the two nearest fields, In-bye and Brookfield, to spend this week in, but they could only use half of In-bye, as the ditch which cut it in half, though blocked and level with the field, was impossible to cross. Brookfield consisted of two half hills, with the main drain, taking the water that flowed from the hill across the road down to the burn, making the boundary between them. The drain was crossed in two places, by a culvert leading to Hill Field and a ford leading north towards Low Knowe and the Bog of Allan. The cows and calves seemed to settle into their new quarters quite easily and spent the week eating off the grass and pondering the rain.

On the Wednesday morning, when they came in to the building for their ration, Richard slipped away round to the back of the shed and shut the gates across, so that they couldn't get back outside again. The vet was expected at 9.30, and just before 9, Marcus arrived to help handle the animals and to show Richard how to administer the copper tablets. These were large oval shaped capsules and Marcus had brought a long handled tool like a pair of forceps to push them down into the cow's stomachs. The vet arrived promptly, and I went into the house and closed the door on the scene. I do not like to see anyone, human or animal, in distress, and I felt sure that there would be plenty of reason for this, that morning. Once again, I felt it would be nice to explain that things were for their own good. I started to busy myself in the house and, switching on the radio and turning up the volume, tried to ignore any noises that were going on outside.

When eventually I ventured out to see if they were ready for coffee, I found that things were not as bad as I had feared. The animals had all been herded into the north half of the shed and, from here, were guided one at a time into the cattle crush. This is a structure of iron poles and metal sheets formed into a crate large enough to hold a cow or a bull, but in a confined way, so that they can be attended to with the least likelihood of injury to either man or beast. Cows are large weighty objects and subject to panic, when they can inflict serious injury or even death on their handlers, and they must be treated with respect at all times. The three men seemed to be working in harmony, with Marcus and Richard guiding the cows into the crush for the vet to inject them and castrate the calves, as they took their turn. I couldn't see what he was doing, but it did not appear to take very long, and the southern half of the shed was filling up with those animals that had been seen to.

I left them to it and had just got back into the house when Richard came to the door. "Can you run down to the vet's in Castle Douglas and fetch some more liver fluke vaccine", he asked, "he hasn't brought enough." I immediately went to get my coat and the car keys, as I knew that it would take me the best part of an hour to get there and back, and that would mean keeping the cattle confined for longer than we had hoped. When I went out to get in the car, the vet was in the yard speaking into his mobile phone, telling the surgery what it was I was going for. He nodded to me and said that they would have it ready.

When I returned with the packages, the vet had gone, leaving Richard to finish off the vaccinations with the stuff I had fetched. Whilst I had been gone, the calves had been taken across the yard into the cattle court. I went to look at them and felt sorry for the forlorn little faces that turned towards me. I spoke to them reassuringly but it didn't seem to make a difference.

It was lunchtime when Richard and Marcus came into the kitchen with the job finished. They were very dirty and thirsty as well as hungry, and I served up the hot soup I had prepared, whilst they cleaned themselves up in the 'wet' kitchen. When we had eaten, we sat at the table, and I stuck the stickers in the right places on the movement 'cheques' and passports, whilst Marcus and Richard had signed in the requisite spaces. Then, Marcus left us and we relaxed for a while after the stresses of the morning.

I then had to start getting to grips with the communication to BCMS to record our 'movements on'. . Marcus was not an 'on-line' customer and so he had taken away his 'movements off' cards to put in the post box on the way home. These movements have to be notified to BCMS within seven days of the movement's taking place, otherwise a fate worse than death is supposed to befall us. I am not sure what it is but I think it will concern having payments withheld, as that is the usual sanction that is threatened.

After a short rest and a few deep breaths, then, I sat down in front of the computer and prepared to 'log on' in earnest for the first time. I had my pile of Registration Certificates to my left hand and, with some trepidation, I entered our User ID and password in the correct place on the BCMS website.

Since 2000 a new system of numbering cattle has been introduced into Britain. This is supposedly to make it easier for them to be traced throughout their lives. Each farm has a six-digit identifying code number, of which ours is 585065, and this is the first half of the identifying number of all cattle born on our farm. There then follows a further six digit number comprising a 'check digit', which apparently 'allows the number to be checked for accuracy very quickly'. This is all we are told, but these digits are one through seven and then begin again at one. The remaining five digits are the animals individual number and, thus, the first calf born on Low Arvie will have the twelve digit identification number 585065 100001 and the next will be 585065 200002 and so on until the eighth, which will be 585065 100008. They will also have a passport bearing this number that has to go with them wherever they go, as a record of their journey from birth to death. All this is very reassuring as a consumer of British beef, to know that each and every animal receives this amount of recording, but as a farmer attempting to follow the stringent rules, there is a lot to remember and a lot to get right, in order to comply.

Our cows, however, were born before the days of this system when things were different, but possibly not much simpler. They still had a holding number and an individual number but their 'passport' was just a Certificate of Registration. The holding numbers were different, each containing letters as well as numbers, and the individual numbers also were alphanumeric. Most of our cows had a holding number, which was D2017, and their individual numbers consisted of two numbers and a letter, thus 37G, 35G and so on. I slowly worked my way through the pile of Certificates, entering in these numbers and letters, and I heaved a sigh of relief as the last letter was typed. All I had to do now was to check in three days time that they had been passed into the system.

Fortunately, I am, at times, impatient and I decided to log on the next day and see what had happened to my entries. I was horrified to discover that all but three of the cows had been rejected, and, in some distress, I called the help line number of BCMS. This just added frustration to my distress, as I steered my way through the various options, pressing the requisite buttons on the telephone, until at last there was a real person at the other end. "Oh yes," she said when I had explained the problem, "it will be because those numbers do not have enough digits to fill all the available spaces, and whoever made the initial entries onto the system will have used a haphazard pattern. In order for the system to accept your entries, you have to match the figures and letters to this initial pattern. If I were you, I would send the cards in by post and let us enter them for you!" So much for twenty-first century technology!

That first night, when I had finished entering the numbers in, I looked at the clock and discovered that it was time the evening meal was ready, and so I left the computer and busied myself in the kitchen. When the potatoes were on and cooking, I decided to go and see how the calves were getting on and nipped along to the cattle court for a peep. What I found there made my heart sink. The calves were all standing still, with their little bodies heaving in and out, and their tongues protruding grotesquely from their mouths. Their breath was making puffs of condensation, and they looked to be in great distress. Quickly, I ran across the yard to the byre, where the smallest bull calf had been bedded down inside with his mother to give him a chance to recover from his castration. I was pleased to see that all was peaceful here, and the little chap was suckling content-edly at his mother's udder. The two smallest heifer calves had also been left with their mothers and were somewhere outside in the dark rainy night, so it was not possible to check on them until morning. I found Richard in the workshop and told him that I was not happy about the calves, and we walked together to look at them. There was no change, and, as I gazed round at the unhappy scene, I noticed one calf that seemed to be in a worse state than the others. He was stand-ing by the far gate, head hanging down, sides heaving in and out and his little black tongue showing in his open mouth. I had no experience of calves, although Richard had reared calves from a few days old, but it was plain even for me to see that there was something very wrong. We decided to leave them in peace while we ate our meal, and then see how they were. If things were still the same, we would ring the vet. We were worried that the little bull calf may be suffering more, because of complications from his operation.

After tea we went back to look at the calves and found them a lot worse. It was very distressing to see them in this way. The little calf that had so concerned me before was in a really bad way, sides heaving, tongue lolling and little eyes shut as though to shut out the misery. We were worried that the castration operation may have caused internal bleeding, and so I hurried in to ring the vet, and she said she would come straight away. When she came, she told us that she was new to the practice having only been here six weeks, and it soon became obvious that she had no answer to offer. She went into the pen and tied the little bull calf to a post to examine it. That must have been the final straw for him, because he gave one convulsive movement and died before our eyes. It was a devastating blow to us in the first week of our venture, and I came inside and wept for the poor little chap. Richard stayed with the vet whilst she did a post mortem, but she found no explanation for the symptoms and, in the end, we put it down to the extreme stress of being castrated and then parted from their mothers, within a week of being moved from their home on the hill. We could do nothing for the remaining calves but see that they had food to eat and water to drink, and, with heavy hearts, we left them and went to bed.

The next morning they seemed a little better, at least they had all survived the night. Gradually, they improved and settled into their new life in the big shed. We fed them a mixture of flaked maize and rolled peas night and morning, and they had access to the haylage Drew and his men had made for us in the summer.

The calves were to stay in the shed all the winter as the land at that side of the farm was so wet and boggy that it was dangerous for the little animals, and we spent many hours in there, over the next few months, feeding them and putting fresh straw down for them to sleep on every few days. I was the one who tended most to their needs, whilst Richard looked after the big cows, and they soon began to take on personalities of their own. Some of them were very amenable to being stroked and touched, whilst others have preferred to remain aloof, but constant contact with them has meant that they are calm and quiet and easy to work with, at the times when it is necessary to treat them for various parasites and vaccines

22

Bulls One and Two

The calves continued to improve slowly and, although we never forgot little 23, we began to feel happier. Life settled down into a pattern of feeding and caring for our new charges. It was very important to get the cows in calf again as quickly as possible, because it would be at least three years before their new calves were saleable, and we began to see any return on our investment. Although we were not entirely dependent on the farm for our income, we did want it to be fairly self-supporting at some time in the future.

It is usual to put the cows to the bull about two months after they calve, but circumstances had meant that our cows were now seven months away from their last calf. Marcus had arranged with a farmer friend of his to hire us his young Galloway bull, and one week later Xingu was duly delivered to the farm. He was very large and black and had a large copper ring through his nose. I was very scared of him at first and kept my distance, but gradually, I realised that what they say is true, the bulls of beef breeds are more docile than the cows. After keeping him in quarantine for a short time, Richard then walked him up to Hill field where the cows were now living.

It was by now winter, and the grass that was left in the fields was pretty poor stuff and low in nutrients, so Richard had bought in some concentrates to give them every morning. In addition, they had barley straw to supplement what they found on the land. It was at this time that the cow with number 57 on her ear tag began to make her presence felt. Checking the pedigree certificates, I discovered that she was Beauty 29th of Dalswinton. Every morning, when Richard appeared carrying the bag of pellets, she would bellow like a bull and dance around him, like some elephantine ballet dancer. At first, this was quite frightening, but soon Richard realised that this was her way of welcoming him and, more particularly, the bag of pellets. He had to be careful, though, as Galloways are large animals and, having back feet attached to half a ton of cow whizzing past your ears, can be a bit hair raising, to say the least.

The first few mornings that Xingu was with the cows, Richard used his trip up with the concentrates to watch for signs of mating activity. At the end of a week, he began to worry about the bull's ability to do the required job. He had seen him 'jumping' the cows a few times, but mostly it was the cows' heads that he attacked and when he did get on the correct end, he did not manage to find the correct orifice in the cows' rear ends, and the 'seeds of life', like those of Onan in the Bible, fell on stony ground, or else they were dispersed into the atmosphere by the wind. This was depressing news for us, because we had been hoping that the cows would get pregnant as soon as possible. One morning, during the first week of Xingu's stay with us, Richard came back from his morning trip even more worried. He had found the bull to be walking as though he had a problem with his left shoulder, and, as if that was not bad enough, one of the cows was lame on a front leg.

When the cow was no better the next day, I rang the vet and asked him to come out. He brought with him a special contraption, which enabled the cow to be immobilised, whilst he dealt with her foot. They took it up to the field and, because the cow was so lame, she was fairly easily caught up and put into this crush. The vet found that a stone had wedged itself between the cow's cleats and was cutting into the soft tissue, causing her great pain. He removed the stone and gave her an injection of long-lasting antibiotic. She wasn't very happy during this operation but, when they eventually let her go, she walked back to the rest of the herd in a less painful way, and gradually, over the next few days, she recovered. We didn't know it then but this was the first of eight times that the vet had to bring out his 'foot crush' over the next few months, as we had a recurring problem with stones in the feet. We still are not sure why it happened, it was only the cows that suffered, and we did not know whether they had picked the stones up before they came to Low Arvie, or whether they had found them here. Thankfully the problem seems to have disappeared now.

While the vet was in the field treating the cow, Richard asked him to look at the bull. They couldn't catch him up to be examined, but the vet watched him walking and thought, like Richard, that the problem was in the left shoulder. The next day things were just the same, and Richard decided to ring the farmer who owned him and ask him to come and look at him. These animals are worth a considerable amount of money, and it was a worry that someone else's animal had fallen sick on our farm. The farmer said that he would come out the next Monday and look at him.

The next morning Richard came back a little happier. The bull, he said, was not just up on his feet, but was trying to jump on anything that stood still for ten seconds. It is the cow that allows the bull to ride her when she is ready. The 'heat' period lasts only for some eighteen hours, and during this time she gives off a scent, which tells the bull that 'things are happening'. It is this that peps him up and attracts his interest in her. Within this eighteen-hour period, the cow will only stand still long enough for the bull to mount her for a short time, and, this particular morning, there was only one cow at this stage of her cycle. The scent she was giving off was obviously having its effect on poor old Xingu, but he didn't appear to know which end was the business end, and even when he got that correct, he was unable to effect penetration. This performance was repeated for the following two mornings, during which time Richard never saw the bull actually fulfil the desired action in the correct manner. After this, Xingu seemed to get very lame again and appeared to be utterly depressed. For the next few days, he was totally disinterested in the cows or breakfast, and just lay lethargically looking into the distance. With a heavy heart, Richard once more rang his owner and arranged for him to be fetched home the next day. Altogether, he had been here three precious weeks, and this meant that our calves would not now be born before October at the earliest, even assuming we could get another bull quickly.

Once again, we called on our friendship with Drew for advice and, once again, he did not fail us. He gave us the telephone number of his wife's cousin, Gordon Gilligan, who is a well-known breeder of Black Galloways in the area and has two or three bulls. We lost no time in phoning him and, unbelievably, the guardian angel was still hovering over us. Gordon had a bull that we could have immediately and, trading still further on Drew's good nature, we arranged to borrow his cattle lorry and fetch the bull the next day. Good farming practice decrees that new stock or visiting animals, such as the hired bull, should remain in quarantine for three weeks before joining the herd. This is to minimise the risk of transferring cattle diseases from one farm to another, as most diseases have an incubation period of three weeks or less and would show up in the quarantine period. However, we could not spare three more weeks and we only kept the new bull, whose name we did not know and whom I christened Hamish for want of something better, for three days before taking him out as an early Christmas gift to the cows on Christmas Eve. I hoped that the guardian angel's bounty would stretch just a little further and keep the bull and cows disease free, and I silently promised that in future we would always abide by the rules!

The farm diary records no evidence of Hamish's prowess as a progenitor. Nothing was seen of his work on Richard's daily visits to take the breakfast up, but we trusted that he was a night owl. Surely there couldn't be two Galloway bulls that didn't know how to perform!

Just about this time, we had received a notice from our vets that they had been asked by SEERAD to perform a brucellosis and tuberculosis test on our cattle, during the month of January. These two diseases are the scourge of cattle breeders, beaten only by the dreaded Foot and Mouth, as the stuff that nightmares are made of. Tuberculosis is well known in humans as well as animals, and is spread in both species by contact. Brucellosis is also known as contagious abortion and causes cows to abort the foetus too early, and therefore lose the farmer's production. It is thought that both TB and Brucellosis come into the cattle population from contact with badgers that live on the same land. Most farmers would dearly love to get rid of all badgers from their land and thus save their cattle from the risk of these two dreadful diseases. The environmental lobby sees the badger as a beautiful animal, which, of course, it is, and a benefit to the countryside, and even denies the evidence that it is responsible for the spread of the diseases. It is not very often broadcast, except in the farming press, that thousands of cattle are slaughtered every year because they have caught these two diseases. Every cow in the country has to be tested every four years for Brucellosis and every two years for TB, and those found to be carrying the diseases are slaughtered immediately. Even so, both diseases are still spreading from their endemic area in South West England. Fortunately, the land on Low Arvie is so wet and peaty that badgers and rabbits and foxes cannot make burrows in it, and so we are spared their presence. However, our cows are still subjected to the two and four yearly tests and, because we had just started up our business, the executive wanted to test the herd as soon as possible. I am so pleased that we bought the herd in its entirety, and did not have to piece one together with cows bought from here and there, because there is much less risk of diseases such as these entering a 'closed herd'. However, this makes it all the more important to follow the rules regarding visiting bulls, as contact with previously unmet bugs can be disastrous. We knew that we were taking a risk in putting Hamish out so quickly but, weighing up the pros and cons, it was one we had decided to take.

And so we rang Roddy, our vet to make the appointment for the TB and Brucellosis testing, and discovered that he has to come twice, once to inject a small quantity of the serum, and then three days later he returns to take blood samples which are tested for reactions. Any reactor cows are then taken away and slaughtered. We had not seen Roddy since the day that he came out to the lame cow and, when Richard rang to sort out the timing of the TB test, he enquired as to the condition of the bull. Richard explained to him that he had got so bad that he had gone back home and that we had been lucky enough to replace him at short notice. Roddy then suggested that when he came out to do the testing, he should bring his scanner and scan the cows to see if any were pregnant. If he waited until the new bull had been out with the cows for thirty days, he would not only be able to tell if any of them were pregnant but, from the size of the foetus, he would know which bull was the sire. This seemed to us to be an excellent scheme.

Because our cows have spent most of their lives living more or less wild out on Bardennoch Hill, they do not take kindly to being handled and treated. We have seen James Herriott on TV walking into a byre, where a cow stands quietly and unconcernedly chewing the cud, while he subjects her to all kinds of examinatory pokes and prods, but the Black Galloways on Low Arvie are made of sterner mettle! When they require to have anything done, they have to be manoeuvred into the cattle crush, from where they cannot escape. The time that Richard has spent walking amongst them, both in daylight and in darkness, talking reassuringly and quietly to them, means that they are now much more manageable than they were. However, I don't think they will ever succumb to the James Herriott treatment and will always need to be put into the crush to be dealt with. Now, after four or five months they are calm enough for Richard to get them into the crush on his own, but, as the TB test was to take place only two months after they had arrived here, it was still a difficult job. The week before it was due Richard rang Drew and asked if we could borrow Peter for the two mornings, and also he arranged for Marcus to come too. The scanning was to take place on the second visit, and we waited eagerly for the day to arrive.

Unfortunately, I had an appointment and was unable to be here to see the scan taking place, but when I returned, Richard told me that they had found seven of the twenty-two cows to be in calf, and all of them were to the second bull. Roddy was certain that none of the foetuses were big enough to belong to poor old Xingu. Two or three, however, looked as though they had formed in the first days of Hamish's stay with us. It was quite amazing to us that Roddy was able to say, with authority, how many days old each foetus was. Hamish had been out in the field for thirty days, and Roddy was able to see all the foetuses that had been created more than twenty days, with the later ones being still too small to spot, so, if seven of the cows had been put in calf in the first ten days, it probably meant that several of the others were already in calf too. We were thrilled and delighted. Also, we could now plan with a great degree of certainty when our calves would be born.

I put the number of days each foetus had been created into my computer program, and it told me that these seven calves would be born in the first eleven days of October, so only eight months to wait!

It seemed to be only of secondary importance that the TB and Brucellosis tests had both proved negative, but, of course, we were very pleased about that too.

The delight was a little tempered by the fact that one of the cows, who had borne a dead calf the year before, had not cleansed properly out on the hill. Some of the placenta had remained inside her and had caused irreversible damage, which meant that she would not be able to bear any more calves. It was a great shame because she was one of the youngest cows.

At this time the fate of poor Snotty Nose was decided too. Every morning when the cows came into the shed for their morning feed, we could hear the rattle of her bronchial tubes, before we even got into the barn. It became clear to us that she was getting thinner and thinner in spite of the kinder conditions of Low Arvie and the good food she was getting. She had to stay with us for sixty days so that we could claim a payment for her, but long before they were up, we realised that it would be a kindness for her not to have to struggle for breath any more. So on the sixty-first day after their arrival, Richard asked David Porteous if he would take her and the sterile cow down to the mart to begin their last journey. It is always a sad time when the cows have to go, but we take some comfort in the fact that their life here with us has been as good as we could make it.

It wasn't until a month later at the February sale of Galloway cattle at Wallets Mart that I spoke to Gordon Gilligan again, and was able to discover that we didn't have Hamish out in our field, but someone much more dynamic sounding. For the bull's real name is Zeppelin. No wonder he put seven cows in calf in the first ten days with a name like that!

23

The Big Freeze

The days passed by very quickly in a haze of feeding and caring for the cattle, for almost as soon as they arrived, the weather turned wintry. We experienced the first frosts in November, and snow covered the ground in early December. It didn't stay long but it made our life at Low Arvie very difficult. We had had so much to do over the months that Richard had not been able to start a log pile. Now that the weather demanded that we gave attention to the temperature level in the house, this became a problem. There was no shortage of wood and burnable material around the farm, but all of it was very wet. Every day became a struggle against the weather in one way or another. The worst days were those where the temperature stayed below freezing.

Hughie McLachlan, who had been a friend of the previous occupants of Low Arvie, having arrived in Corsock at the same time as them, lived in one of the forestry houses that were situated opposite the far end of our land. He had been the person who had had the key and shown prospective purchasers round, when the farm was up for sale. We had seen him on our early visits but had had little conversation with him on those occasions. One day soon after we moved in, Hughie had called in, and Richard and he had had a long chat about the recent history of Low Arvie. The McQuaker family, he told us, had moved here in 1903, and Davie and Jeannie had come into the house when Davie's Uncle had retired to a cottage nearer the village in 1960. They had altered the house by enlarging the windows from the traditional small kind, but they had done very little else to the structure of the house. They had brought up three children here, two girls and one son, and it was the girls from whom we had purchased the farm. The son had died in tragic circumstances some years earlier, and Davie had died in 1995, taking a heart attack one morning in the kitchen and dying before Jeannie could get downstairs. He was only in his mid sixties, but had worked hard all his life to earn enough to bring up his family. We know that Low Arvie isn't a viable farm to do this without some extra income, and Davie had done a lot of contract farming work in the district to make ends meet. Jeannie had lived on in the house after his death, letting out the land to a local farmer, until she had succumbed to a very aggressive cancer, again at an early age, the previous year.

Hughie himself, was now retired from the forestry work and lived with his wife, Gladys, in the house that they had bought from the forestry company. He spent a large amount of time keeping his garden beautiful, and, when we went to the house one day, we saw the vast amount of logs lining the garage walls which gave evidence of his foresting background. We grew accustomed to see him walking past the farm on his way back from the village every morning, having ridden down earlier with Gladys on her way to work in one of the large houses of the area. Sometimes we were lucky enough to entice him in to drink coffee and tell the tale for a while. His conversation is always interesting, and we enjoy his now fairly regular visits to our kitchen.

It was on one of these visits, as the weather was growing colder, that Hughie mentioned the fact that the water pipes, which ran down from the tanks in the west bedroom, came down through the roof of the lean-to kitchen and were very badly lagged. There is a small trapdoor in the ceiling of this kitchen that gives access to the pipes, and Hughie suggested that we lifted this trapdoor in the cold weather to allow the heat from the kitchen to keep the pipes from freezing. It was particularly important when the wind was in the east, he said, as it blew straight into the worst place for the pipes.

It didn't altogether come as a surprise, therefore, when we came down one morning and found no water coming out of the taps downstairs. The temperature outside was down to minus five and, although we had left the trapdoor open and a heater on in the kitchen, whilst closing the door on the 'dry' kitchen to allow the Esse to keep it warm for us, it had obviously not been effective in keeping the pipes free from frost. It was not a total disaster that we had no water downstairs, as the two small tanks of cold water and the tank of hot water under the coomb were still supplying water to the bathroom taps. Therefore, we were not entirely without, but obviously the well pump could not replenish them if we used the water, and there was always the threat of a burst pipe as the frost thawed. We left the tap turned on in the sink and put more heaters on in the cupboard, where the pipes entered the kitchen.

When we went out to feed the calves, we were not surprised to find that the water system in their shed was also at a standstill. There was water in the large storage tanks in the roof of the shed and there was some water in the drinking troughs, but the water in the pipes which joined the two together were frozen and so, as the calves drank, the water would not be replaced. There was a second large trough in the end of the shed that was not connected to the system, and which Richard filled with buckets from the tap underneath the tanks. We were able to unfreeze this tap fairly easily and could, therefore, give the calves water, but as with the house, when the storage tanks were empty, the pump would not refill them. We were able to cope for a while, but it was obvious that something would have to be done to improve things in the long term.

It was about two hours later, as I sat working in the office, that I heard one of the taps in the kitchen begin to drip and, shortly after this, the other one started too. It was a relief to have water once again, and also to discover that no leaks had been caused.

The weather remained wintry and the temperature continuously below freezing for five days. We left the door between the kitchens open all the time to allow the heat to keep the pipes free from frost, but this made the 'Esse kitchen' very cold too, and we struggled to keep the temperature in there up to 60 degrees. The days were spent keeping the cattle fed and watered, as once the water was used up in the storage tanks in the cattle shed, Richard had to carry it to them in buckets from the house.

I strove in vain to keep the house at a viable temperature, in spite of having three electric heaters on all the time and the new bedroom heaters on night and morning. We managed to keep the water flowing most of the time, but, at quite a cost, both to our pockets and our comfort.

When Richard had finished his daily round of seeing to the stock, he gave his attention to wood for the fire. Often, it was dark before he found the time to do this, and the wood he found around the steading was mostly wet and soggy. When he appeared with the log bucket, I would go into the sitting room and try to light a fire. We had very little dry wood even to get it started, and it took me a long time to build up a reasonable fire. Even when we did get it going, we had only wet wood to put on it, and we developed a system of drying out the next days logs overnight in the Esse. However, this took even more heat away from the house.

Eventually, the weather gave us some help, and temperatures returned to the positive side of the thermometer. We were quite lucky with the winter, as there were only three spells of very cold weather, and we had three occasions when the water pipes were frozen, but each time we were able to thaw them out quickly enough not to cause us real hardship; and we kept the cattle well fed and watered throughout. However, I swore that we would not spend another such winter at Low Arvie. At times, it was only the real conviction that this was going to be the lifestyle we both wanted that saw us through the worst of the weather.

As the second winter comes in, we find ourselves still without a central heating system, but the building project is under way and will definitely be finished before next winter, possibly even before the end of this one, and we have a large, dry log pile stacked in the log shed, which has already begun to provide us with large, roaring fires. Also, the conservatory has taken the place of the small porch over the front door and, although it is far from finished, it does keep the draft from the hallway. I hope these three things will be enough to keep us going until we get a real comfort zone in operation!

24

Naming the Calves

When the TB testing was over and the cows were settled in to their new routine and seemed to be quite happy, we turned our attention to thinking about the future. We had twenty-two cows that were going to give us our next crop of calves late in the year, but we also had the seventeen calves, and it was time to plan our strategy where they were concerned. There were several options for both the bullocks and the heifers. The bullocks would go to provide prime Galloway beef, but it was a question of whether we would take them all the way to what is called 'finishing', when they are ready to be killed, or sell them before this time to be finished by someone else. Galloways are fairly slow maturing animals and, whereas some breeds can be 'finished' in a year or even less, it might be two or two and a half years before the Galloway is ready, depending on the feeding regime followed. People have asked me how we can care for these lovely animals, when I know that they are going to end up on the nation's dinner plates. Our philosophy is straightforward. We are raising beef cattle, and those that are going for meat have a life expectancy of two to two and a half years. We will ensure that that time is spent as pleasantly and as happily as possible, that the animals are as free from stress as they can be and that they are cared for in a kind and humane way, until the time comes for them to serve the purpose for which they were bred. They make the rules for their existence and, to a large degree, we fulfil their wishes. If they are hungry, they let us know by shouting to us. They have a shed which is open to them for shelter at all times, and they use it, both in times of bad weather and, also, in the heat of the summer, which is the worst kind of weather for them, with their thick black woolly coats. Hot days are spent almost entirely in the shed, and so we always make sure there is food for them to eat and water to drink in there, even though the grass in the fields is really their summer diet. We feed them once or twice every day, depending on the time of year and, at other times, we walk amongst them. Thus, we are aware of any problems they may have almost as soon as they crop up, and these are attended to. We had most problems at the beginning, when the calves were in the shed. Galloways are sturdy animals, bred for the climate that prevails here. They are provided with thick, woolly coats and beneath these their skin is tough, so that they can remain happily outside in the very severest weather. But, because we had to keep the calves in for the first winter, they became quite ill with pneumonia two or three times during that time. On our morning feeding routine, we began to notice a few of them with snotty noses, and we watched carefully to make sure that these ones still wanted to eat. The worst sign of danger is when the animal stands back from the trough and shows no interest in food. This only happened with one or two animals, but several times they seemed ill at ease and listless, and so we rang the vet and were prescribed with antibiotics to dose them with. The other indicator of ill health in an animal is its temperature, and, several times, we put them through the crush and took temperatures when we were suspicious of their health. Once, we just had the very merest thought that all was not well with them and, when we began to take the temperatures, the first three were all three degrees above normal. Apparently, it is quite common for cattle to become ill when they are housed over the winter, even the breeds that would not fare well outside. So we were very aware that ours were at risk. It is the fact that the germs cannot escape from the building, and so spread quickly from one animal to another that causes the trouble. The cows and the three youngest calves that remained outside were fine, but we dare not let the other calves out, as the field at that end of the farm was so dangerously wet and boggy that we were frightened for their safety. We needed to get the digger in there and do some drainage work, before it would be safe, but the winter was not the right time for this, so they had to remain inside for the time being. If they had been younger they could have remained with their mothers as the little ones had done, but the heifers were by now into the equivalent of teenage years, and Richard was worried that the bull out in the field might be tempted by their young flesh! This would have spoiled them as breeding cattle, as they were far too young to have their first calf.

We had five bullocks that would be our first offering to the meat market. They were now seven months old, and so it would be almost two years before they would be finished. We decided to wait and see what our circumstances were, before deciding whether to finish them ourselves or to sell them to another farmer. The system of subsidies in operation meant that we could get one almost straight away, and there would be a second one due at the beginning of 2004. The system that pertained through the last part of the twentieth century, and the earliest years of this, paid the farmers that were producing Britain's food, and thus subsidised the nation's food bills. We could claim a payment of around £90 on each male beef animal, when they reached the age of seven months, and a second one, of the same amount, when they were twenty months old. In order to qualify for this payment, the animal had to remain on the farm for two complete months after the claim was made and, so that we did not flout these rules, the animals' passports had to be surrendered to the SEERAD office in Dumfries. The subsidy could be claimed at any time after the animal had reached seven months, and farmers worked out the best time for their businesses. Sometimes they sold the calf before they had claimed the subsidy, and this meant getting a higher price, as the new owner could then make the claim, so farm business planning was never straightforward. There were always circumstances to be weighed up, for each farmer to make the best of his individual circumstances.

We had also decided to be an 'extensive' farm. This means the opposite of intensive and, if we kept our animal numbers below a certain figure, this would bring in a further payment on each claimed animal. This figure was worked out on the hectarage of the farm. In our case all the available forage land was measured and, for each hectare, we could have up to 1.4 Livestock Units, and still claim the extra payment. Our land was not good agricultural land, being covered with so many wet areas, but these still counted to our forage land. Each farm animal is given a livestock unit value and in our case, the cows counted as one full unit, calves between the ages of six months and two years counted as 0.6 and younger calves did not count at all. Working out our animals and our hectares—not forgetting to omit all land covered by water, bare rock, tracks and buildings—this gave us a Livestock Unit count of about 0.75 per hectare, which was well inside the permitted figure. This would mean an extra payment of about £50 on each animal. The money would not be paid until November 2003, when they would pay us 60% of it, and the remainder would arrive sometime in mid 2004. It would be a long time before we began to see any return at all on our investment, but we had known this before we started and were prepared. We decided, therefore, to put in our claim for Beef Special Premium on our five 'boys' as soon as they turned seven months old. For the foreseeable future, they would stay here on Low Arvie and any decisions would be taken later.

The twelve heifers had different options. Heifers do go for meat, but they do not attract a premium payment and, since ours are pedigree Galloways, we planned to let them grow into breeding cows like their mothers. We thought we would probably keep them on Low Arvie and increase the suckler cow herd to around thirty, if we found the land could support that many, and then use their offspring as our saleable stock. They were six months old now and would not be ready to go to the bull until they were over two years old, so they would not bring in any revenue for quite a while. They would remain a saleable proposition at any age though, and if we registered them with the Galloway Society, their value would be enhanced. We decided to do this as soon as possible and, on one of my trips down to Castle Douglas, I popped into the Galloway Society office to learn the ropes!

I was greeted by a gentleman who introduced himself as Alex McDonald, and he was, he told me, the secretary of the Galloway Society. I spent an interesting hour learning from him what the Society is, and how it works. There is a Galloway herd book into which all pedigree animals can be entered, and where the ancestry of any animal can be traced. An animal is eligible for entry into the herd book, if both its parents are of pedigree heritage. Apart from this, there are appendices where animals with only one pedigree parent can be entered, as long as their general appearance conforms to the Galloway standard. Animals like this are entered into Appendix 'A' and, if these are put to a pedigree bull, then their offspring is entered into Appendix 'B'. When an Appendix 'B' cow is mated with a pedigree bull, the offspring can then enter the herd book as full pedigree.

Alex was interested to learn that we had bought the Cairsphairn herd of Galloways and told me that he thought they would be a good purchase. I had taken with me the pedigree certificates of those cows that had been registered, and, as he looked through them, Alex told me something of the heritage that they shared. Names that were then unfamiliar to me obviously meant a lot to him, and he told me that there were some famous names in the backgrounds of our cows. Glenapp Trooper, the sire of several of our cows had been a famous Galloway bull, Nether Rusko, Meiklewood, Blackcraig and Penninghame were also names found on the certificates, which obviously meant something in the world of Black Galloways. The calves had been sired by Barlaes Volunteer, the progeny of another famous breeding farm. Fifteen of the cows had been born on the Cairsphairn farm and had Bardennoch Hill as their prefix. These were all registered in the herd book. Six of the remaining seven had been bought from another famous Galloway farm at Dalswinton, but only four of these had been registered. The other two seemed to have the Galloway features, and Alex said he would come out and look at them, to see if they should be listed in one of the Appendices. He also said he would speak to the manager at Dalswinton and see what he could find out about them. The remaining cow was not a pure bred Galloway, but a cross with a Blonde d'Acquitaine French bull, but also may be able to go in the Appendix. We made an arrangement for him to come up to Low Arvie the next week to look at these cattle and register the calves. He said we should decide on our prefix and the names we were going to give the calves before he came.

It was quite exciting to discuss how we were going to name our calves, and, in the end, it was easy. Richard lives a very ordered life and, when he was living alone everything in his house, including the tins of food in his pantry, was placed in alphabetical order. He has files of papers, which he has gathered throughout his life, and they are all neatly arranged according to the alphabet. It is a joke between us that, although he always files in this way, he sometimes forgets which word he has used. For instance, documents to do with the several injections he has had, may be found under I for injection, V for vaccination, I for immunisation, H for Health or M for medical, and he often has to search through several files to find what he is looking for. It was, therefore, natural for him to think of the alphabet when naming the calves, and we opted for the system of a name beginning with A for the oldest calf, B for the next and so on. When they came to have calves of their own, we would give their calves names beginning with the same letter. I felt that our calves were so special that they needed an addition to the name to give them a more aristocratic sound, and we decided that Lady So and so of Low Arvie had a better ring to it than Low Arvie Lady So and so. We then only had to find twelve names beginning with the letters A through L and we were home and dry, and we sat with pen and paper filling in the names from people we knew and liked. Some of them were easy, I have three names and so Ann and Linda were filled in first, the third Mary would have to wait for the first heifer of the next batch. My daughter is Catherine Elizabeth, so that coped with C and E. Hughie's little grand-daughter had been to see us several times and was a lovely little girl of ten so her name, Jade, filled in the J slot. B was for Barbara, Richard's next door neighbour in Sussex whom we had visited several times, and H was Hannah who lived in the bungalow next door, on what had once been a part of Low Arvie land. Catherine's new partner, Morgan, has a daughter named Freya, and that seemed a pretty name to use. G was Gina, whose Bed and Breakfast house, just south of Calais, had become our first and last stop on each of our visits to the continent, D was for Dorothy who is our nearest farming neighbour and who has become a good friend. The wife of David Porteous, whose cattle had been housed in our Eastside field, is called Kathleen and so that was the K. It just left us with I as one that we couldn't fill from friends or family. In the end we opted for Iris as there are irises growing down by the burn on Low Arvie and we have more than our fair share of rainbows here with the rainy climate and Iris is the goddess of rainbows. I sent a picture of Lady Catherine of Low Arvie down to the original Catherine, and was soon inundated with requests from her friends to have calves named for them, so we have plenty of names for future generations.

The bullocks were not going to be registered, as only those males picked out at birth to remain entire and to be grown on as bulls are worth registering, and so we decided to let circumstances suggest names for them. They have become slightly less aristocratically entitled. The first one to be named was number 32, who is very calm and allows me to stroke him without any trouble. I greeted him every morning by giving him a pat and saying, "Hello, my boy," and that has stuck and he is Boy. The calf of the Blonde d'Aquitaine cross cow, number 30, is slightly different to the others both in looks and temperament and is easy to pick out of the line up at the food rail, he has become quite simply Firty. Number 35 was much smaller and weedier than the others, and so we looked for him each morning to give an extra mouthful of food. He, too, was easy to pick out because his back end, as he bent his head to the trough, was so much bonier than the others, and I began to call him Scraggy Bum. The youngest bullock, number 38, was out in the field with his mother until March, when he was brought in, with the two youngest heifers, to join the others. I noticed that his ear tag had been clipped in too high and it weighed down the top part of his ear to give him a funny lop-sided appearance. He immediately became Droopy Lug. The other bullock has simply remained number 22, as nothing has occurred to suggest anything else. He doesn't stand out from the rest in any way.

When Alex came the next week, we were ready to fill in his forms with all the names, and our calves took on their new identities. When we had completed the paperwork, he and Richard went out to look at the cows without registration papers. He had no hesitation in proclaiming them as Galloways, and said he would find out from Dalswinton who their parents were, and then register them along with the calves. He even felt that the Blonde d'Aquitaine cow could go into Appendix A. It wouldn't make any difference initially, as her calf was a bullock, but if she had heifer calves in the future, then they would be Appendix B, and then their calves full pedigree. The fact that Alex thought that the other two were full pedigree was helpful, as it meant that their calves, which might only have been Appendix B, could now be full pedigree. This means that all the cows and calves on Low Arvie, except the crossed one, are full Galloway pedigree. We are very proud of them, and one day I mean to have a sign to hang by the ash tree.

25

Spring works

The winter passed and we somehow managed to keep ourselves from freezing to death, although it was, at times, quite uncomfortable inside the house. In the very coldest weather, I was reduced to wrapping myself up in a blanket and pulling the chairs as near to the fire as I could. There were days at a time when I could not get the temperature above 55 degrees, even with the fire lit. The bedrooms were a little better with the new heaters, but the whole effort to keep warm and unfrozen was very expensive, and a hard won battle. The electricity system runs the whole place through just one meter and, because Low Arvie is a farm, this is charged at business rates, which that winter were much higher than ordinary domestic supplies. With all the heaters we had around the place, I knew the electricity bill would be high, so I was somewhat prepared when it came, to find that the charge for the winter quarter was over £550. I would not have felt so bad if this money had served to keep us comfortable, but to be cold all day every day and then to have to fork out this amount of money came a little hard.

However, cold we might have been, but miserable we certainly weren't. We were both becoming more and more pleased with our purchase of the farm and could see that, once we had sorted a few things out, then life would be very pleasant here. The major worry that my mother's well-being might have been was replaced by the happy knowledge that she was being extremely well cared for in Bothwell House, and was very satisfied with her lot. Hot freshly cooked meals twice a day, company at times throughout the day, a lovely warm room, television and a never-ending supply of books to occupy solitary hours and the church just next door were the ingredients that made her life exceedingly enjoyable. When I was able to visit, as time and circumstances permitted, about twice a week, we never ceased from marvelling at our mutual good fortune in finding the Abbeyfield Society; and I could give my attention to the other things in my life, in the knowledge that she was fine. Richard and I went down on Christmas Day and joined the depleted gathering for a beautiful traditional Christmas Lunch.

Three of the residents had gone off to be with their families, but, even if Low Arvie had been a suitable venue for a 90 year old to spend a few hours, my mother would have still preferred for us to go there. She wanted to go to church in the morning, and then be at ease in her own surroundings for the rest of the day. We paid for our meal, according to the system whenever the guests of residents are accommodated, as Abbeyfield is a non-profit making organisation, but, at £7.50 for a full three course Christmas lunch and then coffee and mince pies afterwards, I know who got the better bargain, and, of course, I was delighted not to have to cook! The arrangement will doubtlessly be repeated!

The Christmas festivities, however, were saddened for us by the death of Richard's mother on the nineteenth of December. She was 98 years old and had never fully recovered from the stroke that she suffered on the day we got Low Arvie. Her death, although leaving her family sad, had brought to an end the long wait she had had to rejoin her friends and most of her family, who had gone before her. She had great faith and was totally convinced that she was going to a better and happier world, and she had been longing for the journey to begin for some considerable time. She was to be buried with her husband in the small churchyard two miles from her home, where my father and so many of the other people she had known were also laid to rest. It was, therefore, with mixed feelings that we drove down to Yorkshire on Boxing Day, for her funeral the next day. It felt wrong to be grieving for her and selfish to grieve for ourselves, and so we gave thanks for her long and happy life and for her new found freedom from the unhappiness that the stroke had brought her.

It was exciting throughout the next few weeks to watch the garden changing at Low Arvie. There did not appear to be much plant life when we had first arrived in the summer, but, as the winter changed to spring, we found a wonderful array of snowdrops appearing, followed closely by beds of wild daffodils. These were all over the lower part of the lawn and in the little wood at the west side of the garden. These last had to be searched out and spotted, just peeping through the tangle of brambles and dead rosebay willow herb stalks, and I vowed that one day they would be able to bloom unhindered by such obstacles.

Slowly the cold receded and the warmer weather began. In early March, we began to let the calves out of the shed during the day time and let them roam in the small paddock between the house and the road. It was grand to see them back outside where they belonged, and they were glad to be there and galloped about kicking their legs in the air. When April was well in and the grass beginning to grow again, we would bring the cows back to the farm from the west end and put them into the boggy Eastside and let the calves out on to the safer fields, where the cows had spent the winter.

Once more it seemed Fate was with us, for 2003 proved to be the driest year ever known in Galloway, and not a drop of rain fell on the farm in the spring-time. Whilst this was a worry for the water supply to the house from the well, with the cattle all out on the land and able to drink from the ditches and the burn, we were happy for the land to dry out a bit. One morning in late March, we were just ready to go and hand one of the interminable forms in to SEERAD in Dumfries, when there was a knock on the door. Hughie McLachlan stood there, with two homemade fire beaters in his hands. "I've come to help you do the burning," he said to Richard, "We have to do it before April—you are not allowed to do it then." Ever glad of an excuse not to leave the farm, Richard checked with me that I was ok to go to Dumfries by myself, and then rushed off upstairs to get changed. This sounded much more promising to him than a trip to Dumfries. Almost before I had picked up the car keys, he was back down, dressed in farm gear, and putting his boots on to join Hughie in the yard. For two or three days, they went out onto the farm land and set light to the dead, dry grass and rushes, which would allow new shoots to appear and grow into strong nutritious plants. Hughie taught Richard the principles of this somewhat danger-ous, but beneficial, act and no doubt he will use the skill he learned in future years. They did not manage to get to every corner of the farmland, but some large portions of it soon lay black and ugly with wisps of smoke still rising from them. It was not long, however, before the ugliness was gone, to be replaced by new bright green growth, which was a considerable improvement from the old dead faded grass and rushes that had been there.

By April, Richard felt it was dry enough to get a digger in to start re-cutting the drains, and we were able to hire one from Hughie Porteous. His digger driver, Tom McSherry, came and operated it. He started work on the drain nearest the house, which had filled in with water and then overgrown with grass and roots, thus preventing any access for either man or beast to the land that bordered the garden. It was amazing to see the water pouring from the bucket, each time Tom lifted it high into the air and swung it round to drop the sodden peat and roots along the bank. Even though we had had no rain for almost three months, that of the previous years was just sitting there, waiting to be added to. All over our land this was repeated, and it was good to get started, at last, on clearing it away. The ditch ran the whole length of the field, and Richard had decided to make a bridge half way along, so that he could get in with the tractor, as the land dried out. This meant remaking the track that ran along the edge of the ditch, and then piping the ditch and levelling it with stones to the same height as the track. It was interesting to watch this engineering project taking shape and, in a surprisingly short time, the ditch was carpeted with polypropylene matting and five huge concrete pipes swung into place, for the water to flow through. Another piece of matting was put on top to prevent the dirt and stones falling through and blocking the pipes, and then stones were placed over the whole structure, large at first and then smaller ones to level the top. We had found out that Andy McQuaker, the brother of Davie who had farmed Low Arvie, had a quarry on his land, and he, and his son Graham, carted load after load the three miles from their farm, and spread it out on the new track and bridge, for Tom to pound into place with his digger bucket. Tom then took his digger over the bridge into the wet land and re-cut the four drains, which we could see had been there by the lines of rushes. This process was repeated again and again all over our fields and, gradually, the land is recovering from its years of neglect and has begun to take on the appearance of a cared for farm again. There is still much to do, but we have made a good start in this first year and most of the worst places are now safe to walk on. I enjoy being able to wander about almost everywhere. There are two new roads cut and waiting for stone, but, now that the winter is upon us again and the weather has begun to be wet, these will wait till next year to be finished.

The cattle have begun to graze the land that was too wet for them to walk on in the early days, and the grassy patches between the rushes are increasing in size every day. Unfortunately we have not trained the cattle to eat the rushes, which would be a very good thing, but Richard was able to start mowing some of them and, in these places, the grass is also growing again. Little by little, we hope to regain the good land from the rushes.

We have also paid attention to the land by the buildings, which so quickly became a morass, when the cattle and the autumn rains arrived simultaneously last year, and there is now a four hundred gallon trough gallantly collecting the rainwater from the workshop roof. This was another fairly big project in the summer, as it was necessary to put a drainage channel in for the overflow. Tom dug out a large area, which Richard filled with stones, for the trough to stand on, and then a channel was made from this down into the wood towards the main drain. A perforated pipe was laid in this and then covered over with earth, and the grass allowed to grow over it again. I thought it would take a long time for the huge trough to fill, but I was surprised both how quickly it did fill and how quickly the cattle emptied it. Suckler cows drink more than fifteen gallons a day, when they are lactating, and twenty-two times fifteen is three hundred and thirty, so, allowing for the bottom few inches that the cows cannot reach, the trough holds only one day's supply. However, the difference it made to the land around it was amazing. The ground remained hard and firm while, once the trough was full, the excess water streamed neatly over the edge straight into the drainage patch and away to the wood. We have not got around to ducting it into the drain yet, and I suppose it is just sitting amongst the tree roots, but that will be sorted out one day. We also put a trough of the same size at the end of the new cattle building, for that side of the farm, and this one fills even more quickly as it takes the rain from a much larger area of roof.

As the spring progressed and the weather remained unusually dry, we continued with the work to change the face of Low Arvie. Tracks were remade and surfaced with load after load of stone, and the digger work continued to improve the drainage potential of the ditches. There were several ditches that came onto the land under the road, and which carried the water from the hill on the other side that was part of the land at Arvie farm. One of these led from the road, along the edge of the small paddock and across the lower edge of the garden. From here it went on to join other ditches from the road and, ultimately, the main drain down to the burn. This drain did not run at all when we first came to the farm, and we could see the water standing amongst the rushes. Then, whenever it rained, the bottom five metres of the garden filled up with water and became impenetrable. When Tom set to work on this stretch of drain, I went out to watch. As he worked his way along towards the garden, digging the large bucket into the sodden land and then lifting it and swinging it round, before tipping the contents onto the side, I watched in wonder at the amount of water that was released from the land. The bucket dug out about two metres at a time, and he dipped it in two or three times at each section, before moving the great machine's tracks on to the next piece. As he got nearer and nearer to the road, the machine dug into the wet peat deeper, and hundreds of gallons of water were freed from their long time prison. At the road, he had to turn right and work away along the roadside wall for about fifty metres, until he came to the place where the ditch came under the road. I stood by the ditch at the bottom of the garden and marvelled as, at each dip in of the bucket, the released water rushed down the newly cut drain. It was obvious that the ditches had been blocked for a long time, and the rain of several years had poured down the hill and under the road, and then was held by the roots of the rushes and the soggy peat, unable to get any further. There was a huge lake sitting just under the surface of the rush cover, and it was good to see its torrents pouring away. Of course, we wouldn't see the benefit for a while as the wet peat had to drain and drain for a long time, until it became firm enough to walk on but, eventually, this would happen.

We were concentrating our efforts to drain the haylage land, as this was the land that would be in the Rural Stewardship Scheme if our application was successful, and we wanted to get all the ditches sorted out in these fields, before the scheme started in the autumn. We would be allowed to keep the present ditches cut and running, but not to cut fresh ones. As most of the present ditches were only marked by long lines of rushes and the stagnant water which sat beneath them, we wanted to get them running again before there could be any danger of it appearing that we were cutting fresh ones. We didn't quite manage to get them all re-cut, but those we did have made a huge difference to the fields. Management of the wetland has to be a careful balance between keeping the rush growth, and not allowing it to become all pervading. The land is low lying and therefore water-holding, and so we have to try and drain as much of the water as we can. There is no way that we could get all of it away, as there is not enough fall in the land to drain it naturally, and so it should not be too difficult to strike a happy medium between wetland habitats and keeping it dry enough for the cattle to graze between the rushes in the spring and autumn. Under the scheme, the wetlands are not to be grazed during the summer months, whilst the birds are nesting. This fits in with the haylage land, which the wetland surrounds, as it is also prohibited for this to be grazed from April until July. These are the months when the grass is growing for our haylage crop, so we would not want the cattle to be in these fields then anyway. The scheme and our regime seem to fit together well. It does mean that the cattle have to be accommodated for these months on the rough grazing lands at each end of the farm, and so this is where our next efforts to drain and recover land needs to be targeted.

26

Meeting the Standards

With the improvement of the infrastructure underway, we turned our thoughts to the long-term prospect of selling the cattle that we were hoping to produce. There is a strict code of practice to follow in order to raise cattle in Scotland, which is in place to keep the kudos attached to Scotch Beef. This is administered by a company called Quality Meat Scotland, and all farms that want to sell meat under the auspices of this company must adhere to a strict regime of good farm practice. Quality Meat Scotland sends inspectors each year to the farms, and they examine the systems and practices under which the cattle are being raised. If a farm is working according to the rules, then they are awarded the accolade of being a Specially Selected Scotch Assured Farm. Stickers are provided, which must be affixed to the passports of the cattle that go for beef, and beef cattle that carry this accolade bring the best prices.

The first rule is that the cattle must be born, bred and raised on a Farm Assured farm. At the moment this can be anywhere in the UK, with the proviso that at least ninety days of its life must be on a Farm Assured farm in Scotland. Shortly the rules are to be changed so that no cattle born outside Scotland, even if they come across the border on day one, are eligible for the scheme. Other rules concern the feeding, veterinary care and welfare of beasts, the biosecurity and good practice on the farm. There are rules concerning the purchase of breeding stock and the choice of hired bulls, the competency of the stockmen and the general level of hygiene practised on the farm. There are even rules concerning the farm dog. In fact, all aspects of good husbandry are addressed in the standards required to achieve certification under the scheme. This is to give an assurance to the public that the highest standards are being maintained in the raising of the food they eat. Similar kinds of schemes pertain to other sectors of the food production industry, and the standards and rules are monitored and upgraded on a regular basis.

It was, therefore, important for us to apply to join the Farm Assurance scheme before we wanted to sell any of our cattle and, accordingly, we sent off our application (and cheque) and awaited events. We received a package detailing the scheme and what we must do to comply with the rules. When the inspection is made, there are three possible outcomes. The first and best is that the farm is fulfilling all conditions and is given Unconditional membership of the scheme. The second is that there are found to be minor non-compliances, which are pointed out to the farmer, and he is then granted conditional membership, upgraded to unconditional, when the faults have been rectified. Where serious non-compliances are found, then deferred membership is given, and the farmer cannot sell his stock as Scotch Assured until he has put right the wrongs, and been re-assessed.

As well as the annual compulsory check, the inspectors are at liberty to make other spot checks throughout the year to make sure that standards are being maintained. Also the SSSFA office will investigate any reports of members failing to comply.

After we had finished work for the day and had our evening meal, we sat at the table and began to go through the standards book together. The booklet was sixteen pages long and contained nine separate sections, to which we must pay attention. The first of these pertained to the farm itself and the steading buildings. I began to read to Richard, "To qualify for Specially Selected Scotch Farm Assurance status, farms must be recognisable as a clean and well-organised primary food production site. The standard of inspection will be the requirement of a retail meat buyer." This seemed fair enough, as he would be selling the meat to the public and was, therefore, in the front line. He needed to be sure that he could promote the product as first class.

We worked our way through the booklet, comparing our farm and practices with those required, and we found that we matched up well. Of course, we have only a very small number of animals compared to other farms, and so it was easier for us to remain aware of the health status and requirements of our animals, and we were always careful, especially in the early days when we were gaining experience, to seek expert advice for any problems. We did encounter some over the first winter. Galloways are a breed, which do not take kindly to being inside, and this gave rise to the illness that the calves suffered this first winter. They have been much better since they have been kept outside. Now that we have drained the land and it is safer for them, they stay outside all year round, and their health is good.

There were a lot of sections in the Farm Assured Book that did not apply to us. We had no sheep and our cattle had no horns, so all the requirements to do with these we could safely ignore. There were guidelines and rules laid down for every process that farmers go through when acquiring and keeping animals, and these all had to be adhered to for entry into the Assurance scheme. Those concerned with the traceability of cattle, we had already met and fulfilled when we bought our stock, those concerned with the treatment of new born calves we would need to comply with when the time came. The rules are all connected with the welfare of the animals and good animal husbandry. When the assessor visited to inspect our holding, he would also satisfy himself as to the capability and fitness of the stockman to treat the animals according to these good practice guidelines.

There was then a large section relating to the feeding of the animals. This, of course, was very relevant after the outbreak of Bovine Spongiform Encephalitis or 'mad cow disease', which hit Britain in the eighties and nineties. This disease happened because the rules were changed about the processing of animal feed. Before this time, it was allowed to put animal protein into the rations fed to bovine animals, which are herbivores, so this was, therefore, not a good thing to do, in any case. But when the rules were changed and this protein was allowed to be processed at a lower temperature, then the BSE prion, or germ, became transmissible to the cows that ate it and, thence, to humans through the food chain. This is a terrible disease, for which there is no cure, and many people suffered terribly and died as a result of this bad practice.

Since the cause has been identified, the feeding of animal protein to cattle has been outlawed and farmers who wish to become 'Farm Assured' must purchase their feed from an approved source. Each section of the food production chain, from feed merchants, farmers, transporters to abattoirs, has its own Assurance Scheme, and the traceability of every animal entering the chain means that the public can be certain that the food marked as UK produce has been through this rigorous system and is, thus, the most safe food to purchase and eat.

We had no problem here, having used an approved haulier to bring our cattle from the Hill, and buying our feedstuff from the local assured supplier. Once the food was brought onto the farm, then our responsibility began. The storage method of the food merited a large section in the book. Having purchased it from an assured supplier, we then had to store it in a way that ensured that it did not become contaminated before the animals ate it. At one of the farm sales, we had purchased a large galvanised bath shaped container, with a sturdy looking wheel at one end and handles at the other. I think its original purpose was to be found in a dairy, but Richard was going to use it for mixing the animals rations. In order to be profitable, a farmer has to be very careful about the cost of feeding his animals, and Richard had spent a great deal of time poring over the price lists from the feed supplier, sorting out the most cost effective way to provide the required nutrients to achieve optimum growth rate. There are various ways to achieve the correct blend of nutritious ingredients, and it was possible to make up one's own mixture, or, alternatively, there were blends which were put together at the feed merchants. Also, the feed merchant would make up an individual mix-ture to one's own recipe. Eventually, Richard decided on the best way to achieve a reasonable protein content, with the requisite amount of vitamins and minerals, and he went along to the feed merchants and re-appeared with several kinds of ingredients. They were all of vegetable origin, and the mixture he made in the large tub contained barley, sugar beet, wheat and soya, with a supplement of vita-mins and minerals. The result looked very much like muesli, and certainly was eaten with relish by our animals. The calves had not eaten any solid food since they were born out on the hill and so, for these, he had bought a special 'baby calf' mix made up at the merchants, which contained all manner of different ingredients. There was flaked beans and peas, soya and maize, sunflower seeds and grass nuts, and this looked like muesli with cornflakes added. At first we scat-tered the flakes along the top of the haylage, but, before long, they had learned that it was tasty, and we were able to give them a separate feed of this, and then the haylage as a second course. This 'baby calf' mix got the calves used to eating this kind of food, and they soon graduated onto the same mixture as the cows.

Richard was meticulous over the storage of this food and kept all the bags tightly tied. He also had made a closely fitting cover for the large tub. When we first arrived at Low Arvie, the buildings had been empty for some considerable time and consequently, they had been appropriated as living accommodation by a large number of crows and jackdaws. These were particularly obnoxious to have as neighbours and co-habitees for the calves, as they left large traces of their nightly visits in the feeding passages for us to clean up in the morning. It was very important to get rid of these pests as soon as we could and, having investigated several ideas, in the end it was very easily achieved. When the spring showed signs of returning, the birds could be seen flying into the shed with their beaks full of twigs, and it was obvious that they had begun to get their nests into habitable order again. Richard got the ladder out and went up to inspect the corners of the roof, and there he found and destroyed more than a dozen nests. After that the birds left and went off to find alternative nesting sites and, thank goodness, haven't returned. As an added safeguard we now have two rodent operatives conducting nightly patrols, and, currently, the only avian inhabitants are a pigeon and a robin. We still sweep the feeding passage out every feeding time, but it is mostly clean to start with.

The letter which accompanied the booklet had said that the inspector would come to make his first visit within four weeks of receipt of the letter but, before we heard from him, we received notice of another inspection from SEPA, the Scottish Environmental Protection Agency. They are concerned with what farmers do with their waste water and other contaminants, and they were in our area because the local beaches had been tested and showed high levels of pollution, some of which was thought to originate on the many farms. They were looking at every farm that lay in the catchment area of the Urr river and they wished to inspect Low Arvie on Thursday of the next week.

Promptly at the arranged time of 2 p.m., a lady drove into the yard and announced herself as the SEPA inspector. As with all visitors, she was offered a cup of tea and refreshment, which she duly accepted, and we chatted in the kitchen whilst this was partaken. Then she made her inspection and identified two areas of concern. Our haylage storage space had an open ditch running along its bottom edge, and she warned us that we were not allowed to store haylage bales within ten metres of this, in case any liquid effluent leaked out of them and got into the watercourse. Also, we were currently feeding the calves in freestanding troughs, as they were not quite big enough to reach into the fixed trough in the building, and she said that these were placed too close to another open drain. Animals have a tendency to take food in at one end and simultaneously part with waste products at the other, and it would be easy for these waste products to get into the watercourse through the drain. Both of these problems were easily solved for us. Indeed, Richard moved the calves' troughs whilst the lady was still here, and the haylage is now stored a little further than the regulation ten metres from the ditch. We later heard that other farmers in the area had also been requested to make adjustments in their working practice to comply with the regulations.

Later in the month, we heard from the Farm Assured inspector and he too came along to look at our set up. Over a cup of tea he chatted away to us about our farm and seemed to satisfy himself as to our fitness to join his scheme, and then Richard took him off to look around the buildings and show him our systems. He also identified a small problem. One side of the cattle crush that Richard used to confine the cows, when he was dealing with them, had begun to rust away at the bottom and the side panel had a sharp edge on which an animal could catch its foot. The inspector advised that this should be repaired. When he left, he said that we would get Unconditional membership as soon as we advised his office that this repair had been done. Within two days, Richard had taken the panel up to the blacksmith's and got it fixed, and our membership number came through the next week. I was very proud that we had had so little problem to be accepted and, when I read in the handbook that qualifying farms could purchase a smart blue and white sign showing membership as a Specially Selected Scotch Assured Farm, I ordered one immediately, and it is now displayed on the cattle shed immediately below the light. We also have little blue stickers to put on the calves' passports.

27

Trials and tribulations of haylage making

We had decided to get our own equipment to mow and bale the haylage, so that we would be independent and able to do the work, as and when things were ready. We worried that, if we had to wait for contractors, the weather could change and life would be stressful. With this in mind, we acquired a mower and hay turner, both second hand and fairly old. Sandy, one of the reps who called in from time to time, offered to get us a baler and wrapper, at reasonable prices. These were the four pieces of equipment required for making haylage, and we were quite happy that we were on track. However, when the baler arrived and Richard tried it out, he found several faults with it. Sandy got the engineer to come out and spend time fixing things on it, but I could tell that Richard was not too happy about it. It is crucial to have all the machines ready to go when the grass is at its peak and the weather is set fair for two or three days, and when the engineer said that the baler was working fine, we eagerly looked at the weather forecast. It seemed as though the gods were with us, as there was no sign of rain on the horizon, and so we planned to 'go for it'. In fact, Richard set off immediately with the mower and proceeded to cut half the grass that evening. He had decided to do only half at a time so that there wouldn't be so much to deal with, until he got used to the new equipment.

All went well and before bedtime, the large field that we call Low Knowe, the field near the house that we call Inbye and half of Brookfield were all covered in long lines of wilting grass. So far, so good.

The next day Richard planned to spread out the mown grass with the hay turner, to allow the sun to get to it and help it to dry out more. The dryer the grass, the better where haylage is concerned. Accordingly, early the next morning, he fixed the turner onto the back of the tractor and set off into Inbye field. The hay turner has two spinning circular wheels, which have eight spikes attached to each of them around the perimeter. If you set these to spin in one direction it spreads the grass out, and then, in the evening, before the dew begins to fall, the wheels are set to spin the other way. This gathers the grass up again into deep piles with a small surface area, so that the dew doesn't wet it too much. There were also two small wheels, which ran along the ground to keep the spinners in the correct position for each of these operations, and the position of these had to be altered too. All went well, and the machine circumnavigated the field, spreading out the grass as it went. As soon as I had watched Richard begin this process and taken the photographs, with which I was compiling a visual record of our life's adventure, I left Low Arvie to shop and visit my mother. This takes quite a while, as the journey is half an hour each way and then I often have quite a few different shops to visit, bills to pay and farm equipment to pick up, as well as enjoying a well-earned cup of tea at Bothwell House. It was, therefore, lunchtime when I returned and, having parked the car and alighted, I stood and listened for the sound of a tractor or machine working, which would tell me where Richard was. All I heard was the braying of a hammer on metal coming from behind the workshop. I looked over at Low Knowe and saw that the grass was still lying in the same lines as when I had left, and so I walked over to see what the problem was.

I found Richard hammering as hard as he could on one of the small wheels that kept the spinners aligned for the tasks they were performing. I enquired tentatively what was happening, and he told me that he had decided to check that the spinners would gather the grass up again, before he spread too much of it out. This wheel, however, was jammed or rusted into the tube in which it should run, and he was having difficulty in freeing it. I left him to it and carried the shopping into the house and began to assemble lunch. I was in quite a hurry, as I had a further appointment that afternoon and, as soon as the lunch was on the table, I called Richard to come and we ate.

At the end of the meal, he informed me that he was giving up his attempt to free the recalcitrant wheel, as it had not shown any sign of moving. He had tried gathering up the grass with the wheel where it was, and the machine seemed to work quite well. He said, therefore, that he was going to spread out the rest of the grass immediately, as it would have to be gathered up again before dark. He went off to his work, and I left the farm once again for my appointment.

On my return, I found the tractor, with the hay turner still attached, parked outside the back door with its engine running, and, as I entered the house, I could hear Richard speaking to someone on the telephone. "Are you sure you can do it now?" he was saying, "That's grand, I'll be along as quickly as I can." Looking at the clock, I saw that it was almost 5.30, when most places close and I cast an enquiring glance. "Can't stop," said Richard, "just rushing up to Tom Corrie's!" With that he strode out of the house and drove off in the tractor. Tom Corrie is the blacksmith at Balmaclellan and, obviously, Richard had just managed to catch him before he closed for the day, and he had agreed to wait and do whatever it was, there and then. Balmaclellan is six miles up the road and, on the tractor, this would take a good quarter of an hour, so it was imperative that Richard left straight away. I would no doubt learn the cause of this all in good time.

While he was gone, I put on my walking shoes and went up to look at Low Knowe to see what had been done. I found that most of it, though not quite all, had been spread out, and, picking up a handful, I found it to be drying nicely and I drank in its sweet smell. I always enjoy walking over the land, and, from the top of Low Knowe, which I think is the highest part of our land, I looked over the rest of our fields towards the farmhouse and enjoyed the view, which always brings balm to my spirit and helps me to put things into perspective in times of stress. On this early summer evening, the sun was slowly making its way around to the west, and, at one end of the farm, I could see the black shapes of the cows and, at the other, the smaller figures of the calves, as they moved slowly over the grass, their heads down, as they grazed gently in the evening air. In the middle of the scene sat the house, the sunlight reflecting warmly from the cream paint of its thick stone walls, and its two chimneys just visible above the top of the steading buildings behind it.

I sat down, leaning my back against the 'dry stane dyke' and thought how my life had changed, and how fate had brought us to this beautiful place and allowed us to call it our own.

My reverie was soon interrupted, however, as the distant hum of cars passing along the road, some hundred metres from me, was suddenly changed into the louder roar of a tractor, and I saw the familiar blue of our 7740, pulling the old yellow hay turner, bouncing along the road towards the track to the house. Jumping up and brushing the wisps of drying grass from my trousers, I began to walk back to the house and I arrived just as Richard had dismounted from the tractor, and we went in the house together.

Over tea, Richard recounted his afternoon! He had set off as arranged after lunch, and the turner and tractor were going well. He had just about completed spreading the grass in Low Knowe, when he noticed that, where the wheel that he had been hammering earlier should have been, there was just a ragged tube projecting downwards from the chassis of the turner. Obviously, the hammering had weakened the already rusted metal of the tube, and, with the bumping ride over the ground, the wheel and the tube had parted company. The wheel was about nine inches in diameter and some of the metal tubing was clearly still attached to it, but the problem that presented itself was: where was the wheel and its tubing now? Low Knowe is a field of some five acres, not large in farming terms, but in terms of locating an object with a maximum dimension of twelve inches, then the proverbial needle and haystack plainly applies! With the hope that the wheel had fallen off fairly recently, Richard switched off the tractor engine and jumped off. He began to retrace his circuits of the field on foot, but his search was hampered by the fact that the grass in Low Knowe was the thickest on the farm, and he had been carefully spreading the lush growth right over the field. The wheel, wherever it was, lay buried under a good thick layer of grass and he had to shuffle his feet along the ground yard by yard. It was very important that the wheel should be found, as an object like that caught up in the baler would have a devastating effect. Suffice to say that quite a portion of the afternoon had passed, before his feet met with the required object and, thankfully, he retrieved the missing wheel. He then came back to the house and phoned Tom Corrie to see if he could weld it back on, and this was where I had come in!

By this time, it was nearing the time for dewfall, and so Richard set off once again in the tractor, this time to gather up the grass again. He had not finished it all, before it became too wet to continue, and some of it had to stay spread out until the morning.

The next day was the day for baling and wrapping the grass. The weather was promising to become unsettled over the weekend, and so we wanted to get the haylage finished by then. Remembering that one field still needed rowing up before the baler could gather it up, we set the alarm clock for five a.m. and retired to bed.

28

Trials continued!

It was a beautiful morning, one of those glorious sunrises that we seem to get more than our fair share of! We have a beautiful open view to the east and the first sight of the sun comes through the bathroom window, and then slowly the rosy fingers stretch around the side of the house to the front. This will be our view from the bedroom and kitchen, when the extension is complete!

We rose at the sound of the alarm clock, and Richard had a hurried breakfast, before going off to finish rowing the field. This, of course, was the summer, when the cattle are out in the grazing fields at the ends of the farm. The grass is plentiful at this time of year and they need no supplementary feed, so the work which fills our winter mornings does not exist, thus enabling us to start straight in on the day's other chores. I busied myself around the house, preparing the day's meals and tidying up, and waited for Richard to return. I wanted to go with him when he started the baling, not only to record the event, but I always try to share in each new step in our farming life. He came in about nine o'clock, and we drank a quick cup of tea and then set off to make our first bale!

There is a tiny second seat in the tractor, which I perch on, and, with some excitement, I climbed up and settled myself on it, whilst Richard started up the engine. He had decided to begin with the middle field, and so we rattled and bumped down the track across Inbye and over the ford to where the drying grass lay. Richard drove the tractor onto the field and straddled the first line of grass with the tractor wheels. Then he sat for a minute or two, checking that the baler was in position and all the controls were set correctly. The baler is a large box that contains big rollers around its outside and an empty space in the middle. The grass is picked up by a roller, which has spikes all around it and which stretches across the full width of the 'box' along its bottom edge. It is then fed into the large empty space and is rolled around into a cylinder, layer upon layer, until it fills the whole inside of the baler. When the bale is big enough, a hooter sounds, and the driver has to stop the tractor to prevent more grass being taken in. Then he presses a button and a couple of layers of stretchy nylon netting is wound, from a reel at the top of the baler, around the outside of the bale to hold it together. When this has finished and been cut, which is all automatically driven by the machine, the operator then presses another button and the back of the baler opens up like the jaws of a large crocodile, and the bale rolls out onto the field. The jaws then close, and the tractor moves on to make the next bale.

As we rode around the field, the spikes stuck themselves into the grass and, looking over my shoulder, I could see it being taken into the baler. Round and round the field we went until, eventually, the hooter blew, and Richard braked the tractor to a stop. He pressed the button, and the reel of 'netwrap' mounted on the top of the baler whirled round and round. All appeared to being going to plan! "Wait a minute," I said, "before you undo the back. Let me get into position to take my photograph!" I climbed off my little seat and carefully made my way down the wrought iron steps of the tractor to the ground, picturing in my mind the email I would send to our families attached to the photo entitled 'The First Bale!' I walked a little way away from the baler and looked through the viewfinder to get the right angle to record the bale rolling out. Our fields are made up of very steep hills and the baler had sounded its hooter for this first bale right at the very highest point, so I knew I would not have a lot of time to record this important moment, as the bale would probably roll off down the hill. When I was in position, I signalled to Richard, and he pressed the button to open the jaws. Slowly, they began to open and I held the camera to my eye, ready to click. But wait a minute, as the baler opened, I could see the bale, but it had no wrapping around it! I took the camera from my face and watched in horror, as the bale of grass plopped out of the drum and rolled off down the hill, unwinding as it went like some giant green toilet roll at a football match!

One look at Richard's face was enough to see that he shared my sense of horror too. It took a minute or two to gather my thoughts together and realise what had happened. When I came to again, Richard was peering under the open jaws of the baler and, fastening them open securely, he stepped inside and swore loudly! This was very unusual, for I seldom heard Richard utter oaths, except very quietly under his breath when he didn't know I could hear him. I stepped nearer and bent down to see what he was looking at under the canopy of the raised back. Then I saw what had caused the swearing! Wrapped round and round one of the rollers was the 'netwrap' that should have been securing the grass on the bale. I could tell that it was really tightly entwined and would be a terrible job to unravel. It had also forced its way in between the roller and the casing of the baler, and there was no way to get at it without taking the baler to pieces. I could think of nothing to say—the second unusual occurrence in five minutes!—and I just stood there looking from the wrapping to Richard and back again. When Richard spoke, it was to add even more anxiety to my already troubled mind. "This is not the only worry we have," he said, "Didn't you hear that loud crack—the chain, which drives the cogs that turn the rollers has broken, and, even if we can free this wrapping, I can't repair that!"

I looked around us in despair. The time had crept past, and it was almost eleven o'clock, and the grass that was to feed our cattle all next winter, was lying in the field, and we had no way of gathering it in. I had taken my mobile phone out with us, but I had not got the number of Sandy's engineer, and so I decided to leave Richard pulling and tugging at the wrapping and walk back to the house and phone him. I had almost got back, when the mobile in my pocket began to ring. It was the very person I wanted to speak to. He was ringing to see if we had started the baler and how it was running! I wailed down the phone to him and told him the tale of the broken chain. "If you can tell me the pitch of it", he said, "I will send someone out with a new link to mend it." Naturally, I had no idea what he meant, and even when he explained that he needed the measurement from the centre of one link to the centre of the next and the measurement across the width of the link, I did not know the answer. Desperately, I turned round and saw the orange baler glinting in the sunshine, and I stared balefully at the half mile of distance that I had just walked and now had to re-cover to find the requisite measurement. I decided to carry on into the house first, and make a flask of tea and pack a sandwich and some cake. Breakfast seemed to have been a long time ago. This done, I set off back to Richard. By the time I arrived, he had taken some of the baler to pieces and was making progress with unwinding the wrapping and the thick wads of grass, which were also caught up in the machine. I explained what the man had said, and he stopped his work, climbed down and took out a measure. Between us, we decided the two measurements were one and a half inches from centre to centre and one inch across the width. Quickly, I dialled 14713 on my mobile and waited for the man to reply. When I had given him the information, he promised to send someone out to us 'in a wee while'!

We sat on the grass and shared the tea and provisions I had taken, but we didn't say very much, each one lost in the same thoughts of our problem and how we could solve it. When we had finished, I decided to go back to the house and ring a few of our farming friends, to see if they could offer a solution. As long as it didn't rain, the grass would be safe out in the field for several days, and I was hopeful that we might be able to find someone to come and bale for us. By this time, we were thoroughly disillusioned with the second hand baler and, I for one, had discounted it ever being fit to do the job.

When I got back to the house, I sat in the office and picked up the phone. As usual when we were in trouble, it was to Drew Brown that we inevitably turned for advice. I rang his mobile number now, and he answered almost immediately. When I had explained our problem and asked if he could offer any help, he said that he and his sons had just begun four days work baling and wrapping the haylage of one of the large farms in the area. This was not a surprise, as I knew that they were always busy at this time of year. However, he did come up with one suggestion, "There's Ian Somerville at Larglea—he said he was doing some contract work this year, you could see if he has time in the next day or two!" I thanked Drew for his help yet again and, picking up the telephone directory, I quickly found the Somerville's number. We had already met Bunty Somerville and, when she answered the telephone, I explained to her the problem we were experiencing and, crossing fingers and toes tightly, awaited her reply. To my delight, she told me that Ian, who was her son, was just in the yard, and she left the phone to go and find him. Two minutes later, the man himself was on the other end of the phone. "Yes, I can come and bale your grass," he said. "What, straightaway?" I asked in astonishment, not daring to believe our good fortune. "Oh well, I'll have to put the baler on the tractor first," he replied! "Do you want it wrapping too?" was his next question. Gratefully, I accepted this offer too, and to cut a long story a bit shorter, by four o'clock that afternoon, sixty-one gleaming black, plastic coated bales were spread out around the fields.

The engineer's 'wee while' turned out to be four hours, and, by the time he arrived, Ian and his mate had almost finished the work. He did mend the baler, and I was quite relieved to see that, when he set it going, the 'netwrap' continued to wrap itself around the roller. This showed that the baler was the culprit, and not anything that Richard had done. Eventually, he managed to get it so that it worked after a fashion, but, by now, our faith in it as a good machine was lost. We had already booked Ian and his friend to come and bale the other half of our haylage in two days time and, as soon as we had had our evening meal, Richard set off on the tractor, this time with the mower attached, to mow the remaining fields.

By the time he got started, it was already into the evening and I knew that he would be working well into the night, if he wanted to get it all mowed. It had been a very long day already, but Richard would keep going as long as there was work to be done. The weather seemed to be set fair for three more days, and it would be wonderful to get the haylage mowed, baled and wrapped before it broke.

There was nothing I could do to help and so, as night began to fall, I went to bed and lay listening to the rhythmic throb of the tractor's engine, as it tracked round and round the fields. I must have drifted off to sleep, as suddenly I woke with a start to the sound of the tractor coming into the yard behind the house. The sky was very dark by now, and I looked at the clock and saw that it was eleven thirty. I was quite pleased, as I thought Richard had done very well to finish by that time. I had thought it would be well past midnight. But, little did I guess that my estimation had been correct, for Richard hadn't finished the mowing at all. When I was about to congratulate him, as he appeared in the bedroom, I bit back the words, as there was a look of such dejection on his face. "Whatever's wrong, now?" I hardly dared to ask. This farming life was proving to be a real emotional roller coaster of a ride.

It appeared that he had got halfway through the last field, when he suddenly began to feel the steering on the tractor change, and strange vibrations come through the transmission. As he turned around, he could just see, in the gloomy light, that the mower was sitting at a strange angle, and when he got off the tractor and lifted its bright yellow cover, which prevented stones from flying all over the place and kept the mown grass in neat rows, he saw that the main metal arm from which the four cutter discs were suspended had completely broken in two!

A perfect end to a perfect day! Wearily, he had disconnected the mower from the tractor and, leaving it perched on the field's hillside at its drunken angle, he made his way back home to bed.

29

All is safely gathered in!

The next morning, we were able to see that there was only about an acre of grass left standing, and so we decided to leave this, until we could get the mower fixed, and then give our equipment one last chance to fulfil its purpose. Over the course of the next two days, Richard took the mower to pieces in the field and removed the broken bar. It was the main frame of the mower and made of heavy steel square section tubing, about three inches by three inches, and all parts of the mower were fixed to it. Once more Tom Corrie's smithing skills were called into action, and he effected a good strong repair.

Meanwhile, Ian and his mate came along and, in no time at all, had fifty-seven more bales decorating our fields. When the wrapping machine had finished with each bale, it tipped its bed and the bale fell off, this action stretched the black wrapping until it tore, and the consequent ragged section was left flapping. It is just a stronger version of the domestic cling film and when it touches itself it sticks, but if the wind were to get hold of this end piece and towse it about, then the wrapping would undo. It became my job, when the machines had finished working, to walk around the fields tucking in these 'tails' and making the bales secure. All that remained now was for the bales to be collected up and stored neatly in their compound—not forgetting to leave a good ten metres of empty ground between them and the ditch! I have said **all** that remained was this collection, but we have no trailer, and, even if we had, it would still be a long job to load them all in the field, and then unload them back at the steading. As it was, all we had that would handle bales was the Matbro telescopic handler. This has several fitments that go on the front telescopic arm, and, among them, is a plate with two arms that move in and out, in a squeezing movement. This allows one bale to be picked up, and the arms then gently move onto it, to hold it firmly, whilst the arm raises it from the ground. It has to be very carefully done as the 'cling film' wrapping is quite delicate and it mustn't be punctured at all, or the air will get in and the grass will not 'pickle' satisfactorily. Richard had to go and pick up every bale in this way, and ferry it carefully back to the farm. He managed an average of five bales an hour, so the collection of the hundred and eighteen bales took three long days. Eight solid hours bumping up and down over our rough farm tracks, carefully balancing precious bales, which each weigh more than half a tonne, is no easy task and we both heaved a sigh of relief, as the last bales were stacked!

The mending of the mower was achieved in and between this carting, and, the next day, I was called into action to help put it back together. This was akin to completing a double sided, thousand piece jigsaw, with one hand tied behind your back and a tight blindfold in place! There were five fixing points along the mended bar and, into each one, there were five connecting rods to be attached. These had to go in the correct order, and they belonged to the cutting discs underneath and the yellow canopy on the top. While you were getting the canopy in the correct position, it was preventing you from seeing the disc connections, and all of these components weighed many pounds. Somehow, after two hours of hard work, we managed to juggle them together in the right way, and Richard was able to bolt all the sections together. The mower was operational once more.

By this time, the grass that remained to be cut was well past its sell-by date, and, in other circumstances, would have been left for the cattle to graze where it stood, but we needed to try out our machinery, and so, that afternoon, Richard went out and mowed it.

Sunday was the big day chosen for the baler to redeem itself. The engineer had done all he could to get it running properly, and this was its big chance! After lunch, the sun had dried the morning dew off the grass, and so Richard set off. Roadside field is just opposite the farmhouse, and so I did not have far to go with the camera, to record the event. I could plainly see the tractor going round the field, and the grass seemed to be disappearing into the baler in correct fashion. I waited with bated breath, as Richard drove round and round the small area—any minute now the hooter should be blowing the signal for Richard to stop and wrap the bale, before opening up the jaws and dropping it onto the field. Yes, the tractor was stopping! I held my breath and waited, even forgetting to take the all-important picture. But what was happening? The baler remained firmly closed, the tractor door was opening and Richard was climbing out. I was not near enough to call out to him, and I watched as his small figure walked round the machines. He didn't appear to touch anything, and then I saw him turn away and begin to walk towards the farm. My heart sank!

When he is upset, Richard becomes even more taciturn than usual, and it took me a while to get from him that something called the shear bolt had broken, and he had no replacement ones. Apparently, these are especially weak areas that give way under tension and save more important parts of the machine from breaking—like the fuse in an electrical circuit. They are easily replaced, and Richard had repeatedly asked Sandy and the engineer to make sure he had some of the correct size for the baler, which they had omitted to do! He went into the workshop to see if he had any which would do the job, whilst I went into the house and guess what! I rang Drew. We had seen his two sons go past the farm earlier in the day, with the baler and wrapper, to work at a farm some miles up the road, and it had occurred to me that they might just be good enough to call on their way home and bale this last grass for us. There would only be six or seven bales and, with proper working equipment, this wouldn't take many minutes. All this worked out wonderfully—we do seem to have lots of luck, in our crisis moments! When Drew rang the boys, they said they were just finished with their job and about to return home, and they would call on us in about half an hour.

Sure enough it wasn't long before Duggie Brown drove up, and entered the field. Not only was he there and ready to bale our remaining grass, but he also had shear bolts of the requisite size. Whilst he got on with one half of the field, Richard replaced the bolt in our baler, and soon, the back door was opening and an absolutely enormous bale was rolling out onto the field. Obviously, the hooter was not operating in time, and the baler was picking up too much grass, which it then couldn't cope with. Richard carried on and tried to make another bale, but now, of course, he had to try and judge when the drum was full enough by guesswork. When he thought he had picked up enough, he pressed the button to release the 'netwrap', but nothing happened. Whatever he did, he could not get the reel to rotate. The reel was operated by something called a solenoid, and this now was found not to be working. Richard had to put the tractor brake on, open the door, climb down and operate a lever on the side of the baler, which did send the reel whirling round and round wrapping the grass inside. When this was done, he then had to get back on the tractor to open back doors and, at last, a reasonably shaped bale escaped onto the ground. It was this same procedure that had to be followed each time: guess, stop, jump out, pull the lever, get back in and open the door, and it soon became obvious that, even with our small operation, it was a non-starter. The baler had to go!

It had taken all afternoon to make just ten bales and Duggie had made five of them in about quarter of an hour! Still, at least they were made and now they needed wrapping. We hadn't yet tried out the wrapping machine, which we had also bought from Sandy. When he brought it, he had given us a demonstration with it, and it did appear to work satisfactorily, but the proof of the pudding was still to be tried!

Richard was able to fetch the unwrapped bales back to the farmyard two at a time. There was another attachment for the Matbro, which consisted of two pointed prongs, and one unwrapped bale could be carried on each of these, so it wasn't too arduous for him to get the ten bales home and lined up in the yard, ready to transfer onto the wrapper.

Ideally, bales should to be wrapped in plastic within two hours of being baled, and so we needed to do this that night. After a quick meal, Richard attached the wrapper to the tractor and set them up in front of the cattle building, near to the bale compound. I was given a quick lesson in how to operate the wrapper, and he jumped into the Matbro and spiked one of the bales onto the wrapping bed. The cling film wrap was fixed in an upright position at one corner of the bed, and the end of this had to be securely tucked into the 'netwrap' on the bale. I then had to raise a small lever slowly, to set the bed and the bale rotating, which pulled the cling film off the roll and wrapped it around the bale. It is quite an ingenious machine, as each rotation changes the angle of the bale and the wrapping slowly covers its whole surface area. We had read that the optimum number of layers to make the best haylage is six and, as it took eleven rotations to cover the whole bale with two layers, I needed to count thirty-three turns for six layers. When this was done, the bed had to be placed in the correct position and another lever tilted it up, and the bale plopped off onto the floor.

We soon had a good rhythm going between us. As I plopped the bale off, Richard was waiting with the next one on the Matbro prongs, ready to place it onto the wrapper bed. I then fastened the cling film to its netwrap and started counting the turns, while Richard gently lifted up the previous bale and carried the few yards to the stack. We worked away steadily, plop, place, fasten, count, plop, place, fasten, count, and, in a very short space of time, all ten bales were wrapped and stacked. The wrapper was a success!

However, we had learned some very salutary lessons from this, our first attempt at the making of our own haylage. We realised that it would not be an easy task, even with good equipment and our small number of acres, for one man to mow, turn, bale, wrap and stack all by himself. With haylage, timing is every-thing, and you are working against the clock and always with one eye on the weather, and so we decided that the best way for us to go would be to get the contractors in, at least to do part of the work.

We sent the baler back to Sandy's firm as unfit for its purpose, but we kept the wrapper, as it is useful to have the facility. Sometimes a bale splits, or becomes damaged, and then it is good to be able to get some more wrapping on it quickly. Haylage is a very precious commodity, and every bale is valuable.

We had intended to get the small amount of manure that the cattle had made over the winter onto the haylage fields, as soon as the bales had been removed, so that the grass would grow again quickly. We needed to take another cut later in the season, to add more bales to the stack, so that we could be sure of having enough to feed the cattle all winter. However, the troubles with the equipment meant that time had slipped by, and it was almost the end of July, before we could get around to thinking about it. We did find somebody to clear out the shed and spread it for us, but Richard felt that it was too late to put it onto the cutting fields. It wouldn't have time to disappear before the grass needed to be cut again, and would thus be baled along with the haylage. In the end we had it spread on some of the grazing land, where it would do just as much good, and bought some ammonium nitrate to try and boost the grass growth for cutting.

We were up against the clock again, as we wanted to get the second cut of hay-lage done at the beginning of September. As the cows were due to begin calving very early in October, we wanted to bring them back near to the steading before this, and we were hoping to let the grass have a few days to recover, after the second cutting, to provide them with some grazing.

I rang Ian Somerville, towards the end of August, to make sure that he would be available to bale and wrap for us. The weather remained good—indeed, it was the driest summer on record, and Richard went off to mow the grass, one day, in the first week of September. He had just finished the largest field and had begun the next one, when disaster struck again! This time it was a mega calamity. The whole under section of the mower collapsed and it was impossible to continue.

It is a tribute to the farming community of Dumfries and Galloway that our grass was cut before the evening. Although busy himself, with his son laid up with a broken leg and their bales to cart back to their farm, our neighbour Tom Corsan put his mower on his tractor, and came immediately to our aid. I really hope that, one day, we can repay all these kind people in a way that will really count for them.

This time when Ian and his mate came to bale and wrap, I asked the wrapper man if he could leave the bales any nearer to the gates. I explained to him that it had taken Richard three full days to move them last time, and he said that it was no problem. Every time he came through the fields nearest to the farm he brought a bale with him and, those that were left in the fields, were all left near to the gates. This time there were only thirty-three bales, and so it was not such hard work to get them back and stacked, and we could relax at last, safe in the knowledge that our winter-feed was safely gathered in.

Of course, we have it all to do again next year!

30

More Water

All summer long, while we had been struggling to get the haylage in, the Ladies had been out at the far end of the farm, spending their days ambling around the grassy field, alternately grazing and resting to chew their cud, and, all the time, our first batch of Low Arvie calves were growing inside them. Zeppelin went home to High Creoch in the middle of May and, one month later, when even the latest of his embryonic offspring would be large enough to show up, we asked Roddy to come back and test the ones that had not been pregnant on his first visit. We would have to think very hard about whether to keep any cows that were not bearing a calf, because as already explained, it costs a lot of money to feed each animal, and one that is not productive is no use to the economic running of a farm. There were the three that had not borne a calf last year, and these were definitely at last chance saloon! Also two had had stillborn calves and one had had a calf that was blind.

It was very encouraging, therefore, to discover that *all* the Ladies were pregnant, and most of them quite well advanced. It was more difficult for Roddy to be specific about dates this time, as he did not scan the cows but just felt the size of the uterus, and so his predictions were only a guide. He thought that most of the calves would be born in October, with just three after this date, one each in November, December and January. There was nothing to do for the cows until they calved, and so we had put them out into the Auchenvey field and left them to the peace and quiet of Galloway! Richard made visits to check on them each day, but otherwise they required no attention.

The young calves were, by now, reaching their first birthday and they were housed in the field we call Eastside. They still came into the shed most days for a feed of their muesli, and then ambled off again on their roundabout route down to the far end and back again. This daily visit to us kept them tame and enabled us to cast an eye over their condition, and look for any problems.

With the haylage in and the Ladies and their progeny requiring little of our attention, we turned it towards our own comfort and improving our lot. The year had been the driest on record, and the level of the water in the well was now a constant worry for us. In the end it never actually got near to drying up, but we were always extremely careful with our usage of the precious commodity. I had worked out that the well filled up to the level of the water table at a rate of three gallons every half hour, but the level of the water table itself was dropping all the time, with the dry weather. The normal level of the water in the well is around fifty inches, which gives us a store of about a hundred and eighty gallons. The lowest level that we recorded in the summer drought was just above thirty inches, which meant there was less than eighty gallons of water. I still continued to use the dishwasher and the washing machine, and we had our baths most days, but I restricted the use of the machines as much as I could and only used one of them in the morning and, if the other one was needed, I would switch that on after lunch. This gave recovery time between usages, and we bathed in the evening. To save the constant drain on the well throughout the day by the use of the toilet, we took to leaving the water in the bath and filled up the toilet cistern from this supply after each flush. The worst thing was to have to ask our visitors to be careful with the water, even though they were all very understanding. In this way, we got through the dry time, but we both agreed that it was no way to have to live in the twenty-first century, and so we began to think about a solution.

There were two possible ways to overcome the problem. One was to get mains water brought in, and the other was to carry on with a private supply, but tap into a better source. We began to investigate both of these options, and both had their pros and cons.

We contacted Scottish Water and asked them what putting mains water into Low Arvie would mean. They were very helpful and sent us detailed maps and information. The nearest Scottish Water pipe is located in the village of Corsock, and it has two possible connecting points for a pipe to Low Arvie. There is one outside the last house in the village, and this is located about 1700 metres from us, along the road. A pipe connected to this point would need to come either under the road or along the side of it. The second point is nearer to Low Arvie by about 400 metres, but the path for this pipe would be across three fields belonging to other people, and then all the way up our Eastside field. It would also need to go under the burn in two places, as well under four dry stone walls.

The second option of a better private supply meant drilling a borehole down to a much greater depth than the well and, hopefully, finding a supply of clean water. I rang the drilling companies that advertised in the local paper, and asked for their advice. This was to get a water diviner out to find some likely spots, and then they would bring a drilling rig and drill a hole some eight inches in diameter down into the water. This would then be lined with steel casing as far as the bedrock, after which only plastic casing was necessary, and a four-inch pump would be lowered down the hole into the water, which would then be piped into the house.

Neither of these options appeared to be easy and, without any knowledge of either process, I was afraid that both would prove to be expensive, and so I set out to find just how expensive. Apart from the cost of instalment, mains water would also incur the ongoing costs of supply, whereas, once the borehole was operational, then the water that that supplied would be free. All this had to be taken into consideration, and we decided the first thing was to contact a water diviner and get his report about the water under our feet.

The drilling company gave us the name of the one that they preferred to work with, and Richard rang him to ask his method of working. It took a while to get hold of him, as he had changed his phone number and not informed the drillers, but when he was eventually tracked down, he told Richard that he would require several maps of the farm, in different scales, and that the initial work would be done at his home, using these. Once he had studied them, he would have an idea where the best supply of water would be found. He would then come to the farm and 'firm up' his opinion on the ground, and mark two or three spots for the drillers to try. The one snag with this was the fact that he lived in Aberdeen, which is hundreds of miles from Low Arvie, and he would charge £500 for the whole amount of the work! I must say that all it sounded pretty strange to us, but his reputation was excellent—he had found wells and boreholes all over the world. We sent off the maps and waited for his call.

We heard nothing for some weeks and then, one day at the end of July, he rang to say that he had to come down to Dumfries and Galloway to 'divine' at one, or possibly two more places. Richard spoke to him about the cost, and he said that, because he had these other places in the vicinity, he would knock a hundred pounds off the price. We still thought this was a bit steep, and so he said that, if the third person decided to go ahead with the divining, he would come for three hundred. We consulted each other and said that we would go ahead at this price. He also told us that he thought he had located a couple of good places just near the house. I don't know about Richard, but I supposed he had looked at geological data for our area.

It was the day of the Dumfries show, which we wanted to go to, so I asked him to come early, so that we would be able to get to the show for lunchtime. He duly arrived at 10 a.m. and, because he was down in the area for a couple of days, he had brought his wife with him for a short break. Ever mindful of my duties as a hostess, I invited her in for a coffee, whilst the men stayed outside poring over maps and talking. I cannot, therefore, write about what happened from first hand experience, but when I went outside again there was a pole being hammered into the ground about ten metres the other side of the cattle shed. This apparently was *the* spot. "Water," said the diviner, "would be found here at a depth of 65 metres, but the borehole should be made 250 metres deep, where a supply of around 400 gallons an hour could be secured." This made our well's six gallon an hour recovery rate seem fairly well down the list of good water sources!

Lying on the bonnet of his car, whilst he was speaking, were two pieces of what appeared to be fibreglass tubing about a centimetre in diameter. We began to discuss the other options for drilling, and he said that the two next best locations were too close to the outflow of the septic tank, and he thought that it might be a good idea just to drill the existing well deeper to see if there was a better supply there. Picking up the fibreglass tubes, he began to walk around the area of the well. I then realised that these were his divining rods. They were fastened together at one end for about four centimetres of their length and he held the unconnected ends, one in each hand pulling them apart about thirty centimetres, with the joined ends out in front of him. Every so often the joined ends would dip down and point at the ground. This, he said, was when he was over the watercourse flowing under our feet. The place to dig a well or a borehole is where two of these fault lines cross, and the water flows in from two directions. He said that our well had been dug in the correct place. He could feel or 'divine' the two lines, but he said they should have dug deeper for a better supply. We asked if he could tell how much deeper, and he took his rods and stood on top of the well cover. He flexed the two rods and again held them out in front of him and, closing his eyes, he began to concentrate very hard. After a few minutes he said that another twenty feet of depth to the well would bring around thirty gallons an hour.

By now, it was lunchtime, and we had abandoned thoughts of getting to the show. Richard extended an invitation to eat with us. Because we had been going out, I hadn't prepared a midday meal, and I hastily added that it would be whatever was in the fridge, to Richard's invitation. Gene and his wife quickly accepted the invitation, but added that they had some provisions in the car, which could be added to the contents of our fridge, and, within a few minutes, we had a very adequate lunch of cheese, pate, bread and salad before us.

We continued to quiz Gene about his art, and he told us that he had found his talent relatively recently, when he had called a diviner, now his boss, to find water on his own land. Since then, they had formed a two-man company and worked all over the world. He said that he could find water just by divining over a map of the area, which is why he needed our maps, and he only travelled to the actual place to fine tune his findings. I believe he said that they had divined over seven hundred wells and boreholes between them, and his personal tally was only four dry holes, that is, after drilling, no water was found. They then began to tell us of the ill effects that sleeping night after night over one of these underground watercourses could have on human health. They told us of chronic health problems, both in their own experience and in other people's, which had been cured simply by moving the bed to a different part of the room, or by sleeping in a different bedroom.

We were just about to start building our extension, and I realised that our bedroom would be right over the two watercourses that crossed in our present well. I spoke these thoughts aloud, and he asked me if we had a plan of the new room. I fetched one from the office, and he spread it out on the table. From his pocket he took out a small cloth bag, which had a pull cord top, and, from this, he extracted a shiny crystal ball some two centimetres in diameter. Attached to the crystal was a thread. Gene held the crystal by its thread over the plan, and we watched in fascination as the crystal swung to and fro over the bedroom. Gene then took a pencil and, every so often, he drew a line under the crystal and then, moving it on slightly, drew another line. When he had finished, there were two lines going through the bedroom, and they crossed about in the middle of the room. This was exactly where the bed would be! I spent the next morning sorting out the optimum place to put the bed, where the lines would not be directly under either of us — just in case!

As Gene and his wife left, he said that he would write out all he had told us in a report, and send it to us in a week or two.

We now had something to give the drilling man, in order for him to give us an estimate of the cost. The worst thing about this process was that no one could absolutely guarantee that water would be found. Gene himself had said that, although he was pretty certain, he couldn't be absolutely sure. Also, there was the chance that, even if water were found, it wouldn't be good water. When a hole is bored and water is found, the water board comes and takes samples for analysis straightaway, and the work is halted, until the results are back from the laboratory. If they don't pass the water as fit for human consumption, then work has to begin again somewhere else. If water is found in sufficient quantity and if it is good water, then it is an excellent way to get one's water, but there are a lot of unknowns.

At the same time, we were investigating the possibility of getting the mains water from the village. The three fields that had to be crossed belonged to two different landowners. The first, nearest the road, belongs to Andy McQuaker, who is the brother of the man who had farmed Low Arvie until 1996. We had dealt with him and his son, Graham, throughout the summer, as they have a quarry on their farm, and we had purchased the stone that mended our tracks from them. We had got to know them quite well and liked all the family. We had been up to their farm at Blackhills to pay bills on two or three occasions, and had been made very welcome. The other two fields belong to Mr Ingall, the owner of the largest house in the village, an imposing mansion called Corsock House, and I rang him and asked if we might call and see him to ask permission to cross his land. We spoke about the problems of a private water supply for a few moments, and he told me that theirs was no problem as they took their water from Corsock Loch—a plentiful supply!—but that some of the people who were his tenants had the same problem as ourselves. In fact, he had just begun the process of putting mains water into one of the houses in the village, and he told me that, because the supply had been contaminated with too much lead, Dumfries and Galloway Council were prepared to give a grant towards the cost of the work. This gave Richard and me food for thought, and I decided to ring the Council the next day and ask if we were eligible also!

After tea, we set off with our maps and information to see Mr Ingall. Corsock House is a beautiful old Scottish Manor House, large and imposing. It is sur-rounded by beautiful grounds and we marvelled at its splendour, as we drove up to it. Mr Ingall came to meet us at the door. He introduced himself and led us into a large room leading off the hall, where we sat and looked at our maps and some that he produced, and we discussed the proposed site of the water pipe. The farm that he owns, on which this land is situated, is managed by a man called Davy Little, and Mr Ingall finished our conversation by saying that he had no objections to us traversing his land, and we would need to liaise with Davy so that stock could be managed around the work. We then went to see Andy McQuaker, and again discussed the route the pipe would take. He also had no objections.

The Council were very helpful too, and a gentleman named Gordon Tilbury came out to see us and, after the usual tea and cake, he told us that because our supply was inadequate, the Council would be prepared to give us a grant of three-quarters of the total cost of the work, up to a maximum of twelve thousand pounds! I don't know what Richard's reaction was to this, as he always keeps his cool in every circumstance, but I was flabbergasted! I had never dreamed of being eligible. This would mean that the cost to us was highly manageable.

We had to fill a form in, and send two quotes for whichever route we chose, and they would pay three-quarters of the cheapest, and, not just the quote, but the whole amount, if the quote turned out to be less than the finished sum for reasonable reasons, such as unforeseen rocks to move or extra drilling depth.

We got four quotes altogether, two for each method, and, in the end, bringing the mains in turned out to be much the cheapest way. Also, in spite of the fact that we would have to pay for the water, it was a certain supply of clean water. Jock Peacock brought his digger and in just nine days, he made a trench fourteen hundred metres long to house our two-inch pipe. I found a super man, named Walter McRobert to do the plumbing part of the job and he worked his week-ends to get the pipe laid out. Once this was done, and the Water Board had been and made a connection to their pipe at the far end, Walter's son came and got the pipe ready to fix to a tap in the farmyard here. The connection to the house was to be made later, when the building work was completed, and, until then, we were just to have this tap in the yard. He left the pipe unattached at first, to run off any dirt that had got into the pipe during its insertion. Then he went off in his van down to the connection with the Scottish Water pipe, and switched the supply on. To travel the fourteen hundred metres of two-inch bore pipe took the water almost three quarters of an hour, and the air that it pushed out of the pipe, as it came, was a really strong current.

In the end, we managed to get it connected into the house at the same time, and so we didn't have to wait for the extension to be ready, before we got the new supply. We kept the well to use for the farm buildings, and the third tap in the kitchen also remains attached to it, and this is the water we use for drinking and cooking, as it has no additives or chlorine. But the day the water came was a real milestone for us and, even now, after four months, I still feel a frisson of thanks-giving as I turn on the dishwasher or washing machine, run a lovely full bath or fill the kitchen bowl with a goodly supply of hot soapy water.

31

Eddy and Lucky

We were by now into September, and the Ladies were approaching their time. At the beginning of the third week, Richard opened the gate from Auchenvey field and allowed them to find their way back into the fields nearer the house. Once they had all left Auchenvey, he closed the gate to keep them in-bye, so that we could watch them more closely. The grass was still growing and there was plenty for them to eat.

We were becoming apprehensive about the approaching births, as people kept telling us how fierce the Galloways are when they have a calf, and the babies had to be tagged in both ears, before they were twenty days old. We thought that perhaps we would need to catch the mothers up and confine them in the crush, whilst this was achieved, and this was another reason that we needed to get them nearer to the buildings. We began to feed them every morning, to get them re-accustomed to coming in. I was still a bit nervous of going into the field with the cows, not really because I was afraid of them, but they were still not used to me, and they could easily be persuaded to stampede, if they were upset. I worried that they might knock me down and trample me, as had happened to one lady we read about not too long ago. And so I left the close watching of them to Richard. They were well used to him walking amongst them and didn't turn a hair, as he approached them.

They were now obviously heavily pregnant, and their gait around the fields was even more ponderous than usual. Looking at them from in front or the rear, we could see huge bulges at either side of their flanks, and Richard began to look for signs of their udders filling. We had Roddy's predictions of the first seven to calve, and so he knew which cows to keep the closest eye on. It was still a surprise, however, when, on September 29th, I went out to feed the cats, early in the morning, and, on the way back into the house, I cast a glance over to far Brook-field, and saw, in the middle of the large black shapes, one small black dot. I rubbed my eyes and looked again, but there was no mistake, there, in the morning sunshine, lay our first born calf. Excitedly, I rushed into the house, shouting to Richard, "We've got one, come and see." Never one to show strong emotions, Richard continued chewing his toast and marmalade and looked at me quizzically, as I entered the kitchen. His expression did not alter, as I told him that there definitely was a new arrival in the field. I could tell, however, that there was a quicker pace to his stride, as he rose from the table and put on his boots. We had prepared a bag with all the necessary requisites for dealing with a newborn, tags and tagging machine, antiseptic spray for navel, towel and cloths to dry and rub warmth into the little body, and he picked this up from the cupboard by the sink and disappeared outside. "Here goes," I thought, "now we shall see how difficult it is to deal with a newborn and its Galloway mother." Rather belatedly and very superfluously, I shouted to Richard to take care, and then I took up station at the farm gate, where I could watch the proceedings. I saw him approach to within about ten yards of the pair, and saw that the other Ladies appeared to pay scant attention to the goings on. At this point, Richard stopped, and I knew that he would be talking to the cow. I knew also what he would be saying, telling her what a clever girl she was and what a fine calf her baby was. I could see him inching nearer to her, and watched with bated breath, as she seemed to allow the approach with nothing more threatening that a slight toss of her head and a further lick to the baby. At that moment, I heard the telephone ring, and I rushed back inside to answer it.

It was Catherine, my daughter, and I could tell from her greeting and the early hour of the morning that something had occurred to upset her greatly. Almost fifteen years previously, she had befriended an old man who lived near to us. His wife had died not long before, and he was very sad. They had had no children of their own, and he came to regard Catherine as a surrogate grand-daughter. When she left home to go to University and ultimately to work in other parts of the country, she remained in constant touch with him. She had just received a phone call from his niece to say that he had died the previous night. Although terribly upset, her grief, she acknowledged, was all for her loss, as she could not be anything other than pleased for Eddy that his wish had been granted and he had at last gone to join his beloved wife.

It seemed somehow appropriate that, if the calf was a boy, we should name him Eddy, as a tribute to this man who had been such a large part of Catherine's life. And Eddy he became.

When Richard re-appeared about half an hour later, he calmly imparted the knowledge that he had been able, not only to put both tags into the little calf's ears, but he had discovered that it was indeed a bull calf, and he had castrated it with a tight rubber band. We had decided on this method, if it could be done soon after birth, as I never wanted to have to go through a night like that when little twenty-three died, ever again. It may sound a bit callous, but it was bloodless, and the little chap would soon lose any feeling that there might be. We discovered with experience that newborn calves sleep for a considerable portion of their first few days and, by the time they were ready to start running about, it was obvious that the castration was not a problem. I asked how the mother had been, and he said that she had been watchful and a bit wary, but that all had gone smoothly and he had not felt in any danger.

I told him about the phone call, and the calf was duly christened Eddy of Low Arvie. I then occupied myself with fulfilling our commitment to register the birth of the calf with BCMS, and found it to be surprisingly easy to achieve.

I was still aware of what we had been told about the mothers, and I kept away from the field for the next few hours, but we watched the mother's behaviour closely. At midday, Richard walked up and found that she had left her calf in the rushes and joined the rest of the herd on their moochings around the fields, and that she appeared not to be giving him a second thought. This concerned us greatly, and we kept looking to see if she went to him. When she did not appear to do so and the herd was several hundred metres away, Richard went and found him, and carried him back to her in the herd. Things seemed to go ok from then on, and the next morning when we went out, they were in a different field from the others and seemed to be getting along well. I watched in wonder, from my station at the farm gate, as the little chap got up on his wobbly little legs, and first of all nuzzled at his mother's dewlap, but finding no sustenance there, eventually found his way to the right place and began to suckle.

I could not settle to any profitable work and kept finding it necessary to go back to the gate, both to see how Eddy was and to see if there were any more black dots. Roddy's prediction had been that two cows would calve on the first of October. Eddy's mother had been one of them, and I began to pester Richard to come into the field with me, several times a day, to keep an eye on the other one. With his infinite patience he always obliged, but the first of October came, and there was no sign of calf number two.

Richard had got into the habit of taking a last look at the mothers-to-be each night, before going to bed, and we had bought a very bright and powerful torch for the purpose. He went round and counted heads, making sure that all twenty-two cows were in view, and all was calm. The evening and night of October 3rd was rainy and cold, and I didn't envy Richard this nightly trip, as he donned waterproofs and boots, at 9p.m., and set off into the dark. I was occupied in the office, catching up with emails, and didn't notice the time passing and that Richard was being longer than usual. "Hi," I called as the door opened, "everything ok?" No answer—instead, there was just a rustling of waterproofs and the clunking of boots being removed. I got up and looked into the kitchen, and found that, instead of taking off his outdoor clothes, Richard had removed his leather working boots and was replacing them with his Wellingtons. "I couldn't find number 26," he said, "and then, when I did, she was down near the brook, where the bank is steep. She has obviously calved, but was looking for the calf everywhere. I couldn't find it either, and I think it must be in the brook." He rushed off out into the night, once more. Number 26 was our oldest cow at twelve and a half years of age, and this would be her eighth or ninth calf. I went upstairs and found an old sheet. If he found the calf in the brook, I couldn't think it would still be alive, but, if it were, he would need more than the towels in his bag to dry it with. I found an old flannelette sheet and a larger towel, and brought them down. As I searched for these, I had heard the tractor rev up and depart through the farm gate—he had taken it for the lights. For want of something better to do whilst I waited anxiously for news, I swung the kettle from the warm hob to the hot one and prepared to make the ever-consoling cup of tea. I filled the flask with a drink for Richard and drank mine as I paced about the house. Then I heard the tractor returning, I had no idea how long he had been, but as he burst into the house, he said, "I've found the calf and its still alive. I'm taking the trailer back for shelter and warmth." I pushed the flannelette sheet, the large towel and the flask into his hands; also I thought of the storm lantern that I had bought at the agricultural supplier's the week before. It was a substantial lamp with a large battery inside and it threw out a good light, and I thought it might be useful in the trailer.

Once again, I was left with my own thoughts, as Richard rushed off out again to fix the livestock trailer to the tractor, and, within a few minutes, I heard the combination leave the yard. I learned later that Richard had jumped into the brook by the fence into the wood, and worked his way back, shuffling his feet along the bottom. The top of the water was covered with the rushes, which were bent over from their roots along the bank, so he was unable to see anything, even with the help of the torch. The bank was steep and vertical for a distance of about fifty yards, and the cow had chosen this dangerous spot to push out her calf. We found out from experience later that, as soon as a calf is born, the mother licks it all over from head to tail, and, within a short time, the calf staggers to its feet on very wobbly legs. We assumed that either the mother had not seen how close the edge of the bank was in the darkness and, in licking it, could have tipped it over the edge, or it may have fallen over when it tried to get to its feet. Anyway, Richard had shuffled his feet about thirty yards along the ditch, when he felt something move against his legs. Reaching down into the water, he felt the shaggy coat of the little chap, beneath the cold water. It had taken all of Richard's not inconsiderable strength to haul the calf out of the ditch and drop it wetly on the top of the bank. He had taken the small towel from the bag and done what he could to dry the black coat, but it was clear that more care was needed, if the calf was to survive his ordeal. He had left the calf to the ministrations of its mother, and driven back to the house for the trailer and sheet and towels.

When he got back, he took the calf into the trailer, in which he had put two or three bales of straw, and set about drying and warming the little chap—for it was another bull calf. When he was satisfied that all had been done that could be done, and the calf appeared to be warm and alert, Richard went out of the trailer to look where the mother was. To his consternation, she was nowhere to be seen and, eventually, he tracked her down back with the herd three hundred yards away. She had obviously got fed up and 'gone home'. In a quandary as to what to do next, but knowing that it was impossible to separate the one cow from the herd and drive her back to the calf, he unhitched the trailer from the tractor and, leaving the calf and the trailer in the field, he came home.

Over another warm drink, we discussed what to do. I wasn't too happy about leaving the calf in the trailer overnight. It is essential that a calf suckle as soon as possible after birth. The first 'milk' that the mother produces is called colostrum and contains many natural antibiotics which, taken in the first hours of life, 'inoculate' the whole of the calf's system, and help it to grow strong and healthy. I didn't think the mother would venture into the trailer to find her calf, and so we decided to go back and see if she had returned to look for him. This time we drove down in the Range Rover, as it was easier to manoeuvre, and we would be able to use the headlights as searchlights. The mother was nowhere to be seen, but the calf was still snug and warm in the trailer. The rain had stopped, and we decided that the best thing to do was to make him comfortable in a bed of straw in the rushes, near to where the mother had last seen him, but well away from the dangerous steep bank, and leave him to her and Mother Nature. In the headlights of the car, we could see the herd on the far side of the field, and we drove across the brook to look for number 26. We found her grazing lazily in the darkness, and we tried to urge her back towards the calf but, as ever, it proved impossible, and we decided to leave her to find her own way.

It was very disturbing to drive away and leave the little creature all by himself in the night, especially after his ordeal and rude introduction to the living world, but there seemed no other way, and we went back to the house and, ultimately, to bed and to sleep.

Anxiety is a terrible thing to wake up with. I had been suffering from chronic anxiety and depression for many years, and that terrible moment when the few seconds of good feeling on waking, are snatched away to be replaced with the gnawing, nagging trauma of worry is one of the worst experiences of my life. It was re-visited the next morning, when the events of the night before disturbed my thoughts, as consciousness came. Unable to rest further, I climbed out of bed and, rushing to drag on a few clothes, I made my way downstairs and out of the house to my lookout post by the gate. I could see the large shapes of the cows, and some way away to the left was Eddy and his mother, but then I looked back to where the herd was, and right up under the far fence, snuggled down behind the grass fringe out of the wind, was a tiny black shape. I went to look at the place where we had left the calf, and found the straw bed empty. So Mother Nature had triumphed, the mother had come back for her baby, and had taken him back to the herd.

I went back into the house to tell Richard and to prepare the breakfast. We felt he couldn't be in too much danger from his immersion in the brook, if he had survived the night, and walked the three hundred or so yards from his bed in the rushes to where he was now. I had already decided that circumstances had chosen his name, and he became Lucky.

We ate breakfast, feeling that the world was a good place and, once more, coincidence had served us well. For if 26 had calved an hour later, or if Richard had gone out any earlier, he might have missed the chance to get the calf out of the ditch that night. With the cold water flowing over him for several hours, there would have been no way he would have survived until the morning, and we would have had our second tragedy.

However, we didn't know it then, but our ordeal around Lucky wasn't yet over. When I made one of my regular trips to cast an eye over the herd for signs of more arrivals, I saw that the herd had moved to the field by the road, but the wee calf was still a tiny black dot up by the far fence. Number 26 had gone off with her sisters, and left him again. All the afternoon he stayed there, whilst she grazed with the others. My trips to the gate got more frequent, and, every time

Richard appeared, we worried together about the situation. I had brought up, from the town, a feeding bottle for emergency use, but had not yet got round to buying the milk powder to put in it. We both felt that it was time that the calf had a feed; we didn't know when, or even if, he had suckled from his mother, and we walked up to look at him together. He was still curled up in the long grass and felt warm to the touch and seemed quite happy, but it was beginning to get dark again, and I don't think either of us could have slept without knowing he had something in his stomach. Looking after animals is very much a process where one has to use one's instincts. We had to realise that we were only the second team, where these new calves were concerned, and their mothers had the same parental feelings as any living thing. But there were human mothers who didn't bond with their offspring and, presumably, this can happen in other species, too. We were heartened by the fact that number 26 had gone back last night and fetched him from his straw bed, but she had shown him little attention all through the day!

I knew that a friend of ours had a sack of milk powder, that he had had for an orphaned calf and, as this was Saturday night and all the shops were by now closed, I determined to run down to his farm and beg a little out of his sack. Accordingly, I ran back to the farm and grabbed the car keys. I crossed the farm-yard and opened the car door. I was just about to climb in, when I cast one more glance over to the calf. In the twilight I could just make out several black shapes plodding across the field and, as I watched, one of them broke ranks and made her way towards the black dot. As she approached, the little calf got up on unsteady legs, and found his way unerringly to the 'milk bar' and began to suckle.

I walked back to the field where Richard was still standing, and together we watched Lucky having his supper. Number 26, whose name is Bardennoch Hill Gladeye turned her 'glad eye' on us and stared at us, giving us a look as much as to say, "Don't try to teach your Grandmother to suck eggs!"

32

Wodan

By the time Lucky was established and doing ok, I realised that my nervousness amongst the cows had disappeared. Through making so many visits to check them, and the night time foray to deal with Lucky's unfortunate beginning, my wish to help Richard keep an eye on the Ladies at this crucial time had completely overtaken my fears, and I suddenly found myself to be an accepted 'member of the herd', as Richard was.

With Lucky suckling well, Eddy being well taken care of by his mother and no other cows showing imminent signs of giving birth, we managed to have a good night's sleep that night. The next day was a Sunday, and there was no activity in the cows' field, and no builders to disturb the calm, so we passed a peaceful day, catching up on those chores that had been forgotten for the previous few days. The weather was still good and dry, and the grass plentiful. The yearlings were still visiting most days, and everything was fine. Eddy was by now six days old, and his mother had begun to return with him to the herd. Old Gladeye had never really left, and Lucky and Eddy began to gallop together around the field. It was fascinating to watch the two youngsters frolicking about, kicking their legs up in the air. We had begun to call the cows into the building each morning, and give them a feed of concentrate. This was really just to tame them and to get them used to coming in again, after their long sojourn out at Auchenvey, over the summer. Richard needed to be able to get them in, just in case any of them required medical attention. I don't think it will ever be possible to drive our cows, but they can be led, if they are sufficiently well bribed! If you get one, you have to have them all, and Richard found it quite easy to work in this way. He got them all in, and then singled out the one needing treatment, before letting the others out. He always kept just one other cow back, as they seemed comforted by the presence of one of their sisters and were easier to deal with. We had had two cows panicked into jumping the gate when they had been left on their own, and this was undesirable on two counts. They could easily injure themselves, and also, we did not want them to get into the habit of jumping obstacles, as our walls are not too high and not too strong!

In the early hours of Monday morning, around four a.m. I woke to the sound of loud mooing outside. With unerring instinct, I knew at once that calf number three was arriving and, as I stirred, Richard woke too and heaved himself out of bed. How glad I was that I had opted for the inside work! He was gone about half an hour, and, when he returned, he told me that number 49, the second cow due on the first of October on Roddy's list, had given birth to our first heifer. The calf had already been born when Richard got to her, and he thought the mooing was just to let everyone know what a clever girl she was! The calf was named Lady Mary of Low Arvie after our mothers and me.

Calf number four appeared the next morning but one, and he was there in the field when we did our first check. He was standing by his mother, and I thought that his front left leg appeared a little strange, but, when they first stand, they are so wobbly that it was difficult to be sure. However, later in the day, we heard a cow giving loud moos, and when we went to look, his mother was calling to him from the other side of the brook. He was trying to get to her, and we could plainly see that he had a problem. His front left leg gave way at the ankle joint every time he put his weight on it, and it bent him forward tipping his nose almost onto the floor. He was a pathetic little sight, trying to keep up with his mum. Once again, we had the quandary of whether to intervene or not. In the end, Richard picked the little fellow up, and carried him to her. Not happy that he had got that far, she then proceeded to try and persuade him through the ditch and up the other side. He did his best but his little leg kept letting him down, and soon he was a pathetic sight, covered in mud. We stood and watched, helplessly, and then, unable to stand it any longer. I left Richard and went back to the house.

Later in the day, she dragged him back to the field where he was born, and we found him curled up in the long grass asleep. His mother had gone wandering off with the herd and, every now and then, gave a loud moo at him as much as to say, "Come on, we're over here now." We were very worried about him, as he seemed to have given up and just lay there miserable and not very warm. Bearing in mind our experience with Lucky and Gladeye, we kept thinking that she would go to him, but there seemed no sign of this happening and, just as it was getting dark, Richard decided to act. First thing on the Monday morning I had been down to Castle Douglas and bought some artificial colostrum. I had spoken to Drew at church on Sunday, and he said that in cases like Lucky's, where the calf had suffered some trauma or other, he always gave the calf a feed of this precious liquid, even if the mother was on hand to feed as well. It just set his mind at rest that the calf had something in its stomach. We went to the kitchen and mixed a batch now, and Richard took it up and fed it to the little calf.

Two more calves, both bulls, had been born that day and, as it was Wednesday, I decided to use a bit of poetic licence and call them Wodan, Woden and Wodin. Woden and Wodin were fine and healthy, and their mothers were looking after them well, but Wodan was a real cause for concern. Richard said that he had taken the feed of colostrum, and so we knew at least that he had some sustenance, but his mother did not approach him at all. He lay there all night on his own, and was still there, next morning. As we looked over, we could see two large black birds hovering close by on the fence, and I feared the worst, for these were the crows, gathering to peck at the tiny body. Richard immediately burst into action. He got the tractor and, having attached the trailer to it, he drove straight up to where Wodan was lying. He put him in and brought him back to the building, where we made a warm bed in the straw. He was still alive and quite warm, but he didn't show any interest in anything at all. Richard gave him another feed of colostrum, but it was a battle to get him to suck.

Then we called the cows in for their morning feed, and Richard managed to manoeuvre Wodan's mother into the end of the shed where Wodan was lying, and shut her in with him. We had to get him suckling if we could. His mother did not show much interest in him, and was not pleased at being shut in, when her sisters finished their feed and went back into the sunshine, but she would have to put up with it, if we were to save her calf. Things did not improve during the day. The little calf lay in his corner and never moved. I had rung the vet earlier in the day, and he had promised to call if he could, but then in the late afternoon, he rang to say he had been held up, and could we take the calf down to the surgery. So just before teatime, we hitched the trailer up to the Range Rover, and Richard put Wodan in and we drove down to Castle Douglas, leaving his mother behind in the shed.

` The vet took his temperature and found it to be normal, but, when he looked at the leg, he found a large and painful abscess had formed, just on the joint where he fell forward onto it, when it gave way. "No wonder he's given up on life," he said, "he's in great pain." He gave the calf an injection of painkiller, which he said would last for three days, until the second injection of antibiotic got to work. He gave us the remainder of the antibiotic and told us to inject him every day for a week. Then he told us that we needed to get some food into him. Because the calf couldn't stand very well, the vet suggested that Richard might milk the cow and feed the calf his mother's milk from a bottle. If the milk were not taken from the cow in one way or another, she would dry up in any case, so she had to be milked. On the way home, we were both quiet, and I was wondering how this new process would be achieved!

However, nothing daunted, Richard put the calf back in the shed and then manoeuvred the mother into the crush and, taking the two litre jug I had fetched from the kitchen, proceeded to squat down behind her. From my position at the other side of the feed barrier, I soon heard the squish, squish of the milk as it was extruded from her udder into the jug. The mother did not make any murmur at this new experience and stood there quite calmly, whilst two pints of the creamiest looking milk I have ever seen was extracted from her. The top half of the jug was a rich yellow colour, but there were long cow hairs and bits of dirt dotted over its surface and, taking the jug from Richard, whilst he flexed and re-flexed his aching fingers, I carried the precious liquid into the house and filtered it through two layers of muslin stretched over my flour sieve. I did this twice, and the milk appeared to be reasonably clean now, so I poured it into the feeding bottle and took it back to the shed. Richard had left the cow in the crush whilst he fed the calf, and this took quite a while, as he still wasn't interested in eating. However, he managed to swallow most of it and then staggered back to his warm bed in the corner, and Richard released his mother.

We gave her plenty of haylage, to keep her hunger at bay, and a large bucket of water, and then we went and had our evening meal.

The next morning Wodan still wanted to stay in his corner, but he did look a little brighter. Richard milked his mother again and fed him with her milk. We decided to feed him half the milk in the morning, and then give him the rest a little later. This seemed to work well, and gradually, he did appear to be taking a bit more notice. As he became a bit perkier, his mother also began to take notice of him. It was heartening to see her go to him and give him a couple of licks. Licking and washing is a very important activity for forging a bond between mother and baby.

During the time we had been so concerned with Wodan, four other calves had been born, and Richard was kept very busy with his bag of tags, trying to make sure he got the calves tagged before they could run away. By this time, we had given the lie to the fiercely protective Galloways that wouldn't let you near. I believe that Richard had won their trust to such an extent, that he was able to spend time with each mother and baby, always being wary, but usually being able to put the tags in and castrate the bull calves, whilst the mother watched. There were one or two hair-raising moments, but by and large, they were very good. As explained earlier the tag numbers are made up of our six-digit Low Arvie number which is 585065, and then a check digit which goes from 1 to 7 and then begins again, followed by the calf's individual number. These begin at 1 and number onwards. Because these numbers have to contain twelve digits, the empty columns are filled with noughts, hence Eddy's ear tag number reads 585065 600001,—I don't know why they started the check digit with 6—Lucky is 585065 700002 and Lady Mary is 585065 100003. The three Wednesday calves are 585065 20004, 585065 30005 and 585065 40006. Richard and I refer to them by the last of these numbers, or by the names that I have given them. The next calf to be born, another bull, had the tag number 50007 so he became James, and number eight was Speedy, as he ran away before Richard could get the second tag in, although only a few hours old. It was only the bull calves that I had to find names for, as the heifers were following the alphabetical pattern begun with the older calves, and they were already decided on. We chose Nikki after my nephew's wife in Canada, Olga for Richard's old boss's wife, P was to be Pete, as this was Richard's mother's pet name, which she always used and introduced herself by. She was only four feet ten inches tall and, like Peter Pan she never grew up. Q presented a problem, but I thought of the Spanish Querida which means 'dearest one', and then I discovered that Zeppelin's mother, the calves' grandmother, was called Querida, so this was fine. R was for Rebecca, a friend of Catherine's, of whom I am very fond and whom I had promised would be included, S became Sharon, my son-in-law's grandmother in America. She is the great grandmother of Freya, who was the reason for our calf named Freya, and she has always expressed an interest in the calves and our farm. T will be Tracey, for more good friends of Catherine, they are called Claire and Nigel, but their surname is Tracey, so that seemed to fit. U will be Ursula, the 'little bear' which the calves resemble so much, and V will be Valerie, a very good friend of mine, W for Wilhelmina for Richard—he is William Richard—and I am still contemplating X, Y and Z.

We seemed to be getting more than our fair share of bull calves, but the next day Lady Nikki appeared, and Beauty gave birth to Lady Olga. By now, we had got the hang of this calving business. We watched out for a cow to go off on her own, and sometimes it would be quite a while before things began. She would just stay alone, grazing and resting. As a general rule, the cows all stay together and where one leads the others follow, the only one who sometimes does her own thing is Spot, but, for calving, they prefer to be alone. I think they must have a method of communication, because the others always knew when a cow needed to be alone, and it was exciting to watch as each, in their turn, sought this solitary space in which to give birth. When the calf is trying to make an appearance, the cow holds her tail straight out, hunches her body up and turns round and round. Having been there and done that, I could feel their pains, as I watched them straining. Then a whitish bubble appears under the tail, and the calf is almost here. Funnily enough, I never actually saw any of the calves being born. Twice I saw the bubble of the sac appear, but each time I had gone somewhere else at the relevant moment.

On Sunday morning, Richard again milked Wodan's mother and fed him. He was holding his own, and had even got up on his feet a few times. His mother was taking more and more interest in him and I was quite hopeful, although Richard was still doubtful about his survival. When Richard fed him the second time that day, he became quite distressed and kept turning his head away from the bottle. It was a worry that he didn't seem too interested in food. When he refused to take any more, Richard let his mother out of the crush, and came round to my side of the feed barrier and we watched them for a few moments. The mother cows make a low, gentle, one note sound to communicate with their offspring, and we heard it now, as the cow went over to her baby and licked him with her rough tongue. All of a sudden, the little chap stood up on his wonky little legs and staggered around his mother, nuzzling his little face into her dewlap. And then as we watched, hardly daring to breathe, he took a few steps towards her udder. All the time, she stood very still and waited patiently. It took him a while, but eventually he found the right place and, to our great delight, he began to suckle. We knew that this was the breakthrough we craved and that he had won the chance to live. His leg was still letting him down, but at least he could suckle. Over the next days, he began to take a real interest in his surroundings. When the other cows came in to the bottom end of the shed, he went to the barrier to look at them. He investigated the perimeter of the pen and chewed at the rope that was tying up the gate. He even tried a few little skips around his mother. He was getting stronger, but his leg was still not holding his weight, and, now that he was more mobile, we noticed that the other front leg was not right either. It wasn't as weak as the left one, but sometimes he would almost fall right over. He was still having his daily antibiotic injections, and we decided to wait until these were finished before we decided what to do about the leg.

On Wednesday, I had to take the car into Carlisle to be serviced, and I was taking the opportunity to go down to Leamington Spa to see Catherine and Morgan. The garage took me to Carlisle station, and I caught a direct train to Leamington, where Catherine met me, and we had the evening together, before I retraced my steps the next day. It was a long way to go for a short time there, but since I had only seen them once in the whole year, it was worth it, especially since I got cheap train tickets by booking well in advance. We were just about to go to bed, having gossiped ourselves to death, when the phone rang. It was Richard. He had just done his nightly round and discovered that three calves had all been born since teatime. Lady Pete had arrived earlier in the day, and then these three. He had not attempted to do anything other than check they were ok, as it was too dark to see properly, but he was just letting me know that they were here.

When I got back the next day, he told me that there were two bulls and Spot had had a heifer. He had tagged them early that morning, and so I went on line and registered them. We had twenty days in which to register them, but I tried to do it as soon as Richard had found out the sex of the calf, and then mistakes were less likely to be made. When BCMS got around to logging these registrations, they then sent out the calves' passports. So I made a point of registering them as early as I could.

Spot had had her calf at the far end of Brookfield, and they had remained there for the first twenty four hours. I liked Spot because she was a character and also the mother of my favourite yearling calf, and so we took in a visit to her on our next little walk. She didn't mind our approach, but just gave the little warning moo to her calf to stay near. We talked to her for a while, and then we watched in surprise as the calf weed onto the grass. Our surprise was not at the liquid, but at the method of its passing, for it was clear that Spot's calf was not Lady Querida at all! We would have to think of a new name for him! Spot's real name is Bardennoch Hill Brownie, and Richard offered the suggestion of Hash (Brown). I agreed, but not because of the hash brown connection, but because Richard had made a hash of telling me the sex, and I had made a hash of the registration! The latter hash was soon put right with an email to Workington, and the calf became Hash. The other two calves born that day are Jack (son of Jill) and Moses, because his mother hid him so well in the rushes after Richard had tagged him, that we didn't find him again for two days!

Two days later, Wodan had finished his injections and, apart from his legs, had made up all his lost ground. We were still worried about his legs, and I felt that some kind of splint on the weakest one would be a benefit. Richard sent for the vet, and together they made one out of two pieces of wood, and strapped it into place with bandage, and then waterproof tape. Wodan seemed to manage fine with this new appendage and was still able to get to the all-important milk bar. We kept them in the shed for two more days, and then put them out into the small paddock, with one of the late calving cows for company. We had to keep the splint in place for two weeks, and we could see that the other leg was gradually straightening, now that the weak leg was not bending all the time. Occasionally he would wobble a bit, but every day saw him gaining more and more strength.

I was attempting to take a really good photograph of the cows and calves to use for a Christmas card and, every time the sun came out, I picked up my camera and rushed into the field. That afternoon I was snapping away, when I suddenly became aware that there was a cow standing near to me, mooing for all she was worth. "OK, ok I've seen you," I said taking a few more photographs, but she just kept on making a terrible racket. Eventually, I took my camera down from my face and looked at her. There were a few calves playing on the grass in front of her, and one of these was lying down, curled up. I idly looked at the numbers, and sorted out in my mind who belonged to who, but when I looked at the curled up calf, I couldn't see a tag. "That's funny", I thought, taking a step nearer to see the other ear. The tags were supposed to go in the left ear, so that the number was easier to see, but Richard had made one mistake and put it in the other ear. I peered at the calf. No, I couldn't see a tag there either. The cow was still shouting at me and, slowly, it dawned on me what she was saying. This was her new calf, just born. Either she hadn't needed to go off on her own like the others, or she hadn't had time, and the calf was born right there amongst the herd. He, for it was yet another bull, was number fifteen and became Quincy—both Richard and I speak Spanish, and quince is Spanish for fifteen.

Sixteen really *was* Lady Querida, and seventeen became Gerald, as I was having a long phone conversation to my friend Janet, when he was born, and Gerald is Janet's beloved husband's name. Eighteen is George, born on my grandmother's birthday, and so named after my grandfather.

33

Wee Boy

These eighteen calves were born in twenty-eight days, and they were amongst the most enjoyable days of my entire life. In spite of the stresses of Lucky's birth and the worry over Wodan, it gave me such immense pleasure to go into the field and walk amongst these tiny creatures and their mothers. The pattern of behaviour was, almost always, the same. The mother would go off to a quiet place for the birth. When the calf was born, the mother would keep it close to the rushes, and the calf spent most of its first day or two curled up deep in a rush bed, safe from the wind and any driving rain. The mother often left the calf alone, as the first cows to calve had done and which had caused us such distress at the beginning, but we became used to the system and, although we kept a watch on things, we began to relax about it. The calf would just emerge to suckle, and then go back into its cosy place. This was why we couldn't find Moses for two days, as his mother had found him such a safe place. We knew the area that he was in, because his mother was grazing nearby but, search though we might, we never found his hiding place. Usually, when we got near to her calf, the mother would exhibit anxious behaviour and begin to make the little warning noise to alert the calf to danger, but Moses' mother barely cast a glance in our direction, as Richard strode up and down through the rushes, and I kept station with him through the fringe growth. We could almost hear her laughing at us and saying, "Look all you like, you'll not find him!" And we didn't. But as soon as we had given up the search and gone off across the field, we would turn to look back and there he would be, enjoying his supper!

After two or three days in this seclusion, the mother would bring her calf back to the herd and introduce him to the others. The older calves would gambol over to the new comer and inspect him all over. The braver ones would move forward to meet this welcome and return the inspection, but the more timid would shrink into their mother's flanks and cower away at first. Soon however, they joined in the galloping games and exhibited the sheer joy of life. We had opened up all the haylage fields to them for this period, and they moved round and round grazing the still growing grass; but always in the morning when we went out, they would be in Inbye waiting for their breakfast. As they saw Richard, the cows would begin to move towards the shed, but somehow they had communicated to their young that they must stay in the field. Richard would feed those mothers that came into the shed, but there were always one or two who stayed outside to guard the babies, and I usually took their portion out to them. I had to be quick because if the ones in the shed finished their share quickly, they would run outside and try to pinch some more, and I can tell you this, it is very difficult to prevent a fully grown Galloway cow from doing what she has in mind!

Then I had to go and feed the cows that were still in calf purdah. This was my favourite job, because the calf would usually stick close to its mother and, while she was eating, I could enjoy being with them. This way the cows gradually lost their wariness of me, and I lost my fear of them. One always has to be careful dealing with animals, especially such large beasts, but I am happy to walk amongst them now.

Once the cows in the shed had finished eating, they seemed to remember their calves again, and they would all rush outside to make sure they were still there. It was really quite funny to see them all rushing about making a great hullaballoo, until they were reassured that all was well. It reminded me of that 'getting to know you' party game where you all go round making different animal noises, until you find someone making the same sound!

Of course, we had the two cows and little Wodan to feed as well, for the two weeks that they were in the small paddock. I usually tried to feed them first, otherwise the cows' bellows would be deafening, by the time we had seen to the others. Everyday, Wodan's right leg seemed to grow stronger, and he began to skip a little around the field sometimes. He did look awkward with the stiff splinted left leg, but we felt that the future looked good for him. When the day came to remove the splint, we opened the gate and the two cows ambled out of the field, with Wodan following behind. Whenever we want to move the cattle from one side of the farm to the other, we always close all the gates around the farmyard and let them wander about, exploring the new environment. Eventually, they will find their way into the place we want them to go, and they never feel the weight of a stick on their backs, or become distressed. This day was no exception and, all in good time, the three of them were back in the shed. Richard trapped Wodan away from his mother behind one of the gates. and. whilst she pawed the ground and mooed her displeasure at being separated from him, Richard cut through the plastic strapping and removed the splints. When he was released into the full space of the pen, he gave his freed leg a few shakes. Then he tried a few tentative steps, and then a few little skips. The leg looked thinner than the other one, but it seemed to hold up straight, and we began to hope that he was cured. We let the companion cow go and left Wodan with his mother in the shed for the rest of the morning, just to keep an eye on him, but when he still seemed fine after lunch, we let them go too. It was a bit nerve racking, as we knew that it would be very difficult to get them isolated again, if his leg gave way and needed further attention, but our worry was needless. In fact we never saw it bend in that distressing way again. Just occasionally, we notice that it is not quite as straight as the other one, but to all intents and purposes, he is just like the others.

By the end of October, there were only four cows without calves, these were the three that Roddy had predicted would be the last, and one that he had thought would calve in the middle of October. He was just about right with the three last ones, and Rebecca made her appearance in mid-November and Sharon at the beginning of December. But this supposed October calver was the one that he got wrong, for she was actually the next to the last, and didn't have her baby until the 7th of December. He was born early in the morning to a white world, thick with frost. By this time, they had ventured back to the far end of the farm and so, when the herd came back to the buildings that night where it was a bit warmer, she kept him out there. It was bitterly cold, and so we took the decision to intervene again, and Richard took out some haylage and water for her and two bales of straw to make a dry bed and a wind break for the calf. He went up just before bedtime to check them again, and was pleased to see that they were both ok and the calf was snuggled up beside the straw bale. The next morning, she had managed to bring him nearer to the farm, but when we went to feed her, we were worried because the little calf kept hunching his back and kicking his legs towards his stomach, showing that he was in pain. The weather was still bitter, and the ground was hard, so we decided to bring them in to the shed. We had taken out some haylage for the mother, and she was munching away, as we discussed our plan of action. This cow was number 46 and probably the most docile of all of them. Her previous calf, Boy, was the tamest of his batch too. Therefore Richard felt reasonably sure that he could carry the calf back and that she would follow quite calmly behind. If he fetched the trailer, she wouldn't be able to see the calf, and would probably get distressed and not even follow. So he picked up the wee fellow—Wee Boy, as he was Boy's brother—and set off across the iron hard ground. The calf might have been Wee Boy, but he still weighed around thirty kilos, and so it was not an easy job to carry him. It wasn't too bad when he kept still, but, when he struggled, it became very difficult. As predicted, his mother watched Richard catch up her son, and she began to walk after him. There was no distress or anxiety, but after going about fifteen yards, she stopped and turned around to look at the pile of haylage that still remained on the grass. She looked once more at Richard's retreating back and once again at the haylage, and then it was clear that the haylage won, for she turned around, walked back and began contentedly munching once more.

By this time, Richard had struggled his way right across the field and was within sight of his goal, but I had to call to him to stop and wait for the mother to come again. If he got out of sight, she would never follow. He put the calf down, but held it between his legs to prevent it from escaping, and waited. The cow seemed determined to finish her breakfast, and unhurriedly chomped away, until every wisp of grass had gone. Only then did she seem to wake up to the fact that her calf was missing! She began to look around for him, and I attempted to steer her in the right direction, calling to Richard to shout her. All to no avail! The silly creature set off to look for him in totally the wrong direction, and there was nothing for it but for Richard to bring the calf back within her ambit!

Eventually, we got her moving in the right direction and we were right about her placid nature, for she followed amiably until we got to In-bye, where the herd was getting sorted out into family groups again. She began to get a bit distressed then, as perhaps she thought it wasn't time for him to join the herd. But we did manage to get them into the shed, and the little chap settled down in the fresh clean straw that Richard spread there for them. It was quite nice to have another customer in Wodan's corner, and I went out often to check on them and to make sure that the mother had enough food and water. Cows need to drink about fifteen gallons of water every day, when they are lactating, so it was essential to keep the bucket filled, as the automatic system which sends water to the drinkers by the trough was frozen up. Wee Boy still seemed to be in pain, and later that day, we phoned the vet and he came out to see him. There didn't appear to be anything drastically wrong, and Roddy gave him a dose of liquid paraffin and suggested we keep him in, until we were sure that food was going in at one end and waste was being produced at the other. Whenever I had a spare minute I went and peeped in the shed, hoping to see him suckling, and I knew that Richard was keeping an eye on them too. We weren't to be rewarded for two full days, as Wee Boy was always in his corner by the bales, whenever we peeped in. But then, on the second night, we looked in together, and there he was, nuzzling his way around his mother's dewlap just as Wodan had done, and, gradually, he found his way to her udder, and we could hear the gurgling sound of the milk going down his throat. That was our first relief, now we had to wait for the other end to become operational, and, each time we went in the shed, we searched the ground for the light brown deposit of a milky calf. Two more days went by without any sign, but Wee Boy was obviously not ill anymore, because he was racing round the shed and showing an interest in everything around him. The weather had relented, the frost had disappeared, and we both felt it was unnecessary to keep them confined any longer. I went into the shed and undid the gate, and the pair walked out in the sunshine. I cast just a slightly anxious eye after them, as we still had not seen the evidence that we wanted. I swung the gate back and walked over to the wall to tie it back and open up the shed again and, as I was tying the rope, I glanced down. There at my feet, still steaming slightly, was the largest, most welcome pile of brownish yellow calf poo any one has ever seen!

34

Tracey

By the time we were sure that Wee Boy was fit and healthy, December was well in and the grass had long since stopped growing. The cows' feet, as they came into the building for their daily feed, were beginning to chop up the Inbye field and make it brown and muddy. The grass cover had to be protected, and so we decided to put the cows and calves over to Eastside, and bring the yearlings over to this west side. They had far fewer feet and were more likely to spend their days in the other fields, picking up what grass they could from the land. They came in for their evening meal and were given straw as well as their muesli ration and, sometimes, they stayed in the shed over night, and only went out again after breakfast the next morning. The cows, on the other hand, stayed near to the shed all the time in the hopes of 'free' food, and so the field got very chewed up.

The land on the Eastside is classified as 'Rough Grazing' and is not used for haylage, so it was not quite so important to keep this right. There were one or two hard areas where Richard would be able to put the feed trailer for the daily bale of haylage, and the cows could use the large shed for eating their ration of muesli. A further advantage of having the cows and calves at this side of the farm is that the calves can reach the feeding passage with their mothers, and thus get used to the system and the food at their own pace and in their own time. Mind you, they have to be quick to get much, before the cows wallop it all down!

Everybody got used to the new homes very quickly, and life settled down into a reasonably easy routine. Much more time is spent with the cattle in the winter, as they have to be fed, but the system worked very well, and, for a month or so, things were calm. Christmas came and went. Once again, we joined Mother at Bothwell House and enjoyed Norma's delicious culinary skills. It was all the more enjoyable because she and her husband and mother joined Richard and me and the three residents who hadn't gone out, and so we shared a very pleasant meal. Also, we were invited to our friends' at Hightae for Boxing Day lunch, so I enjoyed very much having so little cooking and preparation to do. The building work was progressing slowly and, by the time the workmen finished for their fort-night's Christmas break, we just about had the outside shell finished and weath-erproof.

After Christmas, we expected the weather to become cold again and prepared ourselves for another winter of cold fingers and high electric bills. However, we were pleasantly surprised. Although the central heating system was no nearer installation, the enclosures of the conservatory at the front and the porch at the back made the house somewhat less subject to draughts, and the weather was kind to us and did not deteriorate too much. We still had our cold times but, with a goodly supply of dry logs, we managed to keep much warmer than the pre-vious year. The heating will definitely be ready before next winter, and so we can just about say goodbye to the worst of the cold!

Every day, we kept an eye on the one remaining cow to calve. She was Blondie, the only non-pedigree cow, and the vet had put her calving date around the third week of January. She was the largest of our cows, and her bulge never seemed as big as the others' had and, as time went on, I began to wonder if she had a calf inside her at all! However, as her due date approached, she began to wander off, obviously sussing out an appropriate place. For three or four morn-ings, she wasn't in the shed with the others and, when we looked out, she could be seen mooching lazily on one of the several patches of still green grass. The weather at this time was extremely mild, if a little damp, reaching temperatures of around 10 degrees Celsius, and I wished that she would get a move on and deliver the calf, so that it could have its earliest days in the warm.

It was not to be, and the frost had once more hardened the ground, when Richard went out to feed on the twenty-sixth of January, and saw her standing over a small black dot in the distance. Hurrying to feed the remaining cattle, he snatched up the ever ready 'new-born' bag and strode out, across the field, to check on the new arrival. This mother, however, was made of different stuff to the others, either that or she had had to wait so long, watching her sisters with their babies, that there was no way anyone was going to deprive her of her baby. As I have said before, it is so frustrating not to be able to explain our intentions and reassure the animals, and even with all of Richard's patient, calm approaches, Blondie wasn't having any of it. Three times she set herself to defend her calf from his ministrations, and so, checking as much as he could that all was well with the baby and having no doubt as to the fitness of the mother, he left them to their peaceful solitude. The weather that day, although remaining cold, was windless and there was some sunshine, so we weren't too concerned.

Later in the afternoon, hunger drove the mother to leave her baby and make her way to the feed trailer. This was the opportunity that Richard had watched and waited for, and he drove off in the van down the road to a point level with the calf's position, and approached it from there, in order, hopefully, not to arouse the mother's suspicions. I watched him bending low behind the stone wall, keeping as much out of sight as possible. However, the wily mother had moved the calf from the place where they had been earlier, and he had to search through the rushes for quite a while before he found it. The tagging process was achieved quickly, and the little Lady Tracey had her navel sprayed with antiseptic and was given a quick examination, before Richard returned to the van and drove back home. Blondie was still munching happily and was not any the wiser!

When she had finished her meal, Blondie went off back to find her baby still where she had left her, but now sporting a bright yellow tag in one ear and a shiny metal one in the other. She didn't seem to notice, or, if she did, she didn't mind, and we left them to their peaceful night.

The next morning was very bright but bitterly cold, and Blondie was by the feed trailer, when we went out to feed, but Tracey was nowhere to be seen. We fed the other cattle, always keeping an eye on Blondie, hoping to see her march off to her baby and show us where she was now. Eastside is a vast patchwork of grassy patches interspaced with rushy, boggy areas that are impenetrable to all but the bravest adventurer. There is a lot of water lying in the rush roots, and to traverse these areas, it is necessary to tread down a portion of rush stems, before putting your weight down. If you don't do this and you put your feet between the rush plants, you are likely to sink in the bog down to your knees, or beyond. The cattle are experts at knowing where to walk and where not to and, mostly, they find pathways around the rushes. Most of the grassy patches can be reached in this way, but sometimes it is a very contorted route. Richard's long legs were a great advantage to him when walking on this land, as he could stride over the top of the rushes and his large, size 12 feet spread a goodly mat of rushes for his support. It was a very different story for me though, as I have none of Richard's advantages, and I venture into the rushes as little as possible, and, usually, only with Richard by my side to help.

At lunchtime, Blondie was still munching away at the haylage trailer, and, once again, my concern began to surface. Richard made a few sorties to the region where the baby had last been seen, but Blondie's unconcern told us that she was no longer there. These were short days and, by three thirty p.m., the sky was already darkening, and night was falling. That was when Blondie made her move, and the ever-watchful Richard was there to follow. The darkening sky was a help to him, as he was able to stay out of her sight, as she lumbered off down the track.

I was just about to serve our evening meal, when Richard came into the house. I cast an anxious glance in his direction, but was relieved to see a welcome smile on his face. "You'll never guess!" he said. So I didn't try, but waited patiently whilst he carried on. "She's only taken her across to the island!" At the northeast side of our boundary, which for the most part is marked by the burn, there is about half an acre of land that is cut off from the rest of Eastside, as the burn meanders into our land at this point. We call this portion of land 'the island' for this reason, but it is bounded by the 'march dyke' or boundary wall along the far side, so it is only an island to Low Arvie. The other side of the wall is the start of Crogo land. Richard had followed Blondie down the track to the burn and watched amazedly, as she waded into the water, making her soft monotone moo, as she went. As she pulled herself out of the water on the far side, a small black object rose from a bed of rushes and fastened itself contentedly onto her underside.

The next two mornings, we found Tracey huddled into the fallen haylage around the feed trailer, and her mum standing close by, munching away, and, when she had finished eating, Blondie gave her monotone moo, and the little figure struggled up, and the pair trundled off back to the rushes. But on Friday morning, there was again no sign of her. Blondie was there, as unconcerned as ever, but she had no baby with her. That day the weather closed in, and it began to rain, as only it can here in the west. All day and all night, the house echoed to the lashing of the pouring water on the Velux window. My excitement at the new kitchen that was steadily taking shape, with the shiny new four oven Aga taking pride of place, was forgotten, as anxiety over the little calf replaced it. Richard could report no sighting of her on Friday morning, and Blondie did not disappear to go and find her at all. When the same circumstances were replicated again on Saturday, and the rain was still coming down in torrents, anxiety turned to sleep-preventing worry. Eastside is such a vast area, and more than seventy per cent of it is covered by rushes that are impassable at the best of times, but after twenty-four hours of continuous heavy rain, they become a death trap. The little girl was out there somewhere, and we had no chance of finding her, even if we braved the weather and the dark, lowering sky to try, and we passed a miserable day. I kept going out to the fence to see if there was any sign of Blondie fulfilling her motherly duties. I am sure that Richard did the same—he always did things like this surreptitiously in the hope that I wouldn't know how worried he was too,—but it never worked!!. We saw nothing that alleviated our fears all day.

By Sunday morning, the rain had, at last, stopped pouring down, and it was a grey mizzle that met us as we went out to feed. When the animals were all munching away at their muesli feed, I said to Richard that we should at least make an effort to look for Tracey. To find a needle in a haystack would be an absolute doddle, compared to the search we were contemplating, but wading through mud and peering into impenetrable rush cover for some sign of a bedraggled black coat, even whilst envisaging that it might be a lifeless black coat, was better than the repeat of another day's idle worry. We garbed ourselves in wellies and rainproof coats and, armed with stout sticks to lever ourselves out of the mud, we set off to begin our search in the area that we had last seen Blondie go off to, two days before. Needless to say, we found nothing, not any sign of Tracey whatsoever, just yard after yard of wet, dripping rushes, with the standing water in between mocking us at every step of the search. We went everywhere we dared, but it still left acres of land unsearched, and I looked around me in desperation, as Richard called from his searching area behind the cattle shed that we were wasting our time, and had better call it a day and get on with the other chores.

Sadly, I turned for home and was contemplating another anxious day, punctuated by trips to the fence to look for signs of Tracey, when Richard called out to me again. "What number is on the new calf's ear tag?" His memory is filled with the other important things he has to remember, and these administration details are left to me to keep in mind. I am the one who registers the calves and therefore, he was unsure which number was the last one we had used. "She's number 22", I replied miserably, concentrating hard on lifting each welly out of the sticky, muddy quagmire. I didn't take in at first his next words, and he had to repeat them. "Well, she's here with the others!" He was standing in the doorway to the cattle shed and was watching the cows as, having finished their breakfast, they mooched slowly out into the field, with their calves by their side. All the time we had been out in the field, she had been in the shed! We had obviously missed seeing her in the melee that took place at feeding time! I rushed as quickly as it was possible to in the underfoot conditions, and arrived just in time to see Blondie and the tiny youngster, step out of the shed.

It was of no moment whatsoever that mud was plastered all the way up our clothing, that our legs ached with all that lifting and high stepping through the grasping fronds of rushes, that we were soaked from head to toe or that our fingers and toes were so cold they ached. Nothing could keep the joy from our hearts or the tears of relief from our eyes, as I felt Richard's arm slip round my shoulders. We stood together, and watched Blondie amble off down to the burn, with her tiny daughter stepping delicately through the mud by her side.

We (and the Ladies of Low Arvie) had brought our first batch of Low Arvie calves safely to fruition.

Epilogue

I hope you have enjoyed sharing our journey, and that you also enjoyed, with us, the happy outcome.

I add this epilogue to bring our story up to date.

We moved into the new extension in March 2004 and were able to welcome visits from my family, throughout the spring. All the Canadians flew in, at different times, to see Mother and Low Arvie, and we had a happy time. Other guests followed, throughout the year, to test our new facilities, including Janet and Gerald, and Sharon, Morgan's American grandmother, who all came to make acquaintance with their namesakes. The 'guest apartment' works very well and allows both us and our guests to have our own space, as well as the opportunity to gather in the new farmhouse kitchen that has become the heart of our beautiful home

Last winter was a real comfort zone, because the new, super-duper, four oven Aga warms the whole of the new part of the house, and we never used the new heating system there at all. It was a different story, however, in the old part, and the radiators were a real boon. We moved the office into the 'Esse' kitchen and have smart new bookshelves in the old small office. We didn't, in the end, join this onto the sitting room, which is now a cosy room for winter evenings, with its log fire crackling in the grate and its large radiator adding additional heat as well.

Hughie came one day, with protective gear and chainsaw, and set himself on in the copse at the west side of the garden. He had been itching to get that sorted, for all the forty years he had known it. The daffodils now flourish unhindered by brambles, as I promised they would. Soon after this, though, we began to notice Hughie getting thinner, and he complained of not being able to eat. Sadly, he died last September, at the young age of seventy, and we miss his visits very much.

The cattle continue to prosper and, as I write, Lady Freya is tending Lady Flora, born three weeks ago, and Lady Catherine is looking after little Charlie. Lady Jade had to be calved by the vet, as Lady Jayne was a breech presentation, but all is well. Lady Elizabeth has Zvonko (named for the photographer who created the book cover and came out here the day the calf was born). We await the 'first-borns' of the remaining heifers any day now. They were fathered by a young bull named Lucky Strike of Overbarskeoch. The heifers are so tame that Richard has tagged their calves whilst they have been suckling their mother's milk, and neither mum nor baby turn a hair. We have grown accustomed to the fact that the mothers often go and leave their newborn calves cuddled down in the rushes for long periods of time, and our days of panicking are long since over. We make sure to see the calves every day if we can, but none has ever been left to starve! There have been forty-seven calves born on Low Arvie now, so we feel quite experienced.

Beauty has become the 'leader of the pack' of the older cows, who are a separate herd from the heifers. If we want to move these, I just call "Beauty" and she follows me and brings the others with her. She has gone on to provide us with another beautiful heifer, Lady Valerie. X became Lady Xenia. Y is Lady Yvonne-Dear, for the lady in the local pub who serves our meals. She is always called, "Yvonne, dear", by our good friend, Graham, whom we first met when he told us about Ford tractors at the sale. Z is Lady Zafira, just a beautiful Spanish word, meaning sapphire. The cows are currently pregnant with their third Low Arvie calf, all sired by the noble Zeppelin.

We continue to improve the farm, but it is a slow and expensive business. It is in much better heart than when we came, but there is still much to do, to make it perfect.

The promised change to subsidising farmers to farm for the environment has come, ushered in with the New Year of 2005. Gone are the old payments for limiting the production of livestock or crops to the National Quota, and arrived are the payments to help us to keep the green and pleasant land we live in, ever green and pleasant.

Mother, now 93, continues to flourish at Bothwell House, as does Ethel, who reached 100 years of age last December, back in Yorkshire.

Richard and I continue to 'live the farming dream.'

978-0-595-35837-3
0-595-35837-3

Printed in the United Kingdom
by Lightning Source UK Ltd.
125586UK00001B/189/A